DICTIONARY **OF**

Surnames

LESLIE DUNKLING

HarperCollins*Publishers*

HarperCollins*Publishers*
P.O. Box, Glasgow G4 0NB

First published 1998

Reprint 10 9 8 7 6 5 4 3 2 1

ISBN 0 00 472059 8

A catalogue record for this book is available from the British Library

Printed and bound in Great Britain by
Caledonian International Book Manufacturing Ltd, Glasgow G64

CONTENTS

PREFACE

Dictionaries are usually consulted very briefly for what they have to say about a single name or word. Many would apply to them the old joke about telephone directories – they have lots of characters but not much of a story. I think they fail to do their job if that is the case. A dictionary should be a collection of stories, each one briefly told and interesting in its own right. Those stories should be written in plain English, not dressed in academic jargon. The dictionary should, as a result, be a book in which you can happily browse, never being quite sure what you will discover on the next page.

As it happens, Collins have established a tradition of reader-friendliness in their dictionaries which has proved to be very successful. In this work I have gone very deliberately down that 'friendly' path, to the extent of providing from time to time an anecdote, verse or quotation to accompany the linguistic facts. Those facts, of course, are often entertaining in themselves; the anecdotal material is meant to be an icing on the cake.

Surnames are not just words; they are intimately connected with people and with human behaviour in all its variety. Taken as a whole, our surnames show not only where our ancestors lived and how they earned their living; they also record the out-spoken comments our fore-fathers made on their neighbours' physical or mental peculiarities. In our surnames we find a record of life in the Middle Ages and are allowed a glimpse into the medieval mind. Our surnames really do bring the past to life.

Since it is impossible in a book of this size to deal with the huge number of individual surnames that now exist, I have tried to provide as much practical help as possible for those who are trying to trace the origin of an uncommon name. Inevitably that will mean delving into family history, but that is always a rewarding occupation. Researching your own surname leads you back to your ancestors. They are waiting there for you to find them.

INTRODUCTION

We take it for granted today that everyone has a surname, but that was not always the case. Three questions we can usefully ask, therefore, are when, why and how surnames came into being. The answers to the first two questions are closely connected, so we can treat them together.

BLENDED NAMES

Our remote ancestors had a single name, referred to throughout this dictionary as a *personal name*. The Anglo-Saxons and their Germanic cousins usually formed such names by using words that had become conventional name components. Those who make a particular study of names (onomatologists) refer to these name components as *elements*, and they are described as such in the entries which follow. Germanic name elements often referred to abstract qualities such as 'fame' or 'strength.' Some other favourite themes were words meaning 'riches,' 'battle,' 'brave,' 'elf', 'beloved,' 'rule,' 'raven,' 'victory,' 'power,' 'friend,' 'wolf,' 'protection,' 'bright,' 'old,' 'peace,' 'gift.' In forming a name for a child, one of the elements from the father's name might be combined with one from the mother's name to create a new name. It was not necessary for the two parts of the name to complement each other in meaning. *Wulfram*, for instance, was not meant to have an overall sense, linking 'wolf' and 'raven.' That is why it has been necessary in this dictionary to use a rather long-winded formula and say something like 'Wolfram (one of the modern forms of the surname), descendant of someone who bore the Germanic personal name *Wulfram*, composed of elements meaning "wolf" and "raven."'

As it happens, this method of creating a name from parts of other names continues in modern Britain to some extent, though it is normally restricted to minor naming systems. A typical example would be a William and Mary using parts of their names to create *Wilry*, say, or *Wilmar* as a house-name or a name for their boat. Modern formations of this type are usually known as *blends*.

NAME MAGIC

The Anglo-Saxons do not seem to have duplicated personal names within the same community, nor did they re-use the names of distinguished ancestors. That situation changed when the Danes and Norwegians settled in Britain. They brought with them their own names, which were often similar to those of the Anglo-Saxons, but more importantly, they brought with them their own naming philosophy. As Sir Frank Stenton once expressed it, the Scandinavians believed that 'the soul of an individual was represented or symbolised by his name, and that the bestowal of a name was a means of calling up the spirit of the man who had borne it into the child to whom it was given.' Those words could, of course, be used of many modern parents. They name a child after an admired person in the hope that the qualities of that person will somehow be passed on to the new name-bearer.

This belief in name-magic meant that the Scandinavians deliberately re-used the names of famous chiefs or family friends when naming their children. By doing so, they had taken a step towards the modern situation where any number of children born in a particular year are likely to receive the same first name. There is nothing wrong with that system, but it makes a second name essential if an individual Daniel or Laura, say, needs to be identified more precisely.

BY-NAMES

The Normans shared the same ideas as the Scandinavians about re-using names. When they came to England as conquerors in the 11th century their ideas about naming, as well as the names they used, soon began to be adopted by the natives. The Normans had already begun to use secondary names for purposes of legal identification, especially to establish ownership of land. This useful practice became more common, and Englishmen, especially those of high social class and status, followed suit. Over the next two centuries, what had begun as an aristocratic necessity filtered down through the social classes. By the end of the 14th century, families at all levels of society had what we now call a surname. Thesaur- of 'surname,' incidentally, is from Latin *super* 'extra,' though some early writers on the subject insisted that surnames were really 'sirenames.'

An important point about surnames is that they are passed on from one generation to the next. That was not necessarily the case when secondary names were first used. There was a long period during which someone's additional name was a *by-name*, applying only to the person who bore it. John Baker at that time was a baker, but his son might be Robert Johnson. It was only when a man could be called Baker, even though he practised some other trade, or Johnson when his father's name was William, that Baker and Johnson could truly be called surnames.

VARIANT SPELLINGS

There was, then, a fairly lengthy surname-formation period during which surnames slowly evolved, and for purely practical reasons. But the surnames most people bear today have been in existence for some six hundred years. During that time the words that were used to form them in the first place have often changed their meanings, and most names have changed their spelling. For centuries, after all, the names were being written down by semi-literate clerks using their own ideas about how to represent the sound they were hearing. The name-bearers were usually unable to guide them or correct them since most people, at all levels of society, were illiterate. As a result, in their passage through the centuries, individual names may have taken on a wide variety of forms. The lists of variants which accompany many entries in this dictionary make that point.

Not everyone bears a surname that came into existence by the end of the Middle Ages. Many families have understandably adopted a new surname or adapted an existing one, seeing no reason why they should perpetuate the embarrassing nickname of an ancestor. It is easy to see why the names listed in Appendix 1, for instance, have become obsolete. Foundlings were given surnames by parish authorities, often in a whimsical manner, and may only date from the 19th century. Jewish families had their own naming traditions, but were often forced to adopt surnames. It is only by tracing back a family's history that one can be reasonably sure that the surname a family now bears was that of a medieval ancestor.

SURNAME CLASSIFICATION

Let us retrace our steps for a moment and ask how, once the need for additional secondary names had been recognized, they were formed. The easiest way to understand the process is to think of how people might be given a nickname today. A nickname (originally an '*eke* name,' or 'extra name') may comment on someone's physical appearance, such as his or her red hair. It may refer to an aspect of behaviour, such as greediness. Our ancestors were fond of commenting on where someone had originally come from,   as we do occasionally when we nickname someone Paddy or Jock. They were usually far more specific, however, and described someone as from such and such a village, or as the chap who lived at the foot of the hill. They liked names of the Jones the Bread type, which commented on a man's trade or profession. They also liked to describe people in terms of their relationships, as Richard's or Emma's son.

Writers on surnames traditionally refer to such relationship names as *patronymics* (derived from the father or male relative) or *metronymics* (derived from the mother or female relative). Surnames indicating trades and professions are *occupational* names; those which indicate where someone originally lived are either *place names* or *locative names*. Names describing some aspect of appearance or behaviour are lumped together as *nicknames*. These have become established terms, and they are not necessarily as good as they should be, but the four categories do give a general impression of how surnames were formed.

SURNAME LANGUAGES

The simplified summary given above omits at least one vital factor which affects the interpretation of a surname – its language of origin. It may be an Old English name, *Old English* being a technical description of the English language before the 11th century. Between the 11th and 14th centuries, following the huge impact on it of Norman French, the language is known as *Middle English*. From the 15th century onwards we refer to *Modern English*, though as any reader of Shakespeare knows, many words have changed their meanings since his time. Because of the Scandinavian settlers, many of our surnames are based on Old

Norse words. Others are French, specifically the dialect of Old French spoken by the Normans. Some names are Dutch, brought to England by Flemish craftsmen. There are also the many names which have a Celtic origin, in Scottish or Irish Gaelic, Welsh or Cornish. In modern Britain the situation is more complicated still, thanks to our multi-national society.

It is obviously essential to know what language we are concerned with when we are seeking the origin of a surname. If you were asked the meaning of the word *pain* you might say something like 'bodily discomfort.' But if the word is French rather than English, then its meaning is 'bread.' The situation is further complicated in the case of surname, since we need to ask, what did this word mean, in such and such a language, in the Middle Ages. As it happens, *pain* in Middle English often meant 'judicial punishment,' a meaning which has become obsolete other than in one or two fossilized phrases. For a good example of how the original language of a surname can affect its meaning, see the entry at Belcher.

The fact that surnames began life in different languages helped to confuse still further the spelling situation. If an English-speaking clerk was trying to write down something he was hearing from a speaker of Welsh, for instance, he would be completely baffled by Welsh sounds that do not exist in English. French-speaking clerks had equal difficulty with English names; Scottish and Irish Gaelic created difficulties for those who did not speak those languages. One recalls the stories of immigrants arriving at Ellis Island and being given 'American' names by officials who could not understand what was said to them. When asked by other officials what his new name was, one man is said to have replied: *Ich hab vergessen,* 'I've forgotten.' He was registered as Ichabod Fergusson. Another version of this story turns *Schön vergessen* 'already forgotten' into Sean Fergusson.

TRACING THE ORIGIN OF A SURNAME

Given these various complications, how then do we go about tracing the original meaning of a surname. A first step is to consult dictionaries such as this. No single dictionary is able to deal with the huge number of names that exist, and one should always consult as many as possible. The list that follows mentions reference works that have acted as sources for the present dictionary work and give an idea of what exists in print.

A Dictionary of Surnames, Patrick Hanks and Flavia Hodges, Oxford University Press, 1988. This is especially strong on the main European as well as British names. Jewish names are also very well covered thanks to an important contribution from David L. Gold.

The Penguin Dictionary of Surnames, Basil Cottle, Penguin Books, 1967 and later editions. Written in a very condensed style and often assuming that the ordinary reader has the same specialist knowledge as the author. Quirky remarks on many names, and well worth reading.

A Dictionary of British Surnames, P.H.Reaney, Routledge and Kegan Paul, 1958 and later editions. Still available in many reference libraries, and acknowledged as a work of major importance in the field.

The Origin of English Surnames, P.H.Reaney, Routledge and Kegan Paul, 1967. A scholarly discursive work, essential to serious students of the subject.

A Dictionary of English and Welsh Surnames, Charles Wareing Bardsley, reprinted from the original 1901 edition by Genealogical Publishing Co, Inc., 1967. The author spent a lifetime studying the subject and did much pioneering work.

English Surnames, their Sources and Significations, Charles Wareing Bardsley, reprinted from the 1873 edition by David and Charles, 1969. Still highly readable.

Romance of the London Directory, Charles Wareing Bardsley, Hand and Heart Publishing, reprinted by Gryphon, 1971. Entertaining.

A History of Surnames of the British Isles, C. L'Estrange Ewen, Kegan Paul, Trench, Trubner, 1931. An undervalued discursive work, with much to offer.

Homes of Family Names in Great Britain, Henry Brougham Guppy, Harrison & Sons, 1890. Uniquely concerned with the distribution of surnames by county. R.A.McKinley has shown, however, that the names in Norfolk in the 16th century were not necessarily those which still predominated in the 19th century. In other words, Guppy's counts – treated with reverence by eg Basil Cottle – must be treated with some caution. See also Appendix 2 of this book.

English Ancestral Names, J.R.Dolan, Clarkson N. Potter, 1972. This work focuses on 'the evolution of the surname from medieval occupations,' an excellent idea in itself, but a great many names which have other possible explanations have been included.

Family Names J. N. Hook, MacMillan, 1982. Especially concerned with European names in the USA.

New Dictionary of American Family Names, Elsdon C.Smith, Harper and Row, 1956, 1973. This is a collation from the author's vast personal collection of works on the subject. It suffers from accepting rather too easily the explanations of others, but can be very useful as a starting point.

American Surnames, Elsdon C.Smith, Chilton Book Company, 1969. A discursive work.

Surnames, Ernest Weekley, John Albemarle, 1916. A scholarly discursive work, written in a very condensed style. Any serious student of the subject will need to consult it.

Words and Names, Ernest Weekley, John Murray, 1932.

The Romance of Names, Ernest Weekley, John Murray, 1914.

English Surnames, C. M. Matthews, Weidenfeld and Nicolson, 1966. A discursive work in non technical language.

How You Got Your Name, James Pennethorne Hughes, J. M. Dent 1959. A paperback introduction to the subject.

Is Thy Name Wart? James Pennethorne Hughes, J. M. Dent 1965. A paperback dealing with some 'odd' surnames.

An Essay on Family Nomenclature, Mark Antony Lower, John Russell Smith, 1875. Entertaining.

Patronymica Britannica, Mark Antony Lower, John Russell Smith, 1860. A dictionary, still interesting though later scholarship disproved many of the explanations.

British Family Names, Henry Barber, Eliot Stock, 1902. Useful lists of Old Norse and Norman names.

Family Names and their Story, S. Baring-Gold, Seeley & Co, 1910. Discursive.

The Surnames of Scotland, George F. Black, The New York Public Library, 1946. A standard work.

Scottish Surnames, David Dorward, HarperCollins, 1995. An updated work.

Welsh Surnames, T.J. Morgan and Prys Morgan, University of Wales Press, 1985. 'The primary aim of this work is not to explain the "meanings" of Welsh names,' says the Preface. A highly technical work, not easy to read.

The Surnames of Ireland, Edward MacLysaght, Irish University Press, 1969. Fairly technical, a great many names left unexplained.

Irish Family Names, Patrick Kelly, republished by Gale Research, 1976.

A Handbook of Cornish Surnames, G.Pawley White, published by the author, 1972. A useful booklet.

Norfolk Surnames in the 16th Century, R.A.McKinley, Leicester University Press, 1969. Of specialist interest.

English Surnames Series, Yorkshire West Riding, George

Redmonds, Phillimore, 1973.

Suffolk Surnames, N.I. Bowditch, *Trübner* & Co, 2nd edition 1861. An immensely long list of surnames from Boston and its vicinity, without explanations but often useful to check whether a surname has survived.

The Personal Names of the Isle of Man, J.J.Kneen, Oxford University Press, 1937. A scholarly dictionary.

South African Surnames, Eric Rosenthal, Howard Timmins, 1965.

Russian Surnames, B.O.Unbegaun, Oxford, Clarendon Press, 1872.

Dictionnaire Etymologique des Noms de Famille et Prénoms de France, Albert Dauzat, Librairie Larousse, 1951.

Deutsches Namenlexikon, Hans Bahlow, Keysersche,1967.

Unsere Familiennamen, K. Linnartz, *Dümmlers*, 1958.

Particular surnames that have inspired books in their own right include Smith (*The Book of Smith*, Elsdon C. Smith, and *Is Your Name Smith?* by Nicholas Gould). Gould also wrote little booklets about the names Davi(e)s, Williams, Brown(e), Jones and Taylor. James Finlayson long ago wrote a dissertation on the names Buggey and Bugg (see those entries).

The titles mentioned above show only the tip of the onomastic iceberg, and research is constantly in progress. At the Meertens Institute in Amsterdam, for instance, an electronic database of Dutch surnames is being prepared. No doubt computerised research is being undertaken elsewhere. *Personal Names and Naming*, an annotated bibliography, compiled by Edwin D. Lawson, Greenwood Press, 1987, and *More Names and Naming*, 1995, will again need to be up-dated in the near future.

It is necessary to say that an awful lot of nonsense about surname origins has appeared in print, and one must not innocently believe everything one reads. To give just one example, Richard Stephen Charnock, in a book entitled *Ludus Patronymicus*, or the *Etymology of Curious Surnames*, seriously explains the name Shakespeare as a corruption of Jacques Pierre. This carries the 'game of names' a little too far.

RESEARCHING FAMILY HISTORY

If the name that interests you has not already been investigated by a competent researcher, it becomes necessary to do some detective work. It is necessary to trace the male ancestry of the family as far as is possible. The object of the search is to discover as many different spelling forms of the name as possible, so that the sound of the name to those who were recording it can be assessed. Family history research also needs to establish where the family was likely to be living in the 14th century, which in turn indicates the language from which the name is derived.

There are plenty of books available which give advice on how to research family history. There are also professional researchers who can do the job for you, though that can be an expensive option. In most areas there is a Family History Society, and there is a national Genealogical Society. Membership of such societies is well worth while. This kind of historical research soon becomes complex, and helpful advice from others is invaluable.

DEDUCTION

Some may feel that it is worth making an intelligent guess at the origin of a surname by using deduction. Of the four classes of surnames mentioned above, three have been especially well studied. Names which reflect medieval occupations, for example, were also words which were recorded in contemporary literature. They are dealt with in a historical work such as the monumental *Oxford English Dictionary* and find their way into most surname dictionaries. Descriptive nicknames were also normal words, and again have been thoroughly investigated. Patronymics of the Johnson type, including Scottish and Irish *Mac-* names, Welsh *Ap-* or *Ab-*, are well covered in existing works.

Surnames which began as place names, the largest class of surnames, are the ones that give most problems. They may have begun as the names of small settlements or hamlets which were totally unknown fifty miles away. The place names themselves had usually themselves been in existence for centuries and had probably changed their original form. Local pronunciation of many place names, as is still the case today, often varied from what the spelling of the name might suggest. An obscure surname, then, is likely to be a transferred place name, which is why a good place to search for it is often the county by county volumes of the English Place-Name Society. These are available in any good reference library. Such a search should only be made after delving into the family history as described above. Clues as to where to begin may be suggested by Appendix 2 of this dictionary, which gives the main locations of many surnames at the end of the 19th century.

OTHER ASPECTS OF NAMES

Not everyone is concerned with trying to discover the original meaning of a surname. Many American academics now concern themselves very seriously with 'literary onomastics,' a branch of literary criticism which examines how and why authors name their characters. Others have been concerned with eponyms, or proper names that have become words (such as lynch, boycott). Less serious in their approach are the many who content themselves with a collection of 'odd' names. John Train published his findings in *Remarkable Names of Real People* and followed it two years later with *Even More Remarkable Names of Real People*. *Don't Blame the Stork*, by Barbara 'Rainbow' Fletcher, appeared in 1981. It is crammed with 'oddities.' A generally light-hearted approach to names is to be found in *Names*, by Paul Dixon, while a mixture of interesting names information is in Elsdon C. Smith's *Treasury of Name Lore*. That might almost serve as a subtitle to *What's In a Name?* by Leonard R.N. Ashley, and the *Guinness Book of Names*, by Leslie Dunkling. The latter author's *Our Secret Names* discusses onomancy, beliefs in various types of name-divination, such as Numerology. *Signing Off*, by Homer, published by Apogee Publishing, 1980, consists entirely of entries such as '. . . We have the facts and details. Research has been completed and approved. Now, let's go! (Signed) Serge A. Head.'

Perhaps the mention of *Signing Off* should serve as a hint that it is time to bring this introduction to a close. The surnames themselves are waiting in the wings, anxious to show themselves. I have often been asked, in the last thirty years, why I have made a special study of names of all kinds. I hope that this dictionary will help to answer that question, revealing how fascinating names can be.

Leslie Dunkling

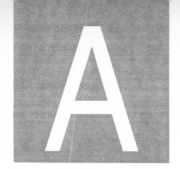

Aaron, Aarons, Aaronson (Eng) Descendant of a man named *Aaron*. Traditionally explained as Hebrew 'mountain of strength,' but this has no evidence to support it. The biblical personage of this name is brother of Moses and Miriam.

Abadam, Adda, Addaf, Atha, Athawes, Badam, Badda, Baddam, Baddams, Badham, Batha, Bathaw, Bather, Batho, Battams (Welsh) *Ab Adam* 'son of *Adam*.' The variety of spellings reflects the efforts of English or Norman scribes as they tried to capture the sound of the name as pronounced by a speaker of Welsh. See ADAM.

Abbé (Fre) Occupational name of someone who was a servant in a priest's household.

Abbett, Abbitt *see* ABBOT.

Abbey, Abbie (Eng, Scot) Occupational name of a worker in an abbey or someone who lived near an abbey.

Abbis, Abbison *see* ABBS.

Abbot, Abbett, Abbitt, Abbotson, Abbott (Eng) Descendant of *Abraham,* or servant in an abbot's household. The frequency of the surname also suggests that it was a nickname for someone who was thought to resemble an abbot in appearance or character.

Abbs, Abbiss, Abbison, Abson (Eng) Son of *Abel* or *Abraham*.

Abe (Scot) Descendant of a man named *Ebenezer,* Hebrew 'stone of help.' In the Bible Ebenezer is the name of a place where there are several confrontations between the Israelites and Philistines. The stone referred to in the name is a memorial of Israel's victory. Ebenezer was used as a given name by the Puritans.

Abel, Abell, Abells, Abelson, Able, Ableson, Abletson, Ablett, Ablin, Ablott (Eng) Descendant of *Abel*, Hebrew 'vapour, smoke,' used to mean 'vanity.' In the Bible Abel is the younger son of Adam

1

and Eve whose offering is pleasing to God. His brother Cain is jealous and kills him.

Abercrombie, Abercromby (Scot) From Abercrombie, a parish in Fife, Scotland, so-named because it is at a confluence of a river, the name of which is based on a Gaelic word meaning 'crooked,' found again in surnames such as CAMERON and CAMPBELL.

Aberdeen (Scot) Descendant of someone who originally came from the Scottish town of this name. The earliest meaning of the place name was 'mouth of the river Don.'

Able, Ableson, Abletson, Ablett, Ablin, Ablott *see* ABEL.

Ablewhite *see* APPLEBY.

Abrach (Scot) Descendant of someone who originally came from Lochaber, Scotland.

Abraham, Abrahams, Abrahamson, Abram, Abrams, Abramson (Eng) Descendant of a man called *Abraham,* a Hebrew name explained in the Old Testament as 'father of a multitude,' though Hebrew scholars believe it means 'the Father loves.' Abraham was originally called *Abram* 'the Father is on high.' He was the first of the Jewish patriarchs.

Absalom, Absolem, Absolom, Absolon, Ashplant, Aspenlon, Aspland, Asplen, Asplin, Aspling (Eng) Descendant of a man named *Absalom*, 'my Father is peace.' In the Old Testament he is the third son of David and is famous for his beauty and hair. He is eventually killed by Joab when his hair is caught in an oak tree.

Abson *see* ABBS.

Acheson *see* ADAM.

Acker, Ackerman, Acreman, Akerman (Eng) Occupational name of a ploughman, worker in a field.

Acket, Acketts, Ackling *see* HAKE.

Ackroyd, Ackeroyd, Acroyd, Akeroyd, Akroyd, Aykroyd (Eng) A mainly Yorkshire name, indicating someone who lived in a 'clearing amongst oak trees'.

Acreman *see* ACKER.

Acroyd *see* ACKROYD.

Acton (Eng) Someone who came from one of the several places so-named because it was a 'settlement near oak trees.'

Adam, Acheson, Adames, Adams, Adamson, Adcock, Addey,

Addis, Addison, Adds, Addy, Ade, Ades, Adie, Adkin, Aiken, Aitchison, Aitken, Atkin, Atkins, Atkinson (Eng, Scot) Descendant of a man named *Adam,* from a Hebrew word meaning 'of red earth.' The biblical Adam dies at the age of 940. *See* DUCK.

Adda, Addaf *see* ABADAM.

Addyman (Eng) Occupational name of *Adam*'s servant.

Adeane *see* DEAN.

Afel (Welsh) Probably a form of ABEL.

Agard *see* HAGGARD.

Agass, Agass, Aggas, Aggis, Aggiss, Aggus, Agus, Aguss (Eng) descendant of *Agace (Agatha)*, Greek 'good'.

Agate, Agates (Eng) Someone who lived at or near a gate, but descendant of *Agatha* is also possible.

Aggas *see* AGASS.

Agget, Aggett, Agg, Agge, Agott (Eng) Descendant of *Agnes* or *Agatha*.

Aggis, Aggiss, Aggus *see* AGASS.

Agnes, Agness (Eng) Descendant of *Agnes,* Greek 'good'.

Agus, Aguss *see* AGASS.

Ahangar *see* FABER.

Aiken *see* ADAM.

Ailby *see* WELBY.

Aimsmith, Ainsmith *see* SMITH.

Airrless, Arliss, Harliss (Eng) Nickname for an 'earless' man, presumably one whose ears were hidden by long hair.

Aish *see* ASH.

Aitchison, Aitken, Aitkens, Aitkin *see* ADAM.

Aizlewood *see* HAZELWOOD.

Akerman *see* ACKER.

Akeroyd, Akroyd *see* ACKROYD.

Alabastar, Alabaster, Albisser, Allblaster, Allyblaster, Arblaster (Fre) An arbalest was a cross-bow. The surname could refer to a maker of cross-bows or a soldier who used this weapon.

Alabone *see* ALBAN.

Alan *see* ALLEN.

Alban, Alabone, Albon, Albone, Alborn, Allbond, Allbones, Allebone, Alliban, Allibon, Allibone, Aubon (Eng) Descendant of

Alban, a Latin name of uncertain meaning. It was the name of the first British martyr.

Albert, Alberts, Albright, Allbred, Allbright, Aubert (Eng) Descendant of a man named *Albert,* a Germanic name composed of elements meaning 'noble' and 'bright.'

Albisser *see* ALABASTAR.

Albon, Albone, Alborn *see* ALBAN.

Albright *see* ALBERT.

Aldefeld *see* OLDFIELD.

Aldersmith *see* SMITH.

Alderson (Eng) Descendant of an 'older son.'

ALDERTON (Eng) Someone who came from one of the several places so-named because it was the 'settlement of *Aelfweard's* or *Ealdhere's* people,' or because it was a 'settlement amongst alder trees.'

Aldington (Eng) Someone who came from one of the several places so-named because it was *'Ealda's* settlement.'

Aled, Allart, Allet, Allett, Allott (Welsh) Resident near the River Aled.

Alefounder, Alfounder (Eng) Occupational name for a man whose task was to inspect and supervise the work of brewers.

He was also known as an ale-conner. Since he was obliged to sample each vessel in which the ale was kept he was likely to show signs of wear after a time. A poem of James I's reign says:

A nose he had that gan show,
What liquor he loved I trow;
For he had before long seven years
Been of the towne the ale-conner.

Alexander, Alshioner, Callister, Callistron, Elesender, Elshender, Elshenar, Elshener, MacAlaster, MacAlester, MacAlister, MacAllaster, MacAllister, MacCalister, Sandars, Sandeman, Sander, Sanderman, Sanders, Sandeson, Sandieson, Sandison, Saunder, Saunders, Saunderson (Eng, Scot) Descendant of *Alexander,* or someone known by a diminutive of that name. The Scottish *Mac-* forms are from the Gaelic MACALASDAIR. Elesender, Elshender etc., represent regional Scottish pronunciations. Callister and Callistron are Manx forms. Alexander is the Latin form of Greek *Alexandros* 'he who protects

4

men.' It occurs in the New Testament, but was mainly associated in medieval times with Alexander the Great, the 4th century king of Macedon.

Alfild, Alfilda, Alfyld (Eng) Descendant of *Alfille,* an Old English personal name composed of the elements 'elf-war.'

Allan, Allanson *see* ALLEN.

Allart *see* ALED.

Allblaster *see* ALABASTER.

Allbond, Allbones *see* ALBAN.

Allbred, Allbright *see* ALBERT.

Allebone *see* ALBAN.

Allen, Alan, Allan, Allanson, Allenson, Alleyne, Allin, Alline, Allinson, Allis, Allison, FitzAlan, Halison (Eng, Scot) Descendant of *Alan,* a Celtic personal name of obscure origin, though usually linked to Gaelic *ailin,* from *ail* 'rock.' However, French first-name dictionaries often explain *Alain* as belonging to the *Alans,* a nomadic tribe originating in Scythia. They were conquered successively by the Roman emperor Justinian and by the Visigoths. A Breton saint of this name made the name popular amongst many of the followers of William the Conqueror. It was then taken up in great numbers in Britain.

The Irish comedian who began life as David Tynan O'Mahoney changed his name to Dave *Allen* simply because he wanted a name that would appear high on any list of available entertainers. Various studies, in fact, have purported to show that children whose surnames begin with a letter which is near the beginning of the alphabet do better than those who have an initial letter near the end. The theory is that names which are always amongst the first to be called out attract the attention of the teachers. The phenomenon, if it is one, was dubbed 'alphabetic neurosis' by the *Chicago Tribune* July 13, 1967: 'If your last name begins with the letters between S and Z you are twice as likely to get ulcers as other people. The rates on heart attacks are three times as high and these people are supposed to be more morose and introspective. One doctor claims that the ulcers result from the strain of waiting for your name to be called. Aplhabetic neurosis can shorten your life by as much as twelve years.' Monica Dickens makes a character in

Mariana comment: 'Mary wished her name did not begin with S. It was so much worse to have to wait one's turn, with one's confidence ebbing away every minute.'

Allerton (Eng) Someone who came from one of the several places so-named because it was a 'settlement near alder trees' or 'settlement of *Aelfweard's* people.'

Allet, Allett *see* ALED.

Alleyne *see* ALLEN.

Allfield *see* OLDFIELD.

Alliban, Allibon, Allibone *see* ALBAN.

Allin, Alline, Allinson, Allis, Allison *see* ALLEN.

Allott *see* ALED.

Allright *see* ARKWRIGHT.

Allweather *see* FOULWEATHER.

Allwright *see* ARKWRIGHT.

Allyblaster *see* ALABASTAR.

Almack (Eng) This is a name which would certainly puzzle surname scholars, but Arthur Bush explains, in his *Portrait of London*: 'About the middle of the 18th century a Scotsman named William Macall married the Duchess of Hamilton's lady's maid. Being a man of ambition he came to London to make his fortune, but, finding that political reasons made Scotsmen unpopular in the capital at that time, he disguised his ancestry by inverting his name; and so *Macall* became *Almack*. He opened his rooms, known as Almack's, in 1765 in King Street.' MACALL itself also occurs as MACCALL, MACCAULL, MACKALL. The name means 'son of *Cathal*,' a Gaelic personal name meaning 'war-wielder.'

Dr Johnson mentions another Scotsman who disguised his nationality by becoming David *Mallet*. His real name was *Malloch*, a nickname for a man with bushy eyebrows.

Alshioner *see* ALEXANDER.

Altham (Eng) Descendant of someone who originally came from the Lancashire place of this name, so-called because of its 'water-meadow with swans.'

Ambler (Eng) Occupational name for an enameller. In rare instances there may be a reference to someone who ambled about.

Amery, Amory, Embery, Embrey, Embry, Emburey, Emerick,

Emerson, Emery, Emory, Hemery, Imbery, Imbrey (Eng) Descendant of someone who bore a Germanic personal name, variously spelt *Amalric, Emaurri, Haimeri* etc., composed of elements meaning 'bravery' and 'power.'

Amore *see* MOORE.

Amory *see* AMERY.

Anable *see* ANNABLE.

Ancel, Anceler, Ancelle (Fre) Occupational name of a serving-maid.

Anchor, Anchorita, Anchorite *see* ANGHARAD.

Anchorsmith *see* SMITH.

Ancoret, Ancret, Ancrete, Ancrite, Ancritt *see* ANGHARAD.

Andrew, Anders, Anderson, Andras, Andress, Andriss, Andrewes, Andrewson, Andro, Andrews, Aunderson, Bandra, Bandrew, Bandrey, Bandro, Dand, Dandie, Dandison, Dando, Dandy, Danson, Drew, Enderson, Gillanders, Kendrew, MacAndrew, Tancock, Tandy (Eng, Welsh, Scot, Irish) All forms derive ultimately from *Andrew,* a Greek name meaning 'manly, warrior-like,' or one of its pet forms. GILLANDERS refers specifically to a devotee of St Andrew. Forms such as BANDRA are from Welsh *ab Andrew*, 'son of Andrew'.

Pamela Andrews was one of the most famous young women of the 18th century, thanks to Samuel Richardson's novel *Pamela, or Virtue Rewarded*. In the book (which is unintentionally hilarious) Pamela protects her virginity at all costs from her would-be seducer, who is also her employer. Virtue is rewarded when he eventually proposes marriage. The underlying message of the novel as Henry Fielding saw it, (roughly speaking, 'don't sell your virginity too cheaply,') prompted him to write *Shamela*, followed by a novel called *Joseph Andrews* in which Joseph, supposedly Pamela's brother, has to defend himself against the advances of his female employer.

Angharad, Anchor, Anchorita, Anchorite, Ancoret, Ancret, Ancrete, Ancrite, Ancritt, Angarad, Angharat, Anghared, Ankaret, Ankret, Ankrift, Ankritt, Enkret (Welsh) Various spellings, by mainly English clerics, of the Welsh feminine name *Angharad* 'much loved one.' The surname indicates a descendant of a woman so-named.

Angliss, Angless, Anglish *see* ENGLISH.

Ankaret *see* ANGHARAD.

Ankelsmith, Ankersmith *see* SMITH.

Ankret, Ankrift, Ankritt *see* ANGHARAD.

Annable, Anable, Annaple, Anniple, Hannibal, Hanniball, Honeyball, Honeybell, Honiball, Honneybell, Honniball, Hunnable, Hunneyball, Hunneybell, Hunnibal, Hunnibell (Eng) Descendant of *Annable,* a woman's name which was originally *Amable* or *Amabel,* from Latin *amabilis,* lovable. Other forms of the name were *Annaple* (Scottish), *Annabella, Arabella, Mabel.*

Anwyl, Annwell, Annwill, Annwyl (Welsh) Descendant of *Anwyl,* which has the basic meaning 'dear one.'

Appleby, Appledore, Appledram, Appleford, Applegarth, Applegate, Applegath, Appleshaw, Applethwaite, Appleton, Appletree, Applewhite, Appleyard (Eng) Someone who originally came from one of the many places so named, in each of which there was originally an 'apple farm or orchard'. **Apple** and **Appleman** also occur, indicating a grower/seller of apples. **Ablewhite** is another form of Applethwaite. **Apley, Appley** and **Apperley** probably refer to a wood with wild apple trees.

Arable *see* ORABLE.

Arasmith *see* SMITH.

Arber *see* HARBER.

Arblaster *see* ALABASTER.

Archer (Eng) Occupational name of a bowman.

The Archers, 'an everyday story of countryfolk' centred on Dan and Doris Archer, has been broadcast since 1950, making it the longest-running BBC radio-serial.

Argue, Argument (Fre) Professor Weekley plausibly suggested in his *Surnames* that *Argument* is a form of the common French place name *Aigremont*, indicating someone who originally came from that place. *Argue* is likely to be from a similar source, eg one of the many French places which begin with an element such as *Aigre* or *Aigue*.

A firm of solicitors in Sligo, Ireland, has attracted a certain amount of publicity at various times because of the partners' names – *Argue* and *Phibbs*.

Arkwright, Artrick, Hartrick, Hartwright, Hattrick (Eng) Occupational name for a 'maker of bins, meal-chests.' Many names ending in *-wright* are of this type, eg BOATWRIGHT, CHEESEWRIGHT, PLOWRIGHT, SHIPWRIGHT, WAINWRIGHT, WHEELWRIGHT, but in some cases this ending has replaced an original *-ric, -rich,* etc., in Old English personal names. Thus *Godric* has become both GOODRICH and GOODWRIGHT; *Aethelric* is concealed in ALLWRIGHT, ALLRIGHT, OLDWRIGHT; *Bealdric* survives as BOLDWRIGHT, BOLDRIGHT.

Arlington (Eng) Someone who came from one of the several places so-named because it was '*Alfred*'s or *Aelfrith's* settlement,' or 'the earl's settlement.'

Arliss *see* AIRRLESS.

Armour, Armor, Armsmith (Eng) Occupational name of an armourer.

Armstrong (Scot, Eng) Nickname for a strong man. The variant **Strongitharm** is also found.

A character in Sir Walter Scott's *Guy Mannering* tells a stranger: 'The folks hereabout are a' Armstrongs and Elliots, and so the lairds and farmers have the names of their places that they live at – as for example, Tam o' Todshaw, Will o' the Flat, Hobbie o' Sorbietrees . . . and then the inferior sort o' people, ye'll observe, are kend by sorts o' by-names, as Glaiket Christie, and the Deuke's Davie or Tod Gabbie, or Hunter Gabbie.'

Arnold, Arnald, Arnason, Arnatt, Arnaud, Arnhold, Arnison, Arnot, Arnott, Arnould, Arnson, Arnull (Eng) Descendant of *Arnold,* a Germanic personal name meaning 'eagle rule.' The name can also refer to an ancestor who came from one of the English places named because of a nearby 'eagle hollow.' The Scottish place name Arnot derives instead from Gaelic *ornacht* 'barley.'

Arrowsmith, Arousmyth, Arowsmith, Arrasmith, Arsmith, Arusmyth (Eng) Occupational name of a maker of arrow heads.

Arrowsmith is a novel by the American writer Sinclair Lewis, about the life of an idealistic doctor, Martin Arrowsmith. Lewis was offered the Pulitzer Prize for the novel but turned it down.

Arthur *see* MACCARTNEY.

Artrick *see* ARKWRIGHT.

Arusmith *see* ARROWSMITH.

Ash, Aish, Asch, Asche, Ashall, Asham, Ashby, Ashcroft, Ashdown, Ashe, Ashenden, Asher, Ashfield, Ashford, Ashley, Ashman, Ashton, Ashurst, Ashwell, Ashwood, Ashworth, Aysh, Daish, Dash, Dashwood, Daysh, Esh, Naish, Nash, Nayshe, Rasch, Tasch, Tesche, Tesh (Eng) Dweller near an ash tree or trees, or someone who originally came from one of the many English places named for its ash trees.

Ashplant *see* ABSALOM.

Ashton, Ashurst, Ashwell, Ashwood, Ashworth *see* ASH.

Aspenlon *see* ABSOLOM.

Aspig, Aspol *see* GILLESPIE.

Aspland, Asplen, Asplin, Aspling *see* ABSOLOM.

Aston (Eng) Someone who came from one of the several places so-named because it was an 'eastern settlement.'

Atack *see* OAK.

Atberry, Atbury *see* BURY.

Atfield *see* FIELD.

Atha, Athawes *see* ABADAM.

Atherden *see* DEAN.

Atherlee *see* LEE.

Atkin, Atkins, Atkinson *see* ADAM.

A private in the British Army became generically known as a *Tommy* or *Tommy Atkins* in the early years of the 19th century, when *Thomas Atkins* was used as a specimen name on Army forms in the same way that *Richard Roe* and *John Doe* were used on legal documents. No one has ever managed to trace a particular Thomas Atkins whose name was borrowed. Kipling has a poem called 'Tommy' in which occur the well-known lines:

Oh, it's Tommy this, an' Tommy that, an' 'Tommy, go away';

But it's 'Thank you, Mr Atkins,' when the band begins to play.

Atlee, Atley *see* LEE.

Atmore *see* MOORE.

Atoc, Attack *see* OAK.

Atterbury *see* BURY.

Attick *see* OAK.

Attle, Attlee *see* LEE.

Attoc, Attock *see* OAK.

Attwood *see* WOOD.

Aubert *see* ALBERT.

Aubon *see* ALBAN.

Auld, Auldson *see* OLD.

Aunderson *see* ANDREW.

Austin, Augustine, Austen (Eng) Descendant of a man named *Austin,* the day to day form of Latin *Augustinus* or *Augustus* 'increasing.' The name was much used in the Middle Ages because of the fame of St Augustine of Hippo, and in England especially, because of St Augustine of Canterbury.

Avann *see* FENN.

Axsmith *see* SMITH.

Aykroyd *see* ACKROYD.

Aysh *see* ASH.

Bacchus, Bacher, Backhouse, Backouse, Backus *see* BAKER.

Badam, Badda, Baddam, Baddams, Badham *see* ABADAM.

Baiker *see* BAKER.

Bailey, Bailie, Baillie, Baily (Eng, Scot, Irish) Occupational name of an official, a bailiff, or an indication that the original name-bearer lived near a bail, the outer wall of a fortification. Bailey 'berry wood' in Lancashire was also the source of the surname for many families.

Bailhache, Ballachey, Ballechett, Ballhatchet, Baylehache (Eng) An English name, but formed from the Old French words *baille hache* 'give axe.' The occupational name of an executioner.

Baitson *see* BARTHOLOMEW.

Baker, Bacher, Baiker, Baxter (Eng) Occupational name of a communal baker. He might also be described as a 'worker at the bake-house,' giving rise to surnames such as **Bacchus, Backhouse, Backouse, Backus, Bakehouse.** The Old French *boulengier* 'baker' led to **Bullinger, Pillinger, Pullinger.** *See* DUCK.

Baldrey, Baldrick, Baldridge, Baudrey, Baudrick, Boldright, Boldwright, Boldry, Bowdery (Eng) Descendant of *Bealdric*, a Germanic personal name composed of elements meaning 'bold' and 'power.'

Baldwin (Eng) Descendant of a man named *Baldwin* 'brave friend.' The assumption that the first element of this name meant 'bald' led to its occasional use In Ireland for a personal name which means 'bald, tonsured.' *See* MILLIGAN.

William Hone relates in his *Every-Day Book* that 'on the twentieth of May, 1736, the body of Samuel Baldwin, Esq., was, in compliance with an injunction in his will, immersed, *sans cere-monie*, in the sea at Lymington, Hants. His motive for this extraordinary mode of interment was to prevent his wife from "dancing over his grave," which this modern Xanthippe had frequently threatened to do, in case she survived him.'

Balismith, Balysmyth *see* SMITH.

Ball, Bald, Balls (Eng) Nickname for a bald man, or indicating an ancestor who lived near a boundary mound.

John Field, in *English Field Names*, cites many instances of *The Ball* as a field name. Such names often give clues to surname origins, preserving as they do earlier senses of words. Field names such as Eighteenpennyworth, Fivepenny, Halfpence, Twenty shilling field, Twopenneworth, indicating the value of the land, may also explain some puzzling 'money' surnames – *see* PENNY.

Ballachey, Ballechett, Ballhatchet *see* BAILHACHE.

Ballaster, Ballester, Ballister, Balster, Bolister (Eng) Occupational name for a crossbow-maker or a soldier armed with one. There is a connection with the word *ballistics*.

Ballock *see* BULLOCK.

Balsillie (Scot) Descendant of someone who originally came from the Scottish village of this name, near Leslie In Fife. It is probably from Gaelic *baile-seilich* 'willow-tree farm.'

Balster *see* BALLASTER.

Bandra, Bandrew, Bandrey, Bandro *see* ANDREW.

Banks, Banker, Bankes (Eng) Descendant of someone who lived near a river bank or on sloping ground. In an Irish context Banks can be the Anglicized form of the Gaelic *Bruachán* 'corpulent,' also found as *O'Brogan*.

Bannister, Banister, Bannester (Eng) Occupational name of a basket weaver.

Barber, Barbour (Eng) Occupational name of a barber, who spent as much time trimming beards as cutting hair. He was also the local doctor and dentist, hence the description:

> His pole with pewter basons hung,
> Black, rotten teeth in order strung,
> Rang'd cups that in the window stood,
> Lined with red rags to look like blood,
> Did well his threefold trade explain,
> Who shaved, drew teeth, and breathed a vein.

Barby *see* BARROW.

Bardon *see* BARNES.

Barebone (Eng) The Little Parliament in Cromwell's time was headed by Praise-God Barebone, His name is variously recorded as **Barbon, Barborne,** which suggests that his ancestors came from Barbourne, in Worcestershire, a place named for its 'beaver stream.'

Barebone's given name *Praise-God* was a typical Puritan slogan name of the 17th century. Two of Praise-God's brothers had the names *Jesus-Christ-came-into-the-world-to save* Barebone and *If-Christ-had-not-died-for-thee-thou-hadst-been-damned* Barebone. The latter was known to most of his contemporaries as *Damned* Barebone, partly because of his immoral behaviour. A special study of such given names was made by Charles Bardsley and published as *Curiosities of Puritan Nomenclature*.

Barfoot *see* PUDDY.

Barham (Eng) Descendant of someone who originally came from one of the places so-named because it was a 'hill homestead.' The Kentish place of this name was instead '*Biora's* homestead.'

Barker (Eng) Occupational name for a tanner, who used tree bark when converting hides into leather. But many Barkers have an ancestor who was a shepherd, the name having absorbed Bircher.

Barnard *see* BERNARD.

Barnes, Barne, Barns (Eng) Descendant of someone who lived near or worked in barns, which were originally places for storing barley. Barnes is also a place in Surrey, named for its 'barns,' where some bearers of the name may originally have lived. The name can also mean descendant of *Barne*, a personal name representing Old English *beorn* 'young aristocrat' or Old Norse *bjorn* 'bear.' In an Irish context Barnes is likely to be an Anglicized form of the Gaelic personal names *Bearán* 'spear,' (found also as **Barrane, Barrington, Barron, O'Barran, O'Barrane**) or *Bardán* 'bard,' (found also as **Bardon**).

Barnet, Barnett (Eng) Descendant of a man named *Bernard,* or someone who came from a place named Barnet. The place name indicated a place where the vegetation had been 'burned' away.

Baron, Barron (Eng, Scot) A nickname for someone who acted in a haughty way; in Scotland a title used for a land-owner.

Barr, Barrs (Eng, Scot, Welsh, French) Descendant of someone who lived by a town or castle gate. He could instead have come from Barr in Ayrshire or Renfrewshire, or from Great Barr in Staffordshire, or from places in France such as Barre-en-Ouche, Barre-de-Semilly. Other possible explanations of this name are 'maker or seller of bars or stakes,' and nickname for a tall, thin man.

Barrane *see* BARNES.

Barras, Barrasford *see* BARROW.

Barrell (Eng) Occupational name of a cooper, maker of barrels or casks, or a nickname for someone who was barrel-shaped. Occasionally a form of **Barwell**, a place in Leicestershire, and indicating someone who originally came from there.

Barrington (Eng) Someone who came from one of the several places so-named because it was *'Bara's* or *Beorn's* settlement.' For the meaning in Ireland *see* BARNES.

Barron *see* BARNES and BARON.

Barrow, Barby, Barras, Barrasford, Barrowby, Barrowden, Barrowford, Barrows, Barugh, Barway, Barwise, Berrow (Eng) Descendant of someone who originally came from one of the many places named for its 'barrow,' a word meaning either a grove of trees or a long low burial mound.

Barrs *see* BARR.

Barsham *see* BASHAM.

Bartholomew, Baitson, Barson, Bart, Bartie, Bartle, Bartleet, Bartlet, Bartleman, Bartlett, Barty, Bason, Bate, Bates, Bateson, Batt, Beatson (Eng) Descendant of a man called *Bartholomew,* an Aramaic name which occurs in the Old Testament. It means 'son of *Tolmai,*' itself another biblical name occurring as *Talmai*.

Film buffs associate the name Bates with *Psycho*, the Hitchcock film based on a novel by Robert Bloch. Anthony Perkins played the part of Norman Bates, killer of a young woman in a much-imitated shower scene.

Barton (Eng) Someone who came from one of the several places so-named because it was a 'settlement where barley was grown.'

The name seems to have appealed to writers: George Eliot

writes about Amos Barton in *Scenes of Clerical Life* and the heroine of Elizabeth Gaskell's *Mary Barton* bears that name. For several years (1946-1951) the adventures of Dick Barton, 'Special Agent,' captivated the British radio audience.

Bartrick, Brightrich (Eng) Descendant of *Beorhtric*, an Old English personal name composed of elements meaning 'bright-ruler.'

Barty *see* BARTHOLOMEW.

Barugh, Barway, Barwise *see* BARROW.

Barwell *see* BARRELL.

Basham, Barsham, Bassham (Eng) Descendant of someone who originally came from one of the places so-named because it was '*Bar's* homestead,' *Bar* being a personal name meaning 'wild boar.'

A Mr Basham of Guernsey who was an osteopath once attracted a certain amount of media attention.

Bason *see* BARTHOLOMEW.

Bass, Bassett *see* FISH.

Bassham *see* BASHAM.

Bastard (Eng) Descendant of an illegitimate child. For obvious reasons bearers of this name tend to change it in modern times. The word itself is avoided because it has become a term of abuse.

Dickens was still able to have Oliver Twist referred to as 'a bastard child,' though he went on to say that the word was a reproach to whoever used the word rather than the person at whom it was aimed.

R.D. Blackmore comments in *Lorna Doone* that 'others were of high family, as any need be, in Devon – Carews and Bouchiers, and Bastards.'

Bate, Bates, Bateson *see* BARTHOLOMEW.

Batha, Bathaw, Bather, Batho, Battams *see* ABADAM.

Batt *see* BARTHOLOMEW.

Battersby (Eng) Someone who came from a place so-named because it was '*Bothvarr's* village.' The *-by* in such names is common in places where Scandinavian invaders settled. It represents an Old Norse *byr* 'village, homestead.' Other typical English place names that became surnames are BOOTHBY, BURNABY, BUSBY, CATESBY, CONINGSBY, DANBY, DERBY, DIGBY, DIMBLEBY,

FRISBY, GOADBY, HORNBY, KEARBY, KIRBY, RIGBY, ROKEBY, SAXBY, SELBY, SLINGSBY, SOWERBY, SWINDERBY, THIRLBY, WELBY, WHITBY, WILLOUGHBY. Occasionally, however, surnames ending in -*by* have a different origin. See, for example, LIBBY, TUBBY.

Baudrey, Baudrick *see* BALDREY.

Bavon *see* EVAN.

Baxter *see* BAKER.

Baylehache *see* BAILHACHE.

Beaconsfield *see* STANSFIELD.

Beadle, Beaddall, Beadel, Beadell, Beadles, Beddall, Beddell, Bedell, Bedle, Beedle, Biddell, Biddle, Biddles, Buddell, Buddle, Buddles (Eng) These are all linked to a 'beadle,' who would have been a junior law official during the surname-formation period. One of his jobs was to make public announcements.

Mr Bumble, the beadle in Dickens's *Oliver Twist*, also takes it upon himself to name the foundlings. 'We name our foundlin's in alphabetical order. The last was a S – Swubble: I named him. This was a T – Twist: I named *him*. The next one as comes will be Unwin, and the next Vilkins. I have got the names ready made to the end of the alphabet, and all the way through it again, when we come to Z.' This explanation evokes an admiring 'Why, you're quite a literary character, sir' from Mrs Mann.

Beak, Beake (Eng) Nickname for a man with a big nose.

Beaker, Beakerman, Beakers, Beekerman (Eng) Occupational name for a potter who made drinking vessels.

Bean, Beane, Beans, MacBain, MacBayne, MacBean, MacVain (Eng, Scot) As an English name, Bean could indicate someone who grew and sold beans, but there was a Middle English word *bene* which meant 'pleasant, kindly' which could have led to Bean as a complimentary nickname. As a Scottish name Bean, MACBAIN etc. refer to a descendant of *Beathan* 'life', a Gaelic personal name. *See* GAVIN.

Beard, Beart *see* WHITBREAD.

Beaton, Beeton (Eng) Someone who originally came from *Béthune* in Normandy.

Beatson *see* BARTHOLOMEW.

Beauclerk *see* CLARK.

Beaulieu, Beaulieux, Bewley (Fre) Someone who came from one of the many French places so-named because it was considered to be a 'lovely place.'

Bewley indicates the pronunciation that became normal in England, a fact commented on by J.C. Keyte in *Minsan*: 'Vernon Beaulieu – and you must pronounce it "Bewley" if you please, or have a half-hour recitation on philology.'

Beauman *see* BOWMAN.

Beausire *see* BELCHER.

Beavan, Beavand, Beaven, Beavin *see* EVAN.

Beavis, Beaves, Beevis, Beves, Bevis, Beviss, Bovis (Eng) A nickname for a 'handsome son.' French *beau fils* now means 'son-in-law,' but this meaning came too late to account for the surname. The latter could, however, indicate someone who originally came from *Beauvais* or *Beauvois*. There are several places with such names in northern France.

Beavon *see* EVAN.

Bedard *see* EDWARDS.

Beddall *see* BEADLE.

Beddard *see* EDWARDS.

Beddell, Bedell, Bedle, Beedle *see* BEADLE.

Bedward, Bedwart *see* EDWARDS.

Bedworth (Eng) Someone who originally came from the place of this name in Warwickshire, so-called because it was '*Beda's* homestead.'

The name is treated rather harshly in J.I.M. Stuart's novel *A Memorial Service*, where a conversation runs: 'Here's a damned impertinent letter from God knows who – calls himself Piddlebed, or some such.' 'Bedworth,' I said. 'Bedworth, Bedpan – I don't give a fart for the fellow's name.'

Beeton *see* BEATON.

Beevis *see* BEAVIS.

Belcher, Belshaw, Belsher, Bewcher, Bewshaw, Bewshea, Bewsher, Bowsher (Eng) This seems to have become confused with a common medieval term of address, roughly equivalent to 'fair sir,' found as BEAUSIRE, BOWSER, BELSIRE, though it began independently as Norman French *bel chere* 'fair face.' No one has ever suggested that Belcher might occasionally have something to do with eructation, though medieval nicknames were not concerned with politeness. This is presumably because the name was usually pronounced *Belsher*. Also, the Old English verb *bealcian* 'to belch' is not recorded as a noun until the 16th century. However, the voidance of wind from the lower region is certainly commented on in English surnames such as PETARD, PETTER, PETHARD and the French names PETAIN, PETON, PETOT. It would be surprising if someone's habit of belching frequently was not commented on by his medieval contemporaries.

Bell, Beller, Bellman (Eng, Scot) *Bell* is a common name because it is derived from many sources. John *atte Bell,* who is mentioned in a medieval document, lived near a public bell or at the sign of the bell. John *le Bel* would have been a 'handsome' fellow, but other Bells were descended from an *Isobel,* or were bell-ringers, or made bells.

Bellingham (Eng) Descendant of someone who originally came from one of the places so-named because it was '*Beora's* homestead' or 'homestead on or near a bell-shaped hill.'

Bellis, Bellison *see* ELLIS.

Bellman *see* BELL.

Bellsmith *see* SMITH.

Bellyse *see* ELLIS.

Belshaw, Belsher, Belsire *see* BELCHER.

Belsire *see* BELCHER.

Bennett, Bendick, Benedict, Bennedick, Bennet, Bennet, Bennetts (Eng, Scot) Descendant of a man named *Benedict*. This was the name of several saints, the most influential being the 5th century monk who founded the Benedictine Order. Professor Reaney remarks that the Latin name *Benedictus* 'blessed' was invariably used in the Middle Ages in its colloqial French form *Beneit,* which led directly to Bennett. He wonders therefore whether surnames such as Benedict and Benedick, which clearly derive directly from the Latin word, were not nicknames for someone whose favourite saying was '*Benedicte!*' 'bless you!' Speakers in the Middle Ages used a wide variety of oaths, such as 'God wot!' 'by my troth!' 'for God's sake!' Several of these 'oath names' became English surnames. Bennett is the English form of this name, Bennet is more usual in Scotland.

Benson, Bennison, Bennsson (Eng) Descendant of a man named *Benedict,* see BENNETT. However, Benson is also an Oxfordshire place name '*Banesa's* settlement' from which the ancestors of some families of this name may have come.

Bentham (Eng) Descendant of someone who originally came from one of the places so-named because it was a 'homestead on bent (reedy) grass.'

Bernard, Barnard (Eng) Descendant of a man named *Bernard.* This is a Norman form of a given name that existed as *Beornheard* in Old English. The first element means 'bear,' the second is 'hardy, brave.'

The *St Bernard* dog commemorates Saint Bernard of Menthon (923-1008), who founded hospices on what are now known as the Great St Bernard Pass and Little St Bernard Pass in the Alps. The dogs were kept at the hospices to help rescue lost travellers.

Berriman *see* BURY.

Berrow *see* BARROW.

Berry, Berryman *see* BURY.

Berry, as those who bear the surname well know, is one of those names which attracts punning comments. The tradesman named Berry who sent a bill to a Mr Mathews received the following message:

'You have sent in your *bill,* Berry, before it is *due,* Berry; your father, the *elder*, Berry, would not have been such a *goose,* Berry; but you need not look so *black*, Berry, for I don't care a *straw*, Berry.'

Thomas Tryon writes, in his novel *Lady*: 'Miss Berry's first name was Mary, but she was too nice for me to make use of the obvious euphony of her names. Some of the guys from the feed store would walk by hollering "Mary Berry's got beriberi," or "Mary Berry loves Harry Carey," but Miss Berry, whose hearing might have been better, would only nod and smile.'

Bevan, Bevans, Bevens, Bevin *see* Evan.

Beves, Bevis, Beviss *see* BEAVIS.

Bewcher *see* BELCHER.

Bewes (Eng) Someone who came from the Norman town Bayeux. A Welsh family would instead look back to an ancestor who was a *Hugh; ab Hugh* being 'son of Hugh.'

In *Tess of the D'Urbervilles*, a novel in which Thomas Hardy makes much of varying forms of surnames, the author mentions that 'the *Debbyhouses*, who now are carters, were once the *De Bayeux* family.' He also has a character state that: 'our little Retty *Priddle* here, you know, is one of the *Paridelles* – the old family that used to own lots of the lands for miles down this valley.' Retty, however, is a dairy-maid. The *Durbeyfield – D'Urberville* variation is of considerable importance to the story. These Hardy names are not easy to find in directories and may have been his inventions.

Bewley *see* BEAULIEU.

Bewshaw, Bewshea, Bewsher *see* BELCHER.

Bicker *see* BIGGER.

Biddell, Biddle, Biddles *see* BEADLE.

Bigg (Eng) Nickname for a big, strong person.

Bigger (Eng) Possibly a variant of BICKER, an occupational name for a bee-keeper.

Mrs H. Bigger of Wantage, Berks, wrote to a newspaper to say that she was not amused when she was pregnant to hear the oft-repeated remark: 'I see you're getting a little bigger.'

Bigod, Bigot *see* PARDOE.

Bill, Billmaker (Eng) Occupational name of a sword-maker or one who made bill hooks, used for pruning.

Billington (Eng) From one of the places bearing this name, so called originally because it was a 'settlement on a sword-shaped hill.'

Billsmith *see* SMITH.

Binder (Ger) Occupational name of a barrel maker.

Bindless, Bindloes, Bindloss *see* CATCHLOVE.

Bingham (Eng) Descendant of someone who originally came from the place in Nottinghamshire, so-named because it was '*Binna's* homestead.'

Bircher (Eng) An occupational name, but not of an educationist, as Weekley remarks in his *Surnames*, a joke which might well be lost on modern children. The origin is French *berger*, 'shepherd'.

Bird, Bride, Burd, Byrd (Eng) Occupational name of a bird-catcher, especially finches. Since *burde* in Middle English referred to a young girl, the surname may in some instances have begun as a nickname for someone thought to have girlish qualities. *See* DUCK.

Birdseye (Eng) At first glance this name appears to be a variant of BIRDSEY, referring to someone who lived on a 'birds' island.' However, no such English place name appears to exist, and the surname is in any case found in America rather than Britain. The name is likely to be a translation of a German locative name: the *Langenscheidt German-English Dictionary,* for instance, glosses *Vogelaugenholz* as 'bird's eye wood.' Professor Weekley, however, in *Surnames*, thought that 'the compounds of the physical eye are numerous and have not hitherto been recognized as such.' He cited BLACKIE, a nickname for someone with black eyes, and the analagous BRIGHTEY, BROWNIE, DOVEY, GOLDIE, GOLDNEY, GOOSEY, HAWKEY, LITTLEY, SHEEPY, SILVERY, SMALLEY, WHITEY, WILDEY, where the second element in each case is 'eye.' Birdseye, for Weekley, fitted easily into this group.

A man named *Victory* Birdseye was a New York senator in 1827.

Clarence Birdseye (1886-1956) founded the Birdseye Seafoods company in 1923. He used to relate to anyone who would listen that one of his ancestors had been a page boy to a queen and used to go hunting with her. One day a hawk swooped towards the queen, whereupon the page boy shot an arrow into its eye. The queen immediately named him *Birdseye* and the family had been 'stuck with it' ever since.

Birtwistle (Eng) Descendant of someone who originally came from a place so-named because of 'birds gathering at the junction of a stream.'

Bishop (Eng) Occupational name of a bishop's servant, or nickname for someone of 'ecclesiastical appearance,' as Bardsley expresses it. He goes on to say: 'Nevertheless, most of our Bishops owe their title to the custom of electing a boy-bishop on St Nicholas' Day.'

The Rev. Thomas Bishop of Johannesburg has said that ecclesiastical names run in his family. 'My great-grandfather was a Mr

Church. He married a Miss *Dean* and their daughter married a Mr *Bishop*.'

Black, Blacke, Blackman, Blake, Blakeman (Eng) A nickname based on the Old English word *blac*, which in modern English has become both 'black' and 'bleach.' The Old English word perhaps had the sense 'absence of colour.' The nickname could therefore have been applied to a person of dark complexion or black hair, but it could equally well have been given to someone who was very pale.

The detective Sexton Blake is the hero of countless stories for boys, written by nearly 200 different authors. He has been described as 'the poor man's Sherlock Holmes,' whom he physically resembles. He also lives in London's Baker Street.

Blackbeard, Blackbird (Eng) Nickname for a man with a black beard. *See* WHITBREAD.

Blackburn, Blackford, Blackpool, Blackwall, Blackwater, Blackwell, Blacon (Eng) Descendant of someonewho originally came from any of the places so-named, each one close to a 'dark stream, pool or spring'. **Blakemere** is a similar name.

Blacke *see* BLACK.

Blackett (Eng) Nickname for a man with a black head of hair.

Blackford *see* BLACKBURN.

Blackie *see* BIRDSEYE.

Blackman *see* BLACK.

Blackpool *see* BLACKBURN.

Blacksmith (Eng) Occupational name of a blacksmith.

Blackwall, Blackwater, Blackwell, Blacon *see* BLACKBURN.

Bladesmith, Blades, Bladsmith (Eng) Occupational name of a cutler.

Blair (Scot, Irish) Descendant of someone who originally came from one of the places so-named. Gaelic *blár* means '(battle)field.'

Blake, Blakeman *see* BLACK.

Blanton This appears to be an English place name, but no trace of the place concerned can be found. The surname nevertheless appears amongst the 2000 most frequent names in the USA.

Blessington *see* HAMILTON.

Bligh, Bly, Blye, Blythe (Eng) Nickname for a happy person, but see BLIGHT.

Blight (Eng) G. Pawley White, in his *Handbook of Cornish Surnames*, says that this is a nickname from Cornish *blyth* 'wolf.' It can have the alternative forms BLIGH and BLYTH.

In *Our Mutual Friend* Dickens comments: 'The office door was opened by the dismal boy, whose appropriate name was Blight.'

Block, Blocker, Blogg, Bloggs (Eng) Occupational name of a maker of blocks, eg for book-binding, shoe-making, hat-making. The wooden blockhead of the hat-maker led to use of that term for a stupid person, and this may be the meaning of the surname Block.

Joe Bloggs, as the name of the average ordinary man, is also Joe *Blow* in American sources, or Joe *Do(a)kes*. In one of her blues numbers Billie Holiday sings: 'But just let me walk out of the club one night with a young white boy of my age, whether it was John Roosevelt, the President's son, or Joe Blow.' This name was originally applied to a horn-blowing musician, then extended to any man. Joe *Soap* is similarly a name applied to a 'dumb' person, a mug, or any very ordinary person. In 1969 the *Guardian* said that: 'Socialists have become over-eager to find out what Joe Soap is doing in order to tell him not to do it.'

Dickens's Blockitt may belong here. In *Dombey and Son* occurs: 'Mrs – ?' 'Blockitt, Sir?' suggested the nurse, a simpering piece of faded gentility, who did not presume to state her name as a fact, but merely offered it as a mild suggestion.'

Bloom, Blomer, Bloomer, Blumer (Eng) Occupational name of an ironworker, who ran the liquid metal into moulds.

James Joyce changed the signification of Bloom for countless readers of his *Ulysses* by making it the name of his central character. The novel deals with the events of one day in 1924, June 16th, a date remembered annually by Joyce fans as 'Bloomsday.' During her long stream-of-conscienceness monologue, Molly Bloom comments 'bloomers. I suppose they're called after him I never thought that would be my name Bloom when I used to write it in print to see how it looked on a visiting card or practising for the butcher and oblige M Bloom you're looking blooming Josie used to say after I married him well it's better than Breen or Briggs . . . ' 'Bloomers' are in fact normally said to have been named for Mrs Amelia Bloomer, a writer on women's suffrage and unjust marriage laws.

Eric Partridge tells us, in his *Name Into Word*, 'that female knicker-bockers owed nothing to Mrs Amelia Bloomer except the fact that it was she who, *circa* 1850, started the earlier fashion from which the dress designers developed the latter.' Mrs Bloomer herself, it seems, habitually wore a short skirt and long loose trousers, gathered at the ankles.

Blower, Bloor, Bloore, Blow, Blowers, Blowes, Blows (Eng) Occupational name of a man who operated bellows, or in some cases, a HORNBLOWER.

Blumer *see* BLOOM.

Bly, Blye, Blythe *see* BLIGH.

Boal, Boaler, Boales *see* BOWLER.

Boatwright, Boatright, Botwright (Eng) Occupational name for a maker of boats.

Bockett *see* BUCKET.

Bodin (Swedish) The Swedish form of BOOTH.

E.V. Cunningham makes a character in *Lydia* say: 'Bodin – it doesn't mean a blessed thing, does it? As a matter of fact, it's another of those small appellative lies that we indulge in so frequently in America. My husband was half-Jewish. His father's name was Bodinski, and the old man changed it.'

Boileau *see* DRINKWATER.

Bold (Eng) Nickname for a courageous man, or from residence in a place called Bold. The place-name derives from an Old English word *bold* 'dwelling, building.'

Boldright, Boldwright, Boldry, Bowdery *see* BALDREY.

Bole, Boler *see* BOWLER.

Bolister (Eng) Probably a form of BALLASTER.

Boll, Boller, Bolles, Bollman *see* BOWLER.

Bolton (Eng) Someone who came from one of the several places so-named because it was a 'settlement with houses.'

Boltsmith (Eng) Occupational name of a man who made crossbow bolts.

Boman *see* BOWMAN.

Bone, Bonn, Boon, Boone, Bown, Bowne, Bunn (Eng) A nick-name for a 'good' person, from French *bon*. Also forms of a Norman name which is sometimes spelt BOHUN, though the pronunciation remains the same. This form rightly hints at a connection with the French place name *Bohon*, indicating an ancestor who came from there.

G.B.Shaw has a class-conscious waiter in *You Never Can Tell* who comments: 'My own name is Boon, sir. By rights I should spell it with the aitch like you, sir, but I think it best not to take that liberty, sir. There is Norman blood in it, sir; and Norman blood is not a recommendation to a waiter.'

Bone also attracts comment in John Wain's *A Travelling Woman*: 'He tucked her name away in his memory: Barbara Bone. He surmised that her maiden name had been something more elegant than Bone.'

Booth, Boothe, Boothman (Eng) Someone who lived in a small hut, or bothy. He would probably have been a shepherd.

While this explanation applies to most bearers of these names, one young lady called Booth was given that name because she was found abandoned in a telephone booth.

Boothby (Eng) Someone who came from a place so-named because it was a 'settlement with huts.'

Boothe, Boothman *see* BOOTH.

Borkett *see* BUCKET.

Bosanquet, Bosanketh (Cornish) *Bos-* in such names (usually transferred Cornish place names) means 'dwelling.' The second element of Bosanquet is probably the personal name *Angawd*. Similar Cornish names include **Boscawen, Bosence, Bosustow, Bosisto, Boswarva.**

Bossom, Bosence, Bosson, Bossons (Eng) Occupational names, forms of bo'sun or boatswain. A Sussex family named Bossom might look instead to an ancestor who came from *Bosham* 'homestead of *Bosa's* people.'

When a Mr Bossom became an MP, Neville Chamberlain is said to have remarked: 'An odd name! Neither one thing nor the other!'

Boswall, Boswell (Scot) Descendant of someone who came from Beuzeville, Normandy.

Botler, Bottel, Bottle *see* BUTLER.

Botwright *see* **Boatwright.**

Bottom, Botham, Bottams, Bottoms (Eng) Someone who lived in a broad valley. See also LONGBOTHAM.

Boucher *see* BUTCHER.

Boudet, Boudin, Boudon, Boudot, Boudeau *see* BUTTON.

Boule, Boules, Bouller *see* BOWLER.

Bouquet, Bouquain, Bouquin, Bouquot, Bouquerel *see* BUCKET.

Bourke *see* BURKE.

Boutcher *see* BUTCHER.

Boutflour, Boughtflower, Bulteflour (Eng) A miller, literally a man whose job was to 'sift flour.'

Bouton *see* BUTTON.

Bovis *see* BEAVIS.

Bowen, Bowing, Bowins *see* OWEN.

Bowler, Boal, Boaler, Boales, Bole, Boler, Boll, Boller, Bolles, Bollman, Boule, Boules, Bouller, Bowle, Bowles, Bowlman (Eng) Occupational name of a maker/seller of bowls (used for drinking). Possibly also a nickname for someone who drank a great deal from bowls.

Bowman, Boman, Beauman (Eng) Occupational name of an archer.

Bown, Bowne *see* BONE.

Bowser, Bowsher *see* BELCHER.

Bowsmith, Bowersmith, Bowyer, Boyersmith (Eng) Occupational name of a maker/seller of bows.

Boyd, Boyde (Scot, Irish) Traditionally explained as a reference to the island of *Bute*, or derived from a Gaelic word for someone with yellowy hair, but no one can be sure of its meaning.

Boyersmith *see* BOWSMITH.

Boys (Fre) Descendant of someone who was a dweller in a wood.

Brace, Brass (Eng) Occupational name of a maker of armour, specifically that which protected the brace, the two upper arms. In some instances the name refers instead to a maker of breeches. A worker in brass was more likely to become a BRASHER, BRASIER or BRAZIER.

Dickens refers in *The Old Curiosity Shop* to 'the legal gentleman, whose melodious name was Brass.' He goes on to joke: 'The dwarf glanced sarcastically at his brazen friend.'

Bracegirdle (Eng) Occupational name of a belt-maker, which girdled a man's breeches.

Bracer, Braisher, Brasher, Brasseur (Eng) Occupational name of a brewer, from French *brasseur*. But Brasher can also mean 'brass-worker.'

Bradley (Eng, Scot) Descendant of someone who came from any one of the many places so-named because of a 'broad clearing, or wood.' Similar place-names which became surnames, where Brad – in each case means 'broad,' include Bradbrook, Bradbury, 'fort', Braddock, 'oak', Braddon, 'hill', Bradfield, Bradford, Bradshaw, 'thicket', Bradwell, 'stream'.

Bradman (Eng) Nickname for a 'broad man.'

Bradshaw, Bradwell *see* BRADLEY.

Bragg (Eng) Nickname for a lively, cheerful person. *See* BRAXTON.

Brampton (Eng) Someone who came from one of the several places so-named because it was a 'settlement where broom grew.'

Brasher, Brasseur *see* BRACER.

Brasier, Brazier *see* BRACE.

Brasnett, Brassett (Eng) Nickname for someone with a 'brazen head,' a head as hard as brass.

Brass *see* BRACE.

Braxton (Eng) Descendant of someone who originally came from a place of this name, which was '*Bracc's* enclosure.'

Harper Lee, in *To Kill a Mockingbird*, mentions 'Mr Underwood, a profane little man, whose father in a fey fit of humour christened Braxton Bragg, a name Mr Underwood had done his best to live down. Atticus said naming people after Confederate generals made slow steady drinkers.'

Bream *see* FISH.

Brenton (Eng) Someone who came from one of the place so-named because it was '*Bryni's* settlement.'

Breton, Bret, Brett, Bretton, Brettoner, Britain, Britner, Britnor, Briton, Britt, Brittain, Brittan, Brittian, Brittin, Brittney, Britton, Brittoner, Britts, Bruttner, Brutton (Eng) Descendant of a Breton, a man from *Brittany*, but *Breton* was also a medieval term of abuse for a braggart.

Brewer, Brewers, Brewster, Broster, Brouwer, Brower, Bruster (Eng) A male or female brewer.

This explanation of his family name did not satisfy Dr Brewer, editor of a *Dictionary of Phrase and Fable*. In the 13th edition of that book he claimed that 'very few ancient names are the names of trades.' He went on to insist that Brewer, 'which exists in France as Bruhiäre and Brugäre, is not derived from the Saxon *briwan* (to brew), but the French *bruyäre* (heath), and is about tantamount to the German Plantaganet (broom plant).' Perhaps one Brewer in a million may trace his name back to a Bruyäre or Labruyäre, but brewing was a very common occupation in the Middle Ages, when beer was probably drunk more often than water.

Brian, Briant, Brien, Bryan, Bryant, MacBrien, O'Brian, O'Brien, O'Bryan (Irish, Eng) Descendant of *Brian,* a Celtic personal name of disputed meaning, borne especially by *Brian Boru,* king of Ireland in the early 11th century. The name may mean 'hill' (with the metaphorical meaning 'eminence'), but 'high, noble' and 'of many qualities' have been suggested by writers on surnames with a knowledge of Gaelic. The final -t in some forms of this name is described by linguists as 'excrescent.' As the name is said the extra sound forms itself of its own accord, as it were.

Brice *see* PRICE.

Brickman (Eng) The official in charge of a toll-bridge.

Bride *see* BIRD.

Bridge, Bridgeman, Bridgen, Bridgens, Bridger, Bridges, Bridgman, Brigg, Briggs, Brigman, Bruggen, Brugger, Brydges, Dealbridge, Delbridge, Dellbridge (Eng) Dweller near a bridge, of collector of bridge tolls. In some instances the reference may be to a Flemish trader from Bruges, Belgium.

Bridson *see* KILBRIDE.

Brien *see* BRIAN.

Brigetson *see* KILBRIDE.

Brigg, Briggs *see* BRIDGE.

Brigham (Eng) Descendant of someone who originally came from one of the places so-named because it was a 'homestead near a bridge.'

Bright, Brightman (Eng) Nickname applied to someone of great beauty.

There are hundreds of limericks which mention particular surnames. A separate book would be needed to do justice to them. One
of the better-known examples is:

> There was a young lady named Bright.
>
> Who could travel much faster than light.
>
> She started one day.
>
> In the relative way,
>
> And came back the previous night.

Brightey *see* BIRDSEYE.

Brightman *see* BRIGHT.

Brightrich *see* BARTRICK.

Brigman *see* BRIDGE.

Brill *see* FISH.

Brisbane, Brisbourne (Eng) A bone-breaker. Reaney mentions a
similar surname CRAKEBONE and suggests that the reference is to
the sheriff's officer who broke the legs of condemned criminals.

**Britain, Britner, Britnor, Briton, Britt, Brittain, Brittan,
Brittian, Brittin, Brittney, Britton, Brittoner, Britts** *see* BRETON.

Broadfoot *see* PUDDY.

Broadhead (Eng) A descriptive nickname.

Brockhouse, Brockis, Brockman, Brockway, Broke, Brokus *see*
BROOK.

Bronson *see* BROWN.

Brontë (Irish) The grandparents of the Brontë sisters lived in
County Down and were known as BRUNTY, a form of PRUNTY or
PRONTY, from a Gaelic name meaning 'bestower, a generous
person.' The girls' father then changed Brunty to Brontë, the Greek
word for 'thunder.'

In her *Life of Charlotte Brontë* Mrs Gaskell remarks that
'about this time, to her more familiar correspondents, she occasionally calls herself Charles Thunder, making a kind of pseudo-
nym for herself out of her Christian name, and the meaning of her
Greek surname.'

**Brook, Brockhouse, Brockis, Brockman, Brockway, Broke,
Brokus, Brookbank, Brookbanks, Brooke, Brooker, Brookes,
Brookfield, Brookhouse, Brooking, Brookings, Brookman,
Brookmire, Brooks, Brooksbank, Brooksby, Brookshank,**

Brookshaw, Bruck, Brucker, Bruckshaw (Eng) Descendant of someone who lived near a brook or someone who originally came from any of the places named for its brook.

Lower also reports that a child found abandoned by the side of a brook, wrapped in a napkin, was duly named 'Napkin Brooker' by the parish authorities.

Roger Brook is the British secret agent hero of a series of novels by Dennis Wheatley. Dorothea Brooke is the rather more complex heroine of George Eliot's *Middlemarch*, which has been described as the best novel written in English.

Broster *see* BREWER.

Brougham (Eng) Descendant of someone who originally came from a place in Cumbria so-named because it was a 'homestead near a fortress.'

Broughton (Eng) Someone who came from one of the several places so-named because it was a 'settlement near a brook, or by a narrow hill, or by a fortified manor.'

Broun, Broune *see* BROWN.

Brouwer, Brower *see* BREWER.

Brown, Bronson, Broun, Broune, Browne, Brownson, Brunson (Eng) A reference to a person's brown hair or skin.

Thomas Hughes waxes lyrical in *Tom Brown's Schooldays* about the part that families named Brown have played in British history. He says that they may be 'quiet, dogged an homespun' but they have done as much for their country as the *'Talbots, Stanleys, St Maurs, and such like folk.'*

Another fictional schoolboy is William Brown, hero of many comic adventures written by Richmal Crompton.

Charlie Brown features with his dog Snoopy, not to mention his friends Linus and Lucy, in the strip-cartoon series *Peanuts*, by Charles M. Schulz.

Chesterton's Father Brown is a priestly detective in many short stories, who would probably have appreciated the epitaph for a dentist named John Brown which runs:

Stranger! Approach this spot with gravity!.

John Brown is filling his last cavity.

Brownie *see* BIRDSEYE.

Brownjohn (Eng) The name derives from a man named John who had brown hair.

Kingsley Amis comments in *Ending Up*: 'Mr Brownjohn's a good man.' 'Unbelievable name, that. I do very much wonder how he came by it – I should say, how his ancestor came by it.'

Brownnutt, Brownhut, Brownutt (Eng) A descriptive nickname, found also as NUTBROWN.

Brownsmith (Eng) Occupational name of a coppersmith.

Brownutt *see* BROWNNUTT.

Bruck, Brucker, Bruckshaw *see* BROOK.

Brugäre, Bruhiäre *see* BREWER.

Bruggen, Brugger *see* BRIDGE.

Brunson *see* BROWN.

Brunty *see* BRONTË.

Bruster *see* BREWER.

Bruttner, Brutton *see* BRETON.

Bryan, Bryant *see* BRIAN.

Bryce *see* PRICE.

Brydges *see* BRIDGE.

Brydson *see* KILBRIDE.

Buchanan (Scot) Descendant of someone who came from the Stirlingshire district of this name, 'house of the canon.'

James Herbert writes, in his novel *Sepulchre*: 'He was Alexander Buchanan, a suitably sturdy name for an underwriter whose firm, Acorn Buchanan Limited, had a 'box' on the floor of Lloyd's of London and company offices near Fenchurch Street.'

Bucher *see* BUTCHER.

Buck (Eng) Probably a nickname for a lecherous man, though some professional connection with stags or goats is also possible. In some instances there may be a reference to residence near a 'beech' tree.

Warwick Deeping presumably had the American slang meaning of buck ('dollar') in mind when he wrote, in *Sorrell and Son*: 'Buck! He did not like the name; it was both too male and too American.'

Bucket (Eng) A well-known character in the BBC television series *Keeping up Appearances* tries to deflect any derision that this name might evoke by insisting that it should be pronounced like the word 'bouquet,' as if it really referred to a bunch of flowers. Bouquet does exist as a French surname, along with its variants Bouquain, Bouquin, Bouquot, Bouquerel, but all are derived, according to Professor Albert Dauzat in his *Dictionnnaire Etymologique des noms de famille et prénoms de France,* from a word meaning 'he-goat.' Such names would have been given to a man who was especially lecherous. BUCKETT is normally taken to be a form of BURKETT, which also has the variants BUCHARD, BURCHATT, BURCHARD, BURCHETT, BURKARD, BURKART, BURKITT, BORKETT, BOCKETT, BUDGETT, BUTCHARD, BUTCHART. These derive from someone named *Burgheard* 'fort-strong,' an Old English personal name. However, G. Pawley White claims in his *Handbook of Cornish Surnames* that Buckett is from Cornish *bos keth* 'dwelling of the serf.'

Students of detective fiction are familiar with Inspector Bucket, who appears in Dickens' *Bleak House* in a relatively minor role. He is perhaps the first fictional detective. Dickens has him introduce himself by saying: 'My name's Bucket. Ain't that a funny name?'

Buckingham (Eng) Descendant of someone who originally came from one of the places so-named because it was *'Bucca's* homestead.'

Buckle, Buckell, Buckler, Buckles, Bucklesmith (Eng) Occupational name of a buckle-maker. However, Weekley suggests that Buckler may on occasion be a form of BEAUCLERK.

Bucklin *see* BUTLIN.

Bucksmith *see* SMITH.

Buddell, Buddle, Buddles *see* BEADLE.

Budgett *see* BUCKET.

Bugg, Buggey, Bugson (Eng) Descendant of *Buggi,* an Old Norse personal name meaning 'fat.' It can also derive from Welsh *bwg*, a word which can variously mean 'bogy, bug-bear, ghost, scarecrow.' Professor Weekley added the suggestion that Bugg might be a shortened form of *Burghart,* a Germanic name meaning 'castle strong.'

The modern form of the name is slightly unfortunate, and Thomas Hood long ago commented:

A name – if the party had a voice –
What mortal would be a Bugg by choice.
As a Hogg, a Grubb, or a Chubb rejoice.
Or any such nauseous blazon?
Not to mention many a vulgar name.
That would make a door plate blush for shame.
If doorplates were not so brazen.

For a further disparaging comment by Matthew Arnold, *see*
HIGGINBOTTOM.

In the 19th century an announcement in *The Times* that a Mr
Bugg was changing his name to *Howard* led to a great deal of comment, including a debate in the House of Commons. As a direct
result, James Finlayson published, in 1863, his booklet *Surnames
and Sirenames, the Origin and History of Certain Family and
Historical Names with Remarks on the Ancient Right of the Crown
to Sanction and Veto the Assumption of Names, and a Historical
Account of the Names Buggey and Bugg*.

Like Bugg itself, Bugson also comes in for its share of disapproval. In *Sorrell and Son* Warwick Deeping writes: 'Personally I
don't like young Bugson; I don't like his name or his face or his
nature, but we have to put up with the Bugsons. They are here –
there – everywhere.'

Bulled, Bulleid (Eng) Nickname for a man with a 'bull head,'
presumably a comment on his impetuous ways.

Bullinger *see* BAKER.

Bullock (Eng) Professor Reaney, in *The Origin of English Surnames*,
says that Bullock might have been a nickname for a young man who
behaved like a bullock, but he adds: 'There can be no doubt that
many a Bullock was once a BALLOCK (Old English bealluc 'testicle').
Occasionally we have a compound, Robert *Blakeballoc*.' He mentions also a Roger *Gildynballokes* 'golden testicles.' *See* GRAY.

A conversation in Elizabeth Gaskell's *Mr Harrison's
Confessions* runs: 'Mr and Mrs Bullock's compliments, sir, and
they hope you are pretty well after your journey.' 'Who would have
expected such kindness from such an unpromising name?'

Bulteflour *see* BOUTFLOUR.

Bumphrey, Bumphries *see* HUMPHREY.

Bunclark *see* CLARK.

Bunn *see* BONE.

Burchard, Burchatt, Burchett, Burkard, Burkart, Burkett, Burkitt *see* BUCKET.

Burd *see* BIRD.

Burfoot *see* PUDDY.

Burgess, Burgiss (Eng) A social title, indicating an inhabitant of a town or borough who enjoyed full municipal rights.

Burke, Bourke, Burgh, De Burgh (Eng) Descendant of someone who lived near a prehistoric hill fort, or in a place named for such a fort.

Burley, Burleigh (Eng) Descendant of someone who lived in any of the places of this name, which at one time would have had a 'fort in a wood.'

In *The Autocrat of the Breakfast Table*, Oliver Wendell Holmes says that Elizabeth I loved to make puns on people's names. He quotes her as saying: 'Ye be burly, my Lord of Burleigh, but ye shall make less stir in our realm than my Lord of Leicester.'

Burnaby (Eng) Someone who came from a place so-named because it was a 'settlement near a stream.'

Burnham (Eng) Descendant of someone who originally came from one of the places so-named because it was a 'homestead near a stream.'

Burns, Burness, Burnhouse (Scot) Descendant of someone who lived (in a house) near a stream.

George Black says in *The Surnames of Scotland* that 'Robert Burns's right name was Burness, but because the name was pronounced in Ayrshire as if written Burns, he and his brother Gilbert agreed to drop Burness and assume Burns in April 1786.'

Burton (Eng) Someone who came from one of the several places so-named because it was a 'settlement near a fortified manor.'

The actor Richard Burton was born Richard Walter Jenkins.

In *South Riding*, Winifred Holtby writes: 'Mr Chairman, I see we have another candidate, Sarah Burton. A good plain name. Let us hope a good plain woman.'

Bury, Atberry, Atbury, Atterbury, Berry, Berriman, Berryman (Eng) These names all have a connection with a 'fort' or 'manor house,' probably indicating someone who worked in such a place (Berriman, Berryman) or lived near one. Since *Bury* is also a place name in its own right, it could mean 'someone who came from a place so-named.' The ancestor of a Cornish Berriman or Berryman, by contrast, might well have come from *St Buryan*.

Busby (Eng) Someone who came from a place so-named because it was a 'settlement amongst shrubs.'

Bush, Bushe, Busk (Eng) Descendant of someone who lived near thick bushes.

Butchard, Butchart *see* BUCKET.

Butcher, Boucher, Boutcher, Bucher (Eng) Occupational name of a butcher or worker in a slaughterhouse.

Butevilain *see* BUTLIN.

Butler, Botler, Bottel, Bottle, Buttle (Eng) A head servant, specifically one who was in charge of the wine-cellar. Occasionally he was responsible for the importation of wine.

Butlin, Bucklin, Butevilain (Fre) Dr Reaney explained this name in his *Origin of English Surnames* as Old French *boute vilain*, 'hustle the churl.' It appears to have been the nickname of an overseer.

Butt, Butson, Butting, Butts (Eng) A nickname for a short, thickset person, or one who lived near, or spent a lot of time at, archery butts. Perhaps also a seller of the flatfish called butt, halibut.

Buttle *see* BUTLER.

Button, Boudet, Boudin, Boudon, Boudot, Boudeau, Bouton Descendant of a man who bore the Germanic personal name *Bodo* or one of its diminutive forms.

There was a Button family on the *Mayflower* when it sailed to America.

Lower reports that there is a sexton's bill in an English parish church which refers to digging a grave for a Mr Button. It reads: 'To making a Button-hole, 4s.6d.'

Butts *see* BUTT.

In *The Newcomes*, Thackeray has the exchange: 'Mr Butts of the Life Guards.' 'Mr Butts – *quel nom!*' (what a name!).

Byfield *see* FIELD.

Bygod, Bygot *see* PARDOE.

Byndloes *see* CATCHLOVE.

Byrd *see* BIRD.

Bywater, Bywaters (Eng) Ancestor of someone who lived near water, such as a lake or river.

Bywood *see* WOOD.

Cadbury descendant of someone who came from one of the places so named because it was *'Cada's* fortress.' The Old English personal name Cada probably meant 'lump,' and was perhaps applied to a fat person.

In the 1820s the Quaker John Cadbury sold tea and coffee in his Birmingham shop. He began grinding cocoa beans to supply a few special customers and went on to make chocolate.

Caldwell, Calwell, Caudell, Caudle, Caudwell, Cauldwell, Cawdell (Eng, Scot, Irish) A fairly common place name meaning 'cold well, spring.' Ancestors of those bearing these names could have come from any one of them.

A member of the American Name Society, some years ago, amused himself by matching surnames with various sports. Caldwell was considered to be suitable for a baseball umpire. Other links were made between LONGFELLOW and FOWLER, basketball; FIELDING, cricket; SITWELL, hunting; UPDIKE, mountaineering. Such a list could be considerably extended.

Caller, Callear, Callier, Callmaker, Caul, Caule, Caules (Eng) Occupational name for a maker of 'cauls,' head-dresses made of net-work.

Callister, Callistron see ALEXANDER.

Callmaker *see* CALLER.

Calwell *see* CALDWELL.

Cambell, Camble *see* CAMPBELL.

Cameron (Scot) In the Highlands a nickname from Gaelic *cam sròn* 'crooked nose.' As a Lowland surname it indicates an ancestor who lived near a 'crooked hill,' or in a place which itself had been named because of the presence of such a hill.

Campbell, Cambell, Camble (Scot) A nickname from Gaelic *cam* *beul* 'crooked mouth.' Popular legend derives the name instead from *de campo bello* 'of the fair field' and equates it with French Beauchamp, but this etymology has no justification.

Cannon, Cannons, Canon, Channon (Eng) Descendant of a canon, a clergyman who lived in a communal house with others of his profession. Perhaps also a nickname for someone who acted like a canon.

As with most surnames, a more individual explanation of its origin is possible. Arnold Bennet writes, in *Hilda Lassways*, that 'Mrs Gailey had married a French modeller named Canonges, and in course of time the modeller had informally changed the name to Cannon, because no one in the five towns could pronounce the name rightly.'

Cape, Cope (Eng) Occupational name for someone who made capes, or a nickname for someone who wore a particularly noticeable one. From the Old English *cape*, retained in northern dialects, or from *cope*, its Middle English development.

Capelen, Capelin, Capeling, Caplen, Caplin *see* CHAPLIN.

Capern, Caperon *see* CAPRON.

Capp, Cape, Capes, Capmaker, Capman, Capper, Capps (Eng) Occupational name of a maker and seller of caps.

Capron, Capern, Caperon, Chape, Chaperon, Chapron (Eng, Fre) Occupational name of a maker of hooded cloaks, of the type worn by monks.

Capstack, Capstick *see* COPESTAKE.

Card, Carde, Carder (Eng) Occupational name of someone who carded (untangled) wool.

Mr Valentine Frank Henry Card, of Chelmsford, Essex, was born on February 14. He once told a *Daily Mail* reporter that he was obliged to take his birth certificate to work on Valentine's Day every year to prove that he really was a living Valentine Card.

Cardrick *see* CARTWRIGHT.

Care *see* KERR.

Careless, Carless, Carloss (Eng) A disapproving nickname for someone who acted in a carefree or careless manner.

Chambers, in his *Book of Days*, quotes an amorous poet who addressed the following to a Miss Careless:

Careless by name, and Careless by nature;
Careless of shape, and Careless of feature.
Careless of dress, and Careless in air;
Careless of riding, in coach or in chair.
Careless of love, and Careless of hate;
Careless if crooked, and Careless if straight,
Careless at table, and Careless in bed;
Careless if maiden, not Careless if wed.
Careless at church, and Careless at play;
Careless if company go, or they stay;
Oh! how I could love thee, thou dear Careless thing
(Oh, happy, thrice happy, I'd envy no king.)
Were you Careful for once to return me my love,
I'd care not how Careless to others you'd prove.
I then should be Careless how Careless you were;
And the more Careless you, still the less I should care.

Carleton, Carlton (Eng) Someone who came from one of the several places so-named because they were 'settlements of free peasants.'

Carloss *see* CARELESS.

Carlyon (Eng) Someone who came from one of the Cornish places bearing this name, probably because of nearby 'earthworks of slate or shake.'

Marie Corelli says of one of her characters in *Delicia*: 'He was absolutely devoid of all ambition, save a desire to have his surname pronounced correctly. "Car-lee-on," he would say, with polite emphasis, "not Car-ly-on. Our name is an old, historical one, and like many of its class is spelt one way and pronounced another".'

Carne (Eng) Descendant of someone who originally lived near a *carn*, a pile of rocks. This word is a common element in Cornish place names.

Carpenter (Eng) Occupational name of a carpenter.

Carr *see* KERR.

Carré *see* QUARRY.

Carrington (Eng, Scot) Someone who came from one of the several places so-named because it was '*Cora's* settlement.'

Carroll, Carrol, Carvil, MacCarroll, MacKarrill, O'Carroll,

O'Carrowill, O'Carvill, O'Carwell (Irish) Descendant of *Cearbhall*, a Gaelic personal name of uncertain meaning, though suggestions include 'hart, stag' and 'hacking.'

Carswell see **Creswell.**

Carter, Charter (Eng) Occupational name of a carter, who transported goods.

Nick Carter is the fictional American detective who appears in over 500 stories, written by many different authors. He is able to disguise himself even more effectively than Sherlock Holmes. He was created as long ago as 1886.

Carton see MacCartney.

Cartwright, Cardrick, Cartrick, Cartridge, Kortwright (Eng) Occupational name for a maker of carts.

Carvil see Carroll.

Casewell, Casswell, Caswall, Caswell, Caswill see Creswell.

Catcher see Catchpole.

Catchlove, Cutliffe, Cutloff, Cutlove (Eng) Occupational name of a hunter. The 'love' in this name is from Old French *loup* or *love* 'wolf'. Hunters or trappers of wolves could also be known as Pretlove, Pritlove, Prykkelove 'prick, kill wolf;' Truslove, Truslow, Trussler 'carry off wolf'; Bindless, Bindloes, Bindloss, Byndloes 'bind wolf'; Spendlove, Spendlow, Spenlow, Spindlowe 'disembowel wolf'; Hachewolf 'hack wolf'.

Catchpole, Catchpoll, Catchpool, Catchpoole, Catchpoule, Chacepol (Eng) Literally, a man who was allowed to 'catch fowl' to offset someone's taxes or other debts. A nickname for a bailiff. He might also be known more simply as a Catcher or Ketcher.

Cater, Cator, Chaytor (Eng) Occupational name for someone who purchased provisions for a large household. Such an official was known in French as an *acheteur* or by the Norman French variant *acatour* 'buyer.' The word *caterer* is from the same source.

Catesby (Eng) Someone who came from a place so-named because it was the 'settlement of *Kati's* people.'

Caudell, Caudle, Caudwell, Cauldwell see Caldwell.

Caul, Caule, Caules see Caller.

Cavalier see Chevalier.

Cawdell see Caldwell.

Cawker *see* CHALK.

Caxton (Eng) Someone who came from a place so-named because it was '*Kakkr's* settlement.'

Chacepol *see* CATCHPOLE.

Chalk, Cawker, Chalke, Chalker, Chalkman, Chaulk (Eng) These names clearly refer to chalk in one way or another. The name-bearers may have been suppliers of chalk, since it was used for various purposes, eg as a whitewash and as a hardening agent by potters. The names could also indicate someone who originally came from one of the many English places named for its chalky soil.

Chamberlain, Chalmers, Chamberlaine, Chamberlayne, Chamberlen, Chamberlin, Chambers, Champerlen (Eng) An occupational name originally designating someone who managed the private chambers of his employer, normally a nobleman or perhaps the king himself. At the highest level he was a very influential official. Later chamber-attendants operated at a much humbler level and were more like chamber-maids.

Popular newspapers were delighted to report on the wedding, in the 1970s, of a Mr Chambers to a Miss Potts. It was inevitably described as 'a marriage of convenience.'

L.G. Pine writes, in *The Story of Surnames*: 'Chamberlain, not in most cases derived from any office of great profit or standing, but from the inn chamberlain, who looked after the arriving guests. The German name, now acclimatised in England, ZIMMERMAN, brings it out better – room man, the fellow who allotted the guests their rooms in the inn.' A German Zimmermann is more likely to have helped build a bedroom or the bed itself. The name means 'carpenter.' *Zimmer* does indeed mean 'room' in modern German, but in the Middle Ages it would have been *Zimber*, a form showing its connection with 'timber.'

Chambly *see* CHOLMONDELEY.

Champerlen *see* CHAMBERLAIN.

Chance *see* HAZARD.

Channon *see* CANNON.

Chape *see* CAPRON.

Chaperlin, Chaperling *see* CHAPLIN.

Chaperon *see* CAPRON.

Chaplin, Capelen, Capelin, Capeling, Caplen, Caplin, Chaperlin, Chaperling, Chaplain, Chapling (Eng) Occupational name for the servant of a clergyman.

Charles Chaplin, in *My Autobiography,* writes: 'I started schooling and was taught to write my name "Chaplin." The word fascinated me and looked like me, I thought.'

Chapman, Chapper, Cheeper, Chipman, Chipper (Eng) Occupational man for a trader, a man who bought and sold articles. The first element in Chapman is from Old English *ceap*, which led to the words 'chap,' 'cheap' and 'chop' (as in 'chop and change.')

Chapron *see* CAPRON.

Charlton (Eng) Someone who came from one of the several places so-named because it was a 'settlement of free peasants.'

Charter *see* CARTER.

Chasselove *see* LOVE.

Chatham (Eng) Descendant of someone who originally came from one of the places so-named because it was a 'homestead near a forest.'

Chatterton (Eng) Probably someone who came from a place named Chadderton, 'settlement near a hill.'

Chatterley, the name made famous by D.H. Lawrence in *Lady Chatterley's Lover*, has much the same meaning. Lawrence was presumably being ironic when he gave his heroine the first name Constance.

Chaucer, Chauser (Eng) Occupational name of a maker of leather leg-wear. Ernest Weekley disliked complicated explanations of a name when a simple one was available, and he agreed that the evidence for the origin of this name from French *chauceor* 'hose-maker' was convincing. He nevertheless suggested that some families of this name might have an ancestor who was a *chauffe-cire*, literally a 'heat wax.' Some English writers (though only from the 17th century onwards) used the term 'chafe-' or 'chaff-wax' to describe the Chancery official who prepared wax that was used to seal official documents. Weekley also suggested that a Chaucer, Chauser might have been a 'chalicer,' a maker of drinking cups or goblets. Of these various possibilities, 'hose-maker' remains by far the most likely.

Chaulk *see* CHALK.

Chauser *see* CHAUCER.

Chaytor *see* CATER.

Cheater, Chetter (Eng) Occupational name of an official *escheater*. He supervised the reversion of estates to the feudal lord when a tenant died without heir. In many cases, surnames accidentally resemble normal words, but in this instance a Cheater really deserved his name, inasmuch as the verbs *escheat* and *cheat* were at one time interchangeable. The development of a new meaning for cheat, namely to 'deprive someone of something by deceit,' was a reflection on the dishonesty of the medieval officials. However, Weekley thought that in some instance this name might be a variant of CATER.

Cheeper *see* CHAPMAN.

Cheesewright, Cheesright, Cherrett, Cherritt, Chessman, Chesswright, Cheswright (Eng) Occupational name for a maker/seller of cheese.

Cheever, Cheevers, Chevers, Chivers (Eng) Occupational name of a goat-herd (from French *chevre,* 'goat'), or a nickname for someone who was thought to be goat-like in behaviour.

Chegwyn, Chegwidden, Chegwin (Cornish) Descendant of someone who originally came from a place named because of its 'white house.'

Cherrett, Cherritt, Chessman, Chesswright see **Cheesewright.**

Chesterton (Eng) Someone who came from a place so-named because it was a 'settlement near a Roman camp.'

Cheswright *see* CHEESEWRIGHT.

Chetter *see* CHEATER.

Chevalier, Cavalier, Chevallier (Eng) A 'knight,' commenting on the fact that he rode a *cheval* 'horse.' This was probably an occupational name for someone who worked for a knight. The noblemen themselves usually had names linked to estates.

Chevers *see* CHEEVER.

Chilton (Eng) Someone who came from a place so-named because it was a 'settlement with children.'

Chipman, Chipper *see* CHAPMAN.

Chivers *see* CHEEVER.

Cholmondeley, Chambly, Cholmeley, Chumley, Chumbly (Eng) Descendant of someone who originally came from the Cheshire place, so-named because it was '*Ceolmund's* wood.'

Weekley remarks that it is 'curious' that a name of this type (ie a very ordinary transferred place name) should have 'acquired an aristocratic flavour.'

Lower, in his *Patronymica Britannica*, pauses to say: 'I cannot refrain from reprobating the curt and absurd pronunciation of this name – *Chulmley* or *Chumley*. Strange that some of our most aristocratic families, who would not willingly concede one jot of their dignity in other respects, should be willing to have their ancient names thus nicked and mutilated. Why should the ST JOHNS submit to be *Sinjen'd*, the MAJORIBANKS to be *Marchbank'd,* the FITZ-JOHNS to be *Fidgen'd*, or the CHOLMONDLEYS to be *Chumley'd*? Why should the contractions of illiterate "flunkeys" be accepted in the places of fine old chivalrous sounds like those?' *See* MARJORIBANKS.

Chopin, Choppen, Choppin, Chopping (Eng, French) Nickname for a heavy drinker. Old French *chopiner* meant 'to tipple,' the verb being derived from a liquid measure called a *chopine,* 'the quantity held in a large ladle.' In France the name also led to Chopine, Chopinel, Chopinnet. Another Old French word *chopin* 'heavy blow' could also have led to this surname, indicating someone who was violently pugnacious.

Chrisp, Chrispin *see* CRISP.

Christian, Christ, Christey, Christie, Christin, Christine, Christison, Christy (Eng) Descendant of *Christian,* a given name of obvious meaning. Christ is a rare form of this name, likely to cause problems for its bearers.

Mr Jay F. Christ, of the University of Chicago, reports that he soon discovered that having a visiting card which simply said "J. Christ," or signing his name in that way, could cause offence.

Christmas, Chrismas (Eng) Descendant of someone born during the Christmas season.

A Surrey publican of this name is said to have thrown a midsummer 'Christmas party,' inviting all those who shared his surname to come along for a free drink.

Christy *see* CHRISTIAN.

Chubb (Eng) A nickname derived from the fish, which is known to be short, fat (chubby) and sluggish. *See* BUGG.

Chumley, Chumbly *see* CHOLMONDLEY.

Churchard *see* CHURCHYARD.

Churchill (Eng) Descendant of someone who came from any of the places, especially in the West Country, which bear this name because of a 'church on a hill.'

Churchyard, Churchard (Eng) Occupational name of a man who worked in a churchyard or indicating an ancestor who lived near one.

Chuzzlewit (Eng) This is a well known name because of Dickens's *Martin Chuzzlewit.* Dickens managed to make it look like a corrupt form of a place-name containing the common Old English element *ceosol* 'gravel, shingle.' He had rejected along the way a number of other possibile names, such as Sweezleden, Sweezleback, Sweezlewag, Chuzzletoe, Chuzzleboy, Chubblewig and Chuzzlewig. In the novel occurs the passage: 'Then Martin is your Christian name?' said Mr Pinch thoughtfully. 'Of course it is,' returned his friend: 'I wish it was my surname, for my own is not a pretty one, and it takes a long time to sign. Chuzzlewit is my name.'

There is also a discussion in the novel about the family's history. Toby Chuzzlewit is asked 'Who was your grandfather?' to which he replies 'The Lord No Zoo.' This is offered as proof that the family is connected to 'some unknown noble and illustrious House.'

Clapham (Eng) Descendant of someone who originally came from one of the places so-named because it was a 'homestead on or near a hillock.'

Clark, Clarke, Clarkin, Clarkson, Clarkstone, Clarson, Clerk, Clerke (Eng) Occupational name of a man, usually a member of a minor religious order who had not taken vows of celibacy and was therefore able to marry, who performed secretarial duties. Later the name came to mean any literate man (in a period when most people, at all levels of society, could neither read nor write). Many of the clerics or clerks, as we would now call them, were in fact only semi-literate by modern standards, often employing their own idiosyncratic spelling systems. Nevertheless, the frequency with which the name now occurs shows that it had high status and was borne proudly as a family name. Some compound names contain 'clerk' as an element. BEAUCLERK is a Norman name that describes a 'handsome cleric' or one who had especially good handwriting. BUNCLARK was a *bon clerc* 'good priest.' MAUCLERC, by contrast, (also recorded as MANCLARK and MOCKLER) was a 'bad priest or clerk.'

Andrea Newman, in *An Evil Streak*, writes: 'Christopher Clark – the very name has a fine solid English ring to it. Lacking the affectation of a final 'e,' it suggests the courage of its own convictions. Insert the prefix 'Dr' and you have a pillar of society, the dependable middle-class professional man, dedicated to doing good and making money, and seeing no contradiction between the two.'

A curiosity about the name Clark is that it appears in correct sequence in the Periodic Table. Elements 17-19 inclusive are Cl (chlorine) Ar (argon) and K (potassium). *See* DUCK.

Clay, Claye, Clayer, Clayman (Eng) Occupational name for someone who worked in a claypit.

Claybrook, Claybrooke (Eng) Descendant of someone who originally came from the Leicestershire place, so-named because of its 'clayey brook.'

Claydon, Clayden (Eng) Descendant of someone who originally came from one of the many places so-named because it was on a 'clayey hill.'

Claye, Clayer, Clayman *see* CLAY.

Claypole, Claypool (Eng) Descendant of someone who originally came from the Lincolnshire place, so-named because of its 'clayey pool.'

Clayton (Eng) Someone who came from one of the several places so-named because it was a 'settlement on clayey soil.'

John Clayton, Lord Greystoke, is otherwise known as Tarzan in the stories of Edgar Rice Burroughs.

Clement, Clemans, Clemence, Clemens, Clemenson, Clements, Clementson, Clemerson, Cleminson, Clemm, Clemmans, Clemmens, Clemmett, Clemmey, Clemmitt, Clemmow, Clemons, Clemonts, Clempson, Clemson, Climance, Climey, Climpson, Clyma, Clymer (Eng) Descendant of *Clement*, from a

Latin word meaning 'merciful.' The name is mentioned only once in the Bible, but it was the name of an early saint and several popes.

Clerke, Clerke *see* CLARK.

Clifton (Eng) Someone who came from one of the several places so-named because it was a 'settlement on a hill slope.'

Climance, Climey, Climpson *see* CLEMENT.

Clocksmith *see* SMITH.

Clog (Eng) Occupational name of a clog-maker. Names like PATTEN and PATTIN belong here, pattens being a kind of clog worn especially by ecclesiastics.

Clout, Clouter, Cloutman, Cloutt (Eng) Occupational name of someone who used 'clouts' or 'patches' to repair holes in clothes or utensils.

Clyma, Clymer *see* CLEMENT.

Cobham (Eng) Descendant of someone who originally came from one of the places so-named because it was '*Cobba's* or *Coffa's* homestead.'

Cock, Cockarill, Cockerell, Cockerill, Cocking, Cocklin, Cockling, Cockrell, Cockrill, Cocks, Cox, Coxe, Coxen, Coxon (Eng) Comparing a young man to a cockerel gave rise to one of the commonest nicknames in medieval times. We might still say that such a person was acting in a 'cocky' way. A cock was also much used as a house sign in the days when most people were illiterate, and the numbering of houses was not yet usual. Cock could therefore refer to someone who lived 'at the sign of the Cock.' In words like 'haycock,' cock means a 'heap, small hill.' The word in this sense could have been used as a nickname for a fat man. The fact that there is a type of small ship's boat called a 'cock' means that the name could have referred to someone who was professionally involved with it. Other possible derivations are from a 'cook,' or from Welsh *coch* 'red,' or from an Old English personal name *Cocca*, the meaning of which might be almost any of the above. It is almost impossible, clearly, to say that a family bearing a form of this name derives it from a particular source. One meaning which is not possible is 'penis,' since cock only acquired this slang meaning long after the surname-formation period.

Basil Cottle mentions the Coxe spelling only to say that it is 'very rare and affected.'

Thackeray had long before commented, in *Cox's Diary*: 'Mr Coxe Coxe (that's the way, double your name, and stick an "e" to the end of it, and you are a gentleman at once). '

Codner, Corden, Cordner, Cordon, Cordwent, Corwin (Eng) Occupational name of a 'cordwainer,' a leather-worker who took his name from the Spanish town of Corduba, where the leather was made from tanned goat-skins. In the Middle Ages he would have been employed by the wealthy to make shoes.

Cohen, Coen, Cohan, Cohn (Jewish) From Hebrew *kohen* 'priest.'

Cointance *see* QUAINTANCE.

Colcock *see* NICHOLAS.

Coldtart *see* COLT.

Cole *see* NICHOLAS.

Coleman, Colman, Coulman (Eng, Irish) Irish families of this name had an ancestor named *Colmán,* a diminutive form of *Columb*, from Latin *columba* 'dove.' The name was very popular in the Ireland of the Middle Ages, thanks to various saints named either Columba or Columban. In an English context the name refers to the occupation of a charcoal burner, or to the servant of a man named *Cole.*

Colin, Colkin, Coll, Collard, Colle, Collens, Collerson, Collet, Collete, Collett *see* NICHOLAS.

Collar, Colleer, Coller *see* COLLIER.

Colley, Collie (Eng) Nickname for a person with 'coal-black' hair.

Collier, Collar, Colleer, Coller, Colliar, Colliard, Collyear, Collyer, Colyer (Eng) Occupational name of a charcoal burner. **Coleman** can also have this meaning.

Collin, Collins, Collinson, Collison, Collisson, Colls, Collyns *see* NICHOLAS.

Collyear, Collyer *see* COLLIER.

Colman *see* COLEMAN.

Colt, Coldtart, Coltart, Colter, Coltman, Coult, Coultate, Coulthard, Coulthart, Coultman (Eng) Occupational name of a colt-herd, though *Colt* may occasionally be a nickname for someone who behaved like a colt.

Colyer *see* COLLIER.

Comfort, Cumfort (Eng) Nickname of someone who provided comfort, probably in the form of support and encouragement. Names of similar meaning are SOLACE and SOLLAS. In some instances Comfort is a later development of *Comport*, formerly a place name in Kent and Surrey.

Comper (Eng) A reference to someone who was a gossip.

Compton (Eng) Someone who came from one of the several places so-named because it was a 'settlement in a narrow valley.'

Coningsby, Conningsby (Eng) Someone who came from a place so-named because it was the 'king's settlement.'

Connor, Connors, O'Conchor, O'Conor, O'Connor, O'Connour (Irish) Descendant of *Conchobhar,* a Gaelic personal name of uncertain meaning. Suggestions as to it significance range from 'meddlesome,' 'dog desiring' or 'dog-lover,' 'wolf-lover,' 'high will.'

Samuel Lover writes in *Handy Andy*: 'The rider was Edward O'Connor; and he was worthy of his name – the pure blood of that royal race was in his heart, which never harboured a sentiment that could do it dishonour, and overflowed with feelings which ennoble human nature, and make us proud of our kind.'

Constant, Constans, Contant, Coutant, Coutans (Eng) Complimentary nickname for someone considered to be 'steadfast, faithful.'

Cooksey (Eng) Descendant of someone who came from the Worcestershire place of this name, '*Cucu's* island.'

Cooper, Cooperman, Copper, Coupar, Couper, Cowper, Cupper (Eng) Descendant of someone who made wooden tubs and casks.

An American woman, Ellen Donna Cooperman, who owned a Long Island feminist film company, attempted in 1978 to have her surname legally changed to Cooperperson. She claimed that the new version of her name would 'more properly reflect her sense of human equality.' The New York State Supreme Court refused to allow the change on the basis that it would lead to an avalanche of similar demands, Manson to Peoplechild, etc. A lower court had previously ruled against Ms Cooperman, saying that the proposed change would hold the women's movement up to ridicule.

Coopersmith *see* SMITH.

Cope *see* CAPE.

Copestake, Capstack, Capstick, Coupstak (Fre and Eng) Occupational name of a stake-cutter. The first part of the name represents French *couper* 'to cut.'

Coppell, Coppayl, Cupples, Curpel, Curtpeil (Eng) Nickname for a man with short hair, from Old French *curt peil*.

Copper *see* COOPER.

Copperfield *see* STANSFIELD.

Coppersmith (Eng) An occupational name of obvious meaning.

Corden, Cordner, Cordon, Cordwent, Corwin see **Codner.**

Corte *see* COURT.

Cosier (Eng) Occupational name of a cobbler.

Cotter, Coterel, Cotman, Cottier (Eng) A villager who lived in a cot or cottage. Those of higher social class were *husbonds* 'householders.'

Coule, Coules, Coull *see* NICHOLAS.

Coulman *see* COLEMAN.

Coult, Coultate, Coulthard, Coulthart, Coultman *see* COLT.

Counter (Eng) Occupational name for a 'keeper of accounts.' He may also have been concerned with taxes.

Coupar, Couper *see* COOPER.

Coupstak *see* COPESTAKE.

Court, Corte, Courtman, Courts, Curt (Eng) Two separate names have blended here. These forms could indicate someone who worked at a manorial court, but they could also be a nickname for a 'short' man.

Richard Court, who died in 1791, had been a blacksmith, as his epitaph reveals:

My Sledge and Hammer lie Reclin'd,
My Bellows too have lost their Wind;
My Fire is out, and Forge decay'd,
And in the Dust my Vice is laid.

Coutant, Coutans *see* CONSTANT.

Covington (Eng) Someone who came from a place so-named because it was the 'settlement of *Cova's* people.'

Cowle, Cowles *see* NICHOLAS.

Cowper *see* COOPER.

Cox, Coxe, Coxen, Coxon *see* COCK.

Crabbe, Crab, Crabb, Crabbie, Crabs, Crabtree (Eng) The form Crabtree makes it clear that these names could sometimes refer to crab-apple trees, or to their fruit. Even then, given the fondness of our ancestors for nicknames drawn from Nature, the name was likely to refer to someone's 'sourness.' If the reference was to the crustacean, a comment was probably being made on someone's shambling gait, his 'crab-like' movement.

Mrs Carol Crabb reported to *Woman* magazine that the midwife who brought her new baby to be fed commented: 'Here you are, Mrs Crabb, your little lobster.' Mrs Crabb was not amused.

The 'lobster' remark will remind avid readers of Charles Dickens of the incident in *Nicholas Nickleby*, when Nicholas falls in love with an unknown girl. He asks Newman Noggs to follow her and find out who she is. When Newman returns he announces: 'The name's Bobster. I remember it by lobster.' Nicholas is taken aback and can only say: 'That must be the servant's name.' He is later greatly relieved to discover that Noggs has followed the wrong girl, and that the object of his affections is really Madeline Bray.

Crackston *see* HAMILTON.

Craft, Crafts *see* CROFT.

Craig, Cragg, Craggs, Craigie, Craik (Scot) Descendant of someone who lived near a rugged mass of rock, a crag.

Crakebone *see* BRISBANE.

Crane (Eng) Nickname presumably commenting on a man's long legs. *See* GREWCOCK.

There is a well-known literary bearer of this name in Washington Irving's *The Legend of Sleepy Hollow*: 'The cognomen of Crane was not inapplicable to his person. He was tall, but exceeedingly lank, with narrow shoulders, long arms and legs, hands that dangled a mile out of his sleeves, feet that might have served for shovels, and his whole frame most loosely hung together. His head was small, and flat at top, with huge ears, large green glassy eyes, and a long snipe nose, so that it looked like a weather-cock, perched upon his spindle neck, to tell which way the wind blew.

Thomas Wolfe also comments on the name in *The Web and the Rock*: 'Nebraska Crane was a fellow that he liked. That was a queer name, sure enough, but there was also something good about it. It was a square, thick, muscular, brawny, browned and freckled, wholesome kind of name, plain as an old shoe and afraid of nothing, and yet it had some strangeness in it, too.'

Crapper *see* CROPPER.

The word crap, 'excrement' or 'defecate', is not derived from this name, in spite of Thomas Crapper's invention of the flush toilet. There was a word *crappe* in Middle English which referred to the 'residue, dregs, chaff,' the meaning of which was extended.

Craswall, Crasswell, Craswell, Crassweller *see* CRESWELL.

Crawcour (Eng) A name which indicates Norman descent. Weekley explained it as a form of a common French place name, Crévecoeur 'heartbreak.' The reference is to land which is heartbreaking for the peasant because it is infertile.

In *Ann Vickers*, a novel by the American writer Sinclair Lewis, the following occurs: 'The name *Crévecoeur* sounded aristocratic. Ann looked it up in the dictionary and announced to Pat, impressively, that it really meant 'heartbreak' and was guaranteed to be romantic. But Pat looked it up in an even bigger dictionary and bawdily announced to Ann that *crévecoeur* also meant 'a French variety of the domestic fowl, heavily crested and bearded, and having a comb like two horns.'

Crawford, Crawforth (Eng) This is a common place name, indicating a ford where crows gathered. Bearers of the name had an ancestor living in such a place in the Middle Ages.

Creighton, Crichten, Crichton, Crighton (Scot) Someone who came from a place so-named because it was a 'settlement near a boundary.'

James Crichton ('Admirable Crichton') of Clunie was a Scottish prodigy in the 16th century. Allusive use of his name sometimes occurs, as when Thomas Hughes writes in *Tom Brown's Schooldays*: 'He was the Crichton of our village boys. He could wrestle and climb and run better than all the rest.' J.M.Barrie later made Bill Crichton butler to Lord Loam in his play *The Admirable Crichton*.

Creswell, Carswell, Casewell, Casswell, Caswall, Caswell, Caswill, Craswall, Crasswell, Craswell, Crassweller, Cressall,

Cressel, Cresswell, Criswell, Kerswell, Kerswill (Eng) Descendant of someone who originally came from one of the many places so-named because because of its 'stream with watercress.' These various spellings occur at the place-name stage, Old English *coerse* 'watercress' having developed in different dialectal ways.

Even when a spelling has become theoretically fixed in its surname form, variations are still likely to occur. A Mr Cresswell of London complained some years ago in a letter to the *Daily Mail* that he had been addressed as Mr Blackwell, Crestfall, Chessman and Watercress.

Crewther *see* CROWTHER.

Crichten, Crichton, Crighton *see* CREIGHTON.

Crisp, Chrisp, Chrispin, Crepin, Crespin, Crespy, Cripin, Crippen, Crippes, Cripps, Crips, Crispe, Crispin (Eng) Nickname for a man with curly hair, or descendant of a man named *Crispin (*which also means 'curly-haired').

Crock, Crockard, Crocker, Crockman, Crocks, Croker (Eng) Occupational name of a potter.

Croft, Craft, Crafts, Crofter, Crofts, Cruft, Crufts (Eng) A 'croft' is a small farm or enclosed field. The word became a place name, especially as **Crofton**, and any of the places so-called could have led to the surname, indicating someone who originally came from there.

Charles Cruft (1852-1938) was born in London. He became a salesman with a company making dog-cakes and saw dog shows as a useful way of selling the product. He organized the first London dog show in 1886 and was guaranteed success when it was patronized by Queen Victoria. However, he ordered that the dogs she had entered were to be judged strictly on their own merits.

Croisier, Croizier *see* CROZIER.

Croker *see* CROCK.

Cromb, Crumb, Crump (Eng) Nickname for a man with a stooping posture.

Crompton (Eng) Someone who came from a place so-named because it was a 'settlement near a bend in the river or road.'

Crook (Eng) Nickname for a man with a crooked back.

Crookshank, Crookshanks see **Cruikshank.**

Cropper, Crapper (Eng) Occupational name of a cropper, mower, sickler.

The English entertainer and singer Lynda Crapper adopted 'Marti Caine' as her stage-name.

Croser *see* CROZIER.

Cross, Crosse, Crossman (Eng) Descendant of someone who lived near a roadside cross, or one that stood in a market place.

Crosser *see* CROZIER.

Crossman *see* CROSS.

Crother, Crothers *see* CROWTHER.

Crousier, Crouzier *see* CROZIER.

Crowther, Crewther, Crother, Crothers, Crowder (Eng) Occupational name of someone who played the 'crowd' or 'rote,' a kind of fiddle used by medieval minstrels, from Welsh *crwth,* Irish *cruit*. In Scottish Gaelic this led to *MacChruiteir* which in turn gave MACCHRUITER, MACWHIRTER.

Crozier, Crosier, Croisier, Croizier, Croser, Crosser, Crousier, Crouzier (Eng, Fre) Occupational name of a maker or seller of crosses; or a man who carried a cross of bishop's crook in ecclesiastical processions; or from residence near a roadside cross. Professor Dauzat has also suggested that the name could refer to someone living at a place where roads crossed.

Cruft, Crufts *see* CROFT.

Cruikshank, Cruikshanks, Cruickshank, Cruickshanks, Crookshank, Crookshanks (Scot) Normally explained as a nickname for someone with crooked leg or legs. In his *Surnames of Scotland*, George Black connects it instead with someone who originally lived near the River *Cruik* in the Grampian region.

Cruise (Eng) Nickname for a bold or fierce man.

Crumb, Crump *see* CROMB.

Cruso, Crusoe (Eng) Timothy Cruso was a Presbyterian minister, born about 1656. He attended Newington Green Academy, where Daniel Defoe was a fellow-student. Defoe's *Robinson Crusoe* was published in 1719, and begins: 'I was born in the year 1632, in the city of York, of a good family, though not of that country, my father being a foreigner of Bremen, who settled first at Hull. He got a good estate by merchandize, and leaving off his trade, lived afterwards at York, from whence he married my mother, whose relations were named Robinson, a very good family in that country, and from whom I was called Robinson Kreutznaer; but by the usual corruption of words in English, we are now called – nay, we call ourselves and write our name – Crusoe.' The English form of the name suggests 'crusader,' *Kreutznaer* being based on the word for 'cross.'

Cumfort *see* COMFORT.

Cunningham, Cuningham, Cuninghame, Cunninghame, Cunnynghame, Cunyngham (Scot) Descendant of someone who originally came from the Scottish territory of this name near Kilmarnock. The name is an ancient one, the original meaning of which is impossible to know. The *-ham* of the name is not the normal English word indicating a homestead.

Cupper *see* COOPER.

Cupples, Curpel, Curtpeil *see* COPPELL.

Curt *see* COURT.

Curtis (Eng) Nickname for someone who was 'courteous,' whose manners were suitable for the royal court. But the name can also be from 'curt hose,' or 'short leggings,' and indicate a short person. The surnames SHORTHOSE, SHORTHOUSE, SHORTIS can also mean 'short hose.'

Cutliffe, Cutloff, Cutlove *see* CATCHLOVE.

Dabbs, Dabinett, Dabs, Dabson *see* ROBERT.

Dackin, Dackine, Dacking, Dackyn *see* DAVID.

Dade, Daffey *see* DAVID.

Daft, Daff, Daffe (Eng) Nickname for a gentle man.

Dafydd, Daid *see* DAVID.

Daile *see* DALE.

Dainty, Dainteth, Daintith, Dentith, Denty (Eng) Nickname for someone who was considered to be 'fine, handsome, pleasant.'

Daish *see* ASH.

Dakin, Daking, Dakins *see* DAVID.

Dale, Daile, Dales, Dallman, Dalman, Deal (Eng) Descendant of someone who lived in a dale.

In *The Egoist*, by George Meredith, a man rhapsodises: 'Laetitia Dale! Your name is sweet English music!' The 'music' of a name seems to depend very much on the ear of a particular listener. 'J. Pierrepoint Finch, there is wonderful music in the very sound of your name' occurs in *How To Succeed in Business Without Really Trying*, by Frank Loesser. J.D. Beresford writes in *Unity*: '"Adrian Gore," she interrupted him. "I'm sure I've never heard that name before, and yet it seems extraordinarily familiar." Indeed it was as if at the music of that name, something within her had faintly sounded an echo.' Mary Johnston, in *Hagar,* makes someone repeat the name 'Rose Darragh' several times and adds: 'It struck through her mind, slow and heavily vibrant, like a deep an melancholy music.' In *Doris*, by Charles Garvice, it is 'Cecil Nevin' which the heroine 'repeated twenty times, and each time it sounded more pleasant and musical.'

Danby (Eng) Someone who came from a place so-named because it was the 'Danes' settlement.'

Dand, Dandie, Dandison, Dando, Dandy *see* ANDREW.

Dane *see* DEAN, DENCH.

Danell, Danells *see* DANIEL.

Dangerfield (Eng) The name should probably be written *D'Angerfield,* since it indicates an ancestor who came originally from one of the French places called *Angerville. See* STANSFIELD.

Sebastian Dangerfield is the American law student hero of J.P. Donleavy's novel *The Ginger Man.*

Daniel, Danell, Danells, Daniell, Daniells, Daniels, Danks, Dannatt, Dannel, Dannell, Dannett, Danniel, Danniels, Dannot, Danson, Denial, Dennell (Eng) Descendant of *Daniel,* a Hebrew name which means 'God is judge.' It is the name of four different men in the Old Testament, but is mostly associated with the young man who explains to King Nebuchadnezzar the meaning of his dream and is given a high rank at court.

Darbinian *see* FABER.

Darcy, D'Arcy, Darcey (Eng) A name indicating Norman ancestry, someone who came from *Arcy* in La Manche. In an Irish context the name has a different possible origin as an Anglicized form of *O Dorchaidhe*, a personal name based on Gaelic *dorcha* 'dark, gloomy.' This Irish name is therefore sometimes Anglicized as DARKY.

Jane Austen's hero in *Pride and Prejudice* is Fitzwilliam Darcy, who seems to combine elements of Norman aristocracy and Irish gloom.

Dark, Darke, Darkes, Derke, Durk (Eng) Descriptive of a man with black hair or a dark complexion.

Darker, Darken (Eng) Occupational name of man who darkened leather.

Darkes *see* DARK.

Darky *see* DARCY.

Darling, Darline, Darlyng, Dearling, Derlyng, Dorling, Durling, Dyrling (Eng) Nickname for a beloved person, from the term of address.

Dash, Dashwood *see* ASH.

Daud, Davage *see* DAVID.

David, Dade, Daffey, Dafydd, Daid, Dakins, Daud, Davage, Davidge, Davids, Davidson, Davie, Davies, Davis, Davison,

Davitt, Davson, Davy, Davys, Daw, Dawe, Dawes, Dawkins, Dawson, Day, Daye, Devitt, Dewey, Dey, Dewi, Doud, Dowson, MacDaid, MacDavid, MacDavie, MacDavitt, MacDavy, MacDevitt, Taffee, Taffie (Eng, Welsh, Scottish, Irish) Descendant of *David*, a biblical name meaning 'beloved.' Its popularity was aided by its being the name of the patron saint of Wales, as well as a royal name in Scotland. In Wales *Dewi* was an early form, *Dafydd* a later one. In their *Welsh Surnames,* T.J. and Prys Morgan say that *Deio* and *Deios* were also synonyms of Dafydd. The sound of these names clearly confused English-speaking registrars, who recorded them variously as **Daus, Dayace, Dayhouse, Dayhus, Dayus, Deios, Deyos, Dias, Diass, Dio, Dios, Dioss, Dyas, Dyass, Dyehouse, Dyhorse, Dyhouse, Dyo, Dyos, Dyoss, Dyous, Dyus**. Welsh diminutive forms of Deio and Deios gave rise to such forms as *Deicyn* and *Deicws,* in turn recorded as **Dackin, Dackine, Dacking, Dackyn, Dakin, Daking, Daykin, Daywyn, Deacon, Deakin, Deakins, Deakon, Dekin, Dekins, Dicken, Dickin, Dykins.** But many of these forms could equally well be associated with RICHARD.

Is Your Name Davi(e)s is a little book by Nicholas Gould published in 1983. It contains interesting anecdotes about famous bearers of the names Davis and Davies, along the lines of: 'The women's world record for non-stop talking is held by Mrs Mary E. Davis, who spoke for 110 hours 30 minutes on the radio in the USA.' (The men's record is some forty hours longer, it seems). The same author also published five other booklets, *(Is Your Name) Brown(e); Jones; Smith; Taylor; Williams.*

Chambers' *Book of Days* quotes the following extract from a last will and testament of 1788: 'I, David Davis, of Clapham, Surrey, do give and bequeath to Mary Davis, daughter of Peter Delaport, the sum of 5 shillings, which is sufficient to enable her to get drunk for the last time at my expense.'

Da Vinci *see* VINCENT.

Davis, Davison, Davitt, Davson, Davy, Davys, Daw, Dawe, Dawes, Dawkins, Dawson *see* DAVID.

Day, Daye, Dayman, Dey, Deye (Eng) In some instances a pet form of *David*, with Dayman being 'David's servant.' Also an occupational name, indicating a farm-worker such as a dairy-maid. Here the word *day* is the same as the *-dy* of the word *lady*, which originally referred to someone who 'kneaded the dough to make bread.' There were also some Old English personal names which began with *daeg* 'day.' A modern Day could be the descendant of someone who bore such a name.

Dayace, Dayhouse, Dayhus, Daykin *see* DAVID.

Daysh *see* ASH.

Dayus, Daywyn, Deacon *see* DAVID.

Deakes *see* DITCH, RICHARD.

Deakin, Deakins, Deakon *see* DAVID.

Dealbridge, Delbridge, Dellbridge *see* BRIDGE.

Deam *see* DEMPSTER.

Dean, Dane, Deane, Deaner, Deen, Denman, Denner (Eng) Descendant of someone who originally came from a dean, or valley. This meaning is reinforced in the surnames ADEANE, ATHERDEN 'at the dene.' In some instances Dean refers to the church official or his servant. It could also be a nickname for someone thought to resemble such a dignitary in appearance or character. Yet another possibility is that it indicates a Danish ancestor, *see* DENCH.

Dearling *see* DARLING.

Death, Dearth (Eng) Descendant of someone who played the part of Death in a medieval miracle play. *See* VERITY. It could also be a nickname for someone who habitually 'looked like Death,' ie sickly or gloomy. It has been said that the name is really *De Ath,* indicating that the original bearer of the name came from a place called *Ath* in Flanders. Bardsley's mild comment on this absurdity is that 'the day of judgement will ask for proof.'

Debbyhouse *see* BEWES.

De Burgh (Eng) *see* BURKE.

Decourcey, De Courcy, de Coursey (Eng) A name brought to Britain by the Normans, indicating ancestors who came from and perhaps owned estates at one of several places in Normandy called Courcy. The place name refers to a personal name *Curtius* 'short.' For a comment on the desirability of a name such as de Courcy, *see* GRAY.

Deeble *see* THEOBALD.

Deek, Deeke, Deeker, Deekes, Deeks, Deetch, Deetcher, Deex *see* DITCH, RICHARD.

Deem, Deemer, Deeming *see* DEMPSTER.

Deen *see* DEAN.

Deios *see* DAVID.

Dekin, Dekins *see* DAVID, RICHARD.

De La Feld, Delafield *see* FIELD.

Dempster, Deam, Deem, Deemer, Deeming, Demer, Demers, Deming, Dome (Eng) A deemer was a person who pronounced a verdict, who decided someone's doom. Dempster was originally a feminine form but was later used for both sexes.

Dench, Dane, Dence, Dennish, Denns, Dennys, Dentch (Eng) Descendant of someone who was 'a *Dane, Danish*,' but Dane and Dennys have other possible explanations, *see* DEAN, DENNIS.

Denham (Eng) Descendant of someone who originally came from one of the places so-named because it was a 'homestead in a valley.'

Denial *see* DANIEL.

Denis, Denison *see* DENNIS.

Denman *see* DEAN.

Dennell *see* DANIEL.

Denner *see* DEAN.

Dennis, Denis, Denison, Dennison, Denniss, Dennisson, Denny, Dennys, Tenison, Tennyson (Eng) Descendant of a man named *Denis , Dennis,* contracted forms of *Dionysios*. Dionysios was a Greek god whose name is of uncertain meaning. Since St Denis was the patron saint of Paris, the name was popular amongst the Normans. They introduced it to Britain where it enjoyed modest popularity in the surname-formation period. Dennys may sometimes be 'Danish,' *see* DENCH.

Dennish, Denns *see* DENCH.

Dennys *see* DENCH, DENNIS.

Dentch *see* DENCH.

Dentith *see* DAINTY.

Denton (Eng) Someone who came from one of the several places so-named because it was a 'settlement in a valley.'

Denty *see* DAINTY.

Derby (Eng) Someone who came from a place so-named because it was a 'settlement near a deer park.'

Derke *see* DARK.

Derlyng *see* DARLING.

Dermott, Kermode, MacDairmond, MacDarmid, MacDearmid, MacDermaid, MacDermid, MacDerment, MacDermont, MacDermot, MacDermott, MacDiarmid (Irish) Descendant of a man who bore the Gaelic personal name *Diarmait,* of disputed meaning. Suggestions that have been made include 'freeman' and 'free from envy.' The name figures strongly in the Celtic legend describing the elopement of *Dermot* and *Grania* and their pursuit by *Fingal*, who was supposed to marry Grania himself. It was also the name borne by several early Irish kings and saints. KERMODE is a Manx form of this name.

Despenser *see* SPENCE.

De Troys *see* TROHY.

De Vincenzo *see* VINCENT.

Devitt, Dewey *see* DAVID.

Dey *see* DAVID, DAY.

Deye, Deyos, Dewi *see* DAY.

Dexter *see* DYER.

Dias, Diass *see* DAVID.

Dibble, Diboll *see* THEOBALD.

Dick, Dickason, Dicke, Dickels *see* RICHARD.

Dicken *see* DAVID, RICHARD.

Dickens, Dickenson, Dickerson, Dickeson, Dicketts *see* RICHARD.

Dickin *see* DAVID, RICHARD.

Dickings, Dickins, Dickinson, Dickison *see* RICHARD.

Dickman *see* **Ditch**, though 'servant of Richard' is also possible.

Dickons, Dicks, Dickson *see* RICHARD.

Digby (Eng) Someone who came from a places so-named because it was a 'settlement with a dyke.'

Digg, Diggan, Diggen, Diggens, Digges, Diggin, Diggins, Diggle, Diggles, Diggon *see* RICHARD.

Digman, Dike, Dikes *see* DITCH.

Dimbleby (Eng) Someone who came from a place so-named because it was a 'settlement near a ravine.'

Dio, Dios, Dioss *see* DAVID.

Disher, Dishman *see* DITCH.

Disraeli (Jewish) Benjamin Disraeli, in a biographical note attached to Isaac Disraeli's *Curiosities of Literature*, remarks that his grandfather's ancestors 'had dropped their Gothic surname on their settlement in the Terra Firma, and grateful to the God of Jacob who had sustained them, assumed the name of Disraeli, a name never borne before, or since, by any other family, in order that their race might be for ever recognised.' The name is obviously linked to *Israel,* a Hebrew name meaning 'May God struggle, show his strength' or 'may God reign, be Lord.' This was the name given to Jacob at the time of his wrestling with God.

Dister *see* DYER.

Ditch, Deakes, Deek, Deeke, Deeker, Deekes, Deeks, Deetch, Deetcher, Dickman, Digman, Dike, Dikes, Ditcher, Dyke, Dykes (Eng) Occupational name of a 'ditcher,' or 'dyker,' or from residence near a dyke. DISHER and DISHMAN may sometimes belong here, though normally they would indicate a 'dish-maker.' Professor Reaney preferred to associate Deakes, Deek, etc., with RICHARD.

Ditchburn (Eng) Descendant of someone who originally came from the Northumbrian place, so-named for its 'dyke' and 'stream.'

Ditchfield *see* STANSFIELD.

Ditton (Eng) Descendant of someone who originally came from one of the many places so-named because it was a 'settlement surrounded by a dyke.'

Dix, Dixon, Dixson *see* RICHARD.

In *Septimus*, by William Locke, a man named Dix proposes to a woman who remarks that he is 'giving her his name.' He responds: 'It's so short. I've always thought it such a silly name.' Jim Dixon is the comic anti-hero of *Lucky Jim*, by Kingsley Amis. George Dixon was also the name of a trustworthy policeman in a long-running BBC television series, *Dixon of Dock Green*.

Dobb, Dobbe, Dobbie, Dobbin, Dobbing, Dobbings, Dobbins, Dobbinson, Dobbison, Dobbs, Dobby, Dobbyn, Dobey, Dobie, Dobieson, Dobing, Dobinson, Dobson, Doby, Dobyn, *see* ROBERT.

Dodge, Dodgen, Dodgeon, Dodgin, Dodshon, Dodshun,

Dodgson, Dodson, Doidge, Doige *see* ROGER.

Dodge is one of those names that attract puns, even in a cemetery:

> Here lies Bill Dodge
> Who dodged all good,
> And dodged a deal of evil,
> But after dodging all he could,
> He could not dodge the Devil.

Dolittle, Doolittle (Eng) A man with a reputation for idleness. FAYPEW is a similar name from French *fait peu*, 'does little.'

Eliza Dolittle is the Cockney flower-seller who is given elocution lessons by Professor Higgins in *Pygmalion*, by George Bernard Shaw. In its musical version this later became *My Fair Lady*.

Eliza is not related to Dr John Dolittle who lives in Puddleby on the Marsh and talks to his animal friends. The doctor was the creation of Hugh Lofting.

Dome *see* DEMPSTER.

Don *see* DUNN.

Donald, Donaldson, Donnell, Macdonald, MacConnal, MacConnel, MacConnell, MacDonell, MacDonnell, O'Donnel (Scot, Irish) Descendant of a man called *Donald*, Gaelic *Domhnall*, from Celtic elements meaning 'world' and 'might, rule.'

Donavan, Donavin *see* O'DONOVAN.

Donegan, Doonican, Dunegain, Dunnigan, O'Donegaine, O'Donegan, O'Dungan (Irish) Descendant of *Donnagán, Donnucán,* Gaelic diminutives of *donn* 'brown.'

Dongan *see* DUNCAN.

Donn, Donnan, Donne *see* DUNN.

Donnell *see* DONALD.

Donovan *see* O'DONOVAN.

Doole *see* DOUGAL.

Doolittle *see* DOLITTLE.

Doonican *see* DONEGAN.

Dopson *see* ROBERT.

Dorling *see* DARLING.

Doubleday (Eng) This name has puzzled most surname scholars. Lower can only say 'it baffles my ingenuity; 'Weekley says 'impossible of explanation.' Bardsley agrees that it is difficult, but suggests that it might be a form of *double-dent*, indicating a man with two prominent teeth. The Lancashire name SINGLEDAY could then mean a man with one tooth. But the surname TWICEADAY exists, which suggests that the *-day* refers to a dairy worker who was called upon to work both morning and evening. *See* DAY.

Doud *see* DAVID.

Dougal, Doole, Dougall, Dowell, Doyle, Dugall, Dugald, MacDougal, MacDougall, MacDowall, MacDowell, MacDuall, MacDugald, O'Douill, O'Dowill, O'Dowilly, O'Doyle (Scot, Irish) Descendant of a man named *Dubhgall*, a Gaelic personal name meaning 'black stranger,' with reference to Danish invaders.

Douglas, Douglass (Scot) Descendant of someone who lived in one of the Scottish places named for its 'black stream.'

Dovey *see* BIRDSEYE.

Dowell *see* DOUGAL.

Down, Downe, Downes, Downing *see* DUNN.

Gillian Bebbington writes, in her *London Street Names*: 'Downing Street was built by Sir George Downing (1623-1684), diplomat. He sat in both parliaments called by Cromwell, but changed his allegiance when the Restoration was imminent, and hurriedly assured Charles II of his support. Sir George was not popular with his contemporaries, who thought him obsequious, treacherous and mean; Pepys said he was 'a perfidious rogue' and 'so stingy a fellow I care not to see him.'

Dowson *see* DAVID.

Doyle *see* DOUGAL.

Drake *see* DUCK.

Drayton (Eng) Someone who came from one of the several places so-named because it was a 'settlement near a slipway.'

Drew *see* ANDREW.

Drinkale, Drinkall, Drinkald, Drinkhale, Drinkhall, Drinkell, Drinkill, Drinkhill (Eng) From a man's common use of the phrase 'drink hale,' meaning 'drink good health, good luck.'

Drinkwater (Eng) The name means what it says, but the reason for the bestowal of this nickname is unclear. It could have referred to someone who for one reason or another drank only water, but could equally well have referred sarcastically to someone who never drank it. BOILEAU is the French equivalent of the name.

Dryden (Eng) Descendant of someone who lived in a 'dry valley.' *See* SETTLE.

Dubber (Eng) Occupational name, probably of someone who repaired clothes, though 'embellisher of dresses with gold lace' and 'trimmer or binder of books' has also been suggested. Old French *adubeour* meant 'repairer.'

Dubbin, Dubin *see* ROBERT.

Ducat, Duckett *see* PENNY.

Duck (Eng) This term has long been used as an affectionate term of address, but the name could also be a nickname taken from the bird, perhaps referring to a manner of walking. The diminutive form DUCKETT also exists, sometimes being a watered down form of 'duck head.' DRAKE was bestowed on some individuals as a bird-nickname, but descendants of those who bore the Old English name *Draca* 'dragon, snake' would also have become Drakes.

There is an Alabama high school principal whose name is Donald Duck. He once explained that his father named him Donald 'because that's what everyone would have called you anyway.' As it happens, there are many surnames which traditionally attracted a nickname. In the armed forces, at one time, men named WHITE would have been known as *Chalky, Blacky* or *Blanco* regardless of their first names. Similar pairs of names were *Bunny* Warren, *Chipper* Wood, *Dicky* Bird, *Doughy* Baker, *Fanny* Adams, *Lefty* Wright, *Muddy* Walters, *Needle* Cotton, *Nobby* Clark, *Nosey* Parker, *Spud* Murphy, *Slider* Cross, *Smudger* Smith, *Spider* Webb, *Topsy* Turner, *Tug* Wilson. Many more such names are fully discussed by Julian Franklyn in his *Dictionary of Nicknames*. There is also a list of them in the *Guinness Book of Names*, by Leslie Dunkling.

Dudgeon, Dudson *see* ROGER.

Dugall, Dugald *see* DOUGAL.

Duggan *see* QUAGGIN.

Duncan, Dongan, Duncanson, Dunkinson (Scot, Irish) Descendant of *Donnchad*, an early Gaelic personal name where the first element means 'brown.' The second element has variously been interpreted as 'warrior,' 'head' and 'lord.' In Ireland the Gaelic name also emerged as DONEGAN.

Dunegain *see* DONEGAN.

Dunkinson *see* DUNCAN.

Dunkley (Eng) Descendant of someone who came originally from Dinckley, Lancashire. The place name is recorded as *Dunkythele* in the 13th century. Its meaning is uncertain.

Dunklin, Dunkling (Eng) Descendant of someone who originally came from *Dunclent*, near Stone, Worcestershire, 'settlement at the foot of the Clent hills.' The place name was given as *Dunklyn* on a 16th century map and was mentioned as *Dunklin* in a 17th century register. The final -*g* of Dunkling was added unnecessarily by over-zealous registrars who thought that -*lin* was an uneducated pronunciation of -*ling*. Since DUNKLEY was far more commonly found than Dunklin, Dunkling, the latter names were often recorded as Dunkley in early registers.

Dunn, Don, Donn, Donnan, Donne, Down, Downe, Downes, Downing, Dunne, Dunnet, Dunning, O'Dunn, O'Dunne (Scot, Irish) Descendant of *Donn* 'dark, brown,' a Gaelic personal name that would originally have indicated someone with dark hair or a swarthy complexion. The name would have much the same meaning in an English context. In Scotland, earlier forms of the name such as *de Dun* point to a place name origin, eg Dun in Tayside, named for its 'fort.' *See* GAVIN.

Dunnigan *see* DONEGAN.

Dunning *see* DUNN.

Dunton (Eng) Someone who came from one of the several places so-named because it was a 'settlement on a hill.'

Duparc *see* PARK.

D'Urberville, Durbeyfield *see* BEWES.

Durham (Eng) Descendant of someone who originally came from the city so-named because it was a 'hill island.'

Durk *see* DARK.

Durling *see* DARLING.

Dyas, Dyass *see* DAVID.

Dybald, Dyball, Dybell *see* THEOBALD.

Dyer, Dexter, Dister, Dyers, Dyson, Dyster (Eng) Occupational name of a dyer. Dexter and Dyster were originally feminine forms.

Dyhorse, Dyhouse, Dykins, Dyo, Dyos, Dyoss, Dyous *see* DAVID.
Dyke, Dykes *see* DITCH.
Dykins *see* RICHARD.
Dyrling *see* DARLING.
Dyson, Dyster *see* DYER.
Dyus *see* DAVID.

Ead, Eacock, Eaddy, Eade, Eades, Eadie, Eads, Eady, Eakin, Eakins, Eason, Easson, Eddison, Ede, Edes, Edeson, Edison, Edkins, Edson (Eng) Descendant of *Edith*, an Old English personal name composed of elements meaning 'prosperity' and 'strife.'

Eagan, Eakin *see* HIGGINS.

Eame, Eames, Emes, Heams, Hemes, Neam, Neame (Eng) Descendant of a maternal uncle, one who acted as guardian to children.

Earl, Earle, Earles, Earll, Harle, Hearl, Hearle, Hurle, Hurles, Hurll (Eng) Occupational name for a servant in an earl's household or ironic nickname for someone thought to behave like a nobleman.

Earnshaw (Eng) Descendant of someone who originally came from the Lancashire place, so-named because it was the 'eagle's nook.'

    This is also a famous literary name thanks to Emily Brontë's *Wuthering Heights*. Catherine Earnshaw is the girl whose passionate love is famously expressed in the words 'I am Heathcliff.'

Earthroll, Earthrowl (Eng) Professor Reaney agrees with Lower that this name, two examples of which were listed in the *London Directory* of 1852, must mean 'ear-hole.' He adds that, like Lower, he 'cannot begin to guess how or why it became a surname.'

Eason, Easson *see* EAD

East, Eastend, Eastes, Eastham, Eastland, Eastman, Easton, Este (Eng) Dweller to the east of a village, or someone who originally came from a place named as an eastern settlement. *See* WEST.

Eastall, Eastell, Estall, Estel (Eng) Occupational name of a servant at the East Hall.

Eastbrook, Eastabrook, Easterbrook, Estabrook, Esterbrook

(Eng) Descendant of someone who lived near the eastern stream.

Eastcott, Eastcourt, Escot, Escott, Estcourt (Eng) Descendant of someone who dwelt in the 'eastern cottage.'

Eastell, Estall *see* EASTALL.

Eastend, Eastes *see* EAST.

Eastgate (Eng) Descendant of someone who dwelt near the eastern gate of a town or castle.

Eastham, Eastland, Eastman, Easton *see* EAST.

Eastlake (Eng) Descendant of someone who lived near the 'east lake.'

WESTLAKE occurs as a surname for a similar reason, but Lower remarks rather pompously: 'I have searched in vain for a lake that is either boreal or meridional.' In other words, *Northlake* and *Southlake* do not seem to exist as surnames.

Eastwood (Eng) Someone who originally came from a place named for its eastern wood or lived near the wood to the east of a settlement.

Eaton, Eyton (Eng) Descendant of someone who came from any of the places bearing this name because of a 'settlement on an island' or 'settlement on low-lying ground.'

Eaves, Eaveson *see* EVE.

Eccles, Eccleston (Scot, Eng) Descendant of someone who came from one of the places bearing these names, each named for its 'church.'

Edbro (Eng) Descendant of a man named *Eadburgh*, an Old English personal name composed of elements meaning 'prosperity-fortress.'

Eddison *see* EAD.

Eddowes *see* EDWARDS.

Ede, Edes, Edeson *see* EAD.

Edgerton (Eng) Someone who came from a place so-named because it was a 'settlement on a hillside.'

Edgoose *see* NEGUS.

Edison, Edkins *see* EAD.

Edmund, Edmands, Edmenson, Edminson, Edmond, Edmonds, Edmondson, Edmons, Edmonson, Edmunds, Edmundson (Eng) Descendant of a man named *Edmund*, an Old

English personal name that survived the Norman Conquest thanks to its saintly and royal connections. It is composed of elements which mean 'prosperity' and 'protector.'

Edson *see* EAD.

Edwards, Bedard, Beddard, Bedward, Bedwart, Eddowes, Edward, Edwarde, Edwardes, Edwardson (Eng, Welsh) Descendant of *Edward*, an Old English name composed of elements meaning 'prosperity' and 'guard.' The name was much used in the Middle Ages in honour of Edward the Confessor, a much loved king. The *B-* forms of this name are Welsh, though Edwards is more frequently found in Wales.

Egan *see* HIGGINS.

Eiffel (French, German) Descendant of someone who came from Eifel, a desolate plateau region in Germany between the rivers Rhine, Mosel, Ahr and Our.

Gustave Eiffel (1832-1923) was the constructor of the tower which bears his name. For forty years 'the Three Hundred Metre Tower,' as it was formerly known, was the highest man-made structure in the world. Now a symbol of Paris which is recognized throughout the world, the Eiffel Tower was bitterly attacked by French literati while in the course of construction. Guy de Maupassant called it a 'disgraceful skeleton;' Verlaine said 'I have never seen anything so horrible, it is horrible, ignoble.' A number of other writers, painters and sculptors made a public protest about *l'inutile et monstrueuse Tour Eiffel,* 'the useless and monstrous Eiffel Tower.'

Elcock, Eles, Elias, Elijah, Eliot, Eliott, Elis, Ellacot, Elles, Ellet, Ellice, Ellicock, Ellicott *see* ELLIS.

Elder (Eng) The reference was to the elder of two men bearing the same first name.

Eles *see* ELCOCK.

Elesender *see* ALEXANDER.

Elias, Elijah, Eliot, Eliott, Elis, Ellacot, Elles, Ellet see **Elcock.**

Ellington (Eng) Someone who came from a place so-named because it was the 'settlement of *Ealda's* people.'

Ellis, Bellis, Bellison, Bellyse, Elcock, Eles, Elias, Elijah, Eliot, Eliott, Elis, Ellacot, Elles, Ellet, Ellice, Ellicock, Ellicott, Elliot,

Elliott, Ellison, Elliss, Ellison, Elliston, Elson, Elys, Heelis, Helis, Hellcat, Hellhouse, Hellis, Hellison, Helwys, Hillcoat, Hillhouse (Eng) Descendant of a man called *Elias, Elijah,* a Hebrew name meaning 'my God is Yah.' Elias is the Greek form of Elijah. In Wales *ab Ellis* 'son of Ellis' led to Bellis, etc., though T.J. and Prys Morgan, in *Welsh Surnames,* say that these names are more likely to derive from a separate Welsh personal name, *Elisedd,* the meaning of which they do not explain. Professor Reaney believes that an intermediary form *Hellicate* led to Hellcat, but the latter could also be a form of HALKETT, indicating someone who came from Halkhead in Scotland. Many names which originally ended in *-house* weakened this to *-us, -is* in unstressed positions. Hellhouse and Hillhouse would represent false expansions of what was thought to be a weakened suffix. *See* ARMSTRONG.

The Elliots of Jane Austen's *Persuasion* are mostly proud of their name, but William writes: 'I wish I had any name but Elliot. I am sick of it.'

Elm, Ellms, Elmes, Elmhurst, Elms, Nelmes, Nelms (Eng) These names indicate an ancestor who lived near elm trees.

Elphee, Elvey, Elvy (Eng) Descendant of *Aelfgifu* or *Aelfwig,* Old English personal names composed of elements meaning 'elf' and 'gift' or 'war.'

Elsegod, Elsgood (Eng) Descendant of *Ealhgod,* an Old English personal name composed of elements meaning 'temple' and 'god.'

Elshender, Elshenar, Elshener *see* ALEXANDER.

Elson *see* ELLIS.

Elvey, Elvy *see* ELPHEE.

Elwes (Eng) Descendant of a woman called *Eloise,* a Germanic name composed of elements meaning 'healthy' and 'wide.'

Eloise was the name of the beautiful French woman, distinguished for her attainments in languages and philosophy, who became the pupil, mistress and (secret) wife of Peter Abelard, theologian and philosopher. Her violent guardian had Abelard beaten up and castrated. He became a monk and Eloise became abbess in a convent. Subsequently, their letters to each other, in elegant Latin, expressed their life-long fidelity and devotion.

Elys *see* ELLIS.

Embery, Embrey, Embry, Emburey, Emerick, Emerson, Emery, Emory *see* AMERY.

Emes *see* EAME.

Emson, Hemson (Eng) Descendant of a woman named *Emma* 'entire,' a Germanic name introduced to Britain from Normandy. It was the name of Edward the Confessor's mother.

Enderson *see* ANDREW.

English, Angliss, Angless, Anglish, England, Inglis, Inglish (Eng, Scot) A reference to an Englishman, probably a derogatory term in an area where Normans had settled in some numbers.

Enkret *see* ANGHARAD.

Entwistle, Entissle, Entwisle, Entwhistle (Eng) Descendant of someone who originally came from Entwisle in Lancashire, so-named because of the 'ducks (that gathered) at the joining of two streams.'

L'Estrange Ewen, discussing 'the inconsistent spelling of our forefathers' in his *History of British Surnames,* reminds his readers that, 'as in the middle ages the majority if the people were illiterate and unable to spell their own names, they could not possibly convey the information to a recording scribe, the result being noticeable in the large number of orthographic renderings of a surname in ancient rolls, and to a lesser extent even yet in our directories.' He goes on to say: 'Some names gave more trouble than others; thus in a series of nine North of England inquisitions (AD 1276) relating to same affray, a suspected malefactor was variously named, *Aynetwysel, Ennutwesille, Emmetwesille, Ennetwysel, Hennetwysel, Hennetwisele, Hennethysil, Hennetwysil, Hentwysil, Hennethwisell, Hennethuysil*; its modern guise being Entwisle, Entwistle and Entwhistle.

In *The Dividing Line*, a novel by Baroness von Hutten, there is a reference to 'a merry-sounding name, Ross Entwistle; some-thing thrush-like about it.'

Errable *see* ORABLE.

Esh *see* ASH.

Essex (Eng) Someone who originally lived in the county of Essex.

Estabrook *see* EASTBROOK.

Escot, Escott, Estcourt *see* EASTCOTT.

Esh *see* ASH.

Este *see* EAST.

Estel *see* EASTALL.

Esterbrook *see* EASTBROOK.

Eubank, Eubanks *see* EWBANK.

Evan, Bavon, Beavan, Beavand, Beaven, Beavin, Beavon, Bevan, Bevans, Bevens, Bevin, Evans, Evens, Genyns, Givons, Givvons, Heavan, Heavans, Heaven, Heavens, Janes, Jayne, Jaynes, Javens, Jeanes, Jeavon, Jeavons, Jenings, Jenn, Jennings, Jenno, Jenns, Jenyns, Jevan, Jevans, Jevon, Jevons, Jeyn, Jeynes (Welsh) Descendant of *Ieuan, Ifan, Evan*, Welsh forms of John. *Ab Evan* 'son of Evan' gives rise to the forms beginning with *B*-. Some of the forms with *J*- may be from John itself rather than Ieuan. Lower thought that HEAVEN, HEAVENS, etc., were Cockney forms, but they are found mainly on the Welsh border. *See* JOHN.

Eve, Eaves, Eaveson, Eves, Eva, Evatt, Evelot, Evenett, Evett, Evetts, Evison, Evitt, Evitts (Eng) Descendant of a woman named *Eve,* or of a man who played the part of Eve in one of the medieval pageants. *A Dictionary of Proper Names and Places in the Bible*, by Odelain and *Ségineau*, gives 'living' as Eve's most probable meaning. The name was not much used in medieval times, nor, for that matter, is it especially popular today.

Evens *see* EVAN.

Evett, Evetts, Evison, Evitt, Evitts *see* EVE.

Ewan, Ewen, Ewens, Ewin, Ewing, Ewings, Ewins, Hewin, Hewins, Keown, MacCown, MacCone, MacCune, MacEwan, MacEwen, MacEwing, MacGeown, MacKeon, MacKeown, Yewen, Yewens, Youings (Scot) From Gaelic *Eoghann*, itself a form of Latin *Eugenius*, *Eugene* in its normal English form. The name means 'well born, noble.' The *MacK*- forms of the name are usually Irish.

J.R. Ewing of the American television series *Dallas*, as played by Larry Hagman, became very popular in the early 1980s, in spite of (or because of) his often despicable behaviour.

Ewbank, Eubank, Eubanks, Ewbanks (Eng) Descendant of someone who lived near the banks of a stream where yew trees grew.

Ewen, Ewens, Ewin, Ewing, Ewings, Ewins *see* EWAN.

Eye (Eng) Descendant of someone who lived on an island. *See* BIRDSEYE.

Eyton *see* EATON.

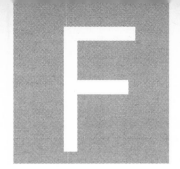

Faber (Lat) An occupational name, equivalent to **Smith**. Faber is a Latin form of the name.

In *The Book of Smith*, Elsdon C. Smith lists forms of Smith in many other languages. They include Arabic *Khaddad*, Armenian *Darbinian*, Assyrian *Nappakhu*, Bulgarian *Kovac*, Catalan *Feffer*, Czech *Kovar*, Danish *Smed*, Finnish *Seppanen*, French *Lefevre*, German *Schmidt*, Greek *Skmiton*, Lithuanian *Kalvis*, Persian *Ahangar*, Polish *Kowal*, Russian *Kuznetzov*, Scottish *Gow*, Spanish *Herrero*, Turkish *Temirzi*. Such names are not as frequently found in the countries concerned as Smith is in the English-speaking world.

Fagan *see* FAGIN.

Faggetter (Eng) Occupational name of a maker of fagots, bundles of firewood.

Fagin (Jewish) Descendant of *Feyge*, a Yiddish feminine name ultimately from German *Vogel* 'bird.'

C.A.Bodelsen, in an article entitled *The Physiognomy of the Name*, said that 'Dickens induced the world to accept an Irish name like Fagin, taken from a friendly boy at Warren's Blacking Factory, as a suitable name for an elderly Jewish criminal (in *Oliver Twist*).' Bodelsen was probably thinking of *Fagan*, an Irish personal name of uncertain meaning.

Fairbairn, Fairbairns, Fairchild (Eng) Nickname for a fair child.

Fairbank, Fairbanks (Eng) Someone who lived near a bank of ferns, or possibly a bank covered with yellow flowers.

Fairbeard, Fairbard (Eng) Descriptive of a man with a light-coloured beard. See also **Whitbread.**

Fairbrother, Farbrother, Farebrother, Fayerbrother (Eng) Probably, as Bardsley suggests, an English rendering of French *beau frère* brother-in-law. Other suggestions have included 'brother of a fair person' or 'the better-looking of two brothers.'

Anthony Powell introduces the unusual name *Sunnyfarebrother* into *A Question of Upbringing*, saying that 'the name "Sunnyfarebrother" struck me as almost redundant in its suggestion of clear-cut, straighforward masculinity. It seemed hardly necessary for Peter to add that someone with a name like that had "done well" in the war, so unambiguous was the portrait conjured up by the syllables.'

Fairchild *see* FAIRBAIRN.

Fairclough, Faircliff, Faircliffe, Faircloth, Fairtlough, Fearcloth, Featley (Eng) Descendant of someone who lived in an attractive clough, a valley with steep sides.

Fairfax, Farefax, Fayrfax (Eng) Nickname for a man with especially noticeable hair, fair and shoulder-length.

Fairfield *see* STANSFIELD.

Fairhead (Eng) A descriptive nickname of someone with a fine head of hair.

Fairman (Eng) Nickname for a handsome man.

Fairtlough *see* FAIRCLOUGH.

Fairweather, Fareweather, Fayerweather, Fearweather (Eng) Nickname for someone of a happy disposition. *See* FOULWEATHER.

Faith, Faithful, Faithfull (Eng) Nickname for a loyal person.

Fallow, Fallowes, Fallows (Eng) Descendant of someone who lived near fallow land. There was also another 'fallow' of different origin which meant a yellowy colour. A nickname for someone with tawny hair is therefore possible.

Fann, Fanning *see* FENN.

Fanner, Vanner, Vannah, Vannar (Eng) From residence near a fen or marsh, or occupational name of a man whose job was to winnow grain - to fan it to remove the chaff.

Faraday, Farraday, Fereaday (Eng) Bardsley suggests that this was the occupational name of a merchant or chapman, someone who travelled about by day.

Fareweather *see* FAIRWEATHER.

Farewell, Farwell (Eng) Descendant of someone who originally came from *Farewell*, Staffordshire.

Farnham (Eng) Someone who originally came from one of the places so-named because it was a 'homestead amongst ferns.'

Farny *see* FERNIE.

Farraday *see* FARADAY.

Farrar, Faro, Farra, Farrah, Farrer, Farrey, Farrie, Farrier, Farris, Farrow, Pharaoh, Pharo, Pharro, Vairow, Varah, Varey, Varro, Varrow, Vary, Varyer (Eng) Occupational name of a 'farrier, smith, iron-worker.'

Farriman *see* FERRY.

Farrington (Eng) Someone who came from a place so-named because it was a 'settlement amongst ferns.'

Farris (Eng, Scot) In England a form of FARRAR, in Scotland of FERGUS.

Farrow *see* FARRAR.

Farthing *see* PENNY.

Farwell *see* FAREWELL.

Fayerbrother *see* FAIRBROTHER.

Fayerweather *see* FAIRWEATHER.

Faypew *see* DOLITTLE.

Fayrfax *see* Fairfax.

Fear, Feare, Fears, Phear (Eng) Nickname for a good companion. As a French name it refers to someone who was proud or bold.

Fearcloth *see* FAIRCLOUGH.

Feare *see* FEAR.

Fearfield *see* STANSFIELD.

Fears *see* FEAR.

Fearweather *see* FAIRWEATHER.

Featherstonehaugh (Eng) Descendant of someone who came from the Northumberland place which formerly had this name, though it is now reduced to Featherstone. The name means 'four stones,' those which made up a so-called *tetralith*, a pre-historic structure like three huge cricket stumps with a single bail across the top. The final element in the name referred to a 'hollow.'

Featherstonehaugh is probably the longest English surname. Names which are either long or complex are known to give difficulty to young name-bearers when they need to be spelt out. *The Reader's Digest* reported in 1977 that a small Indian boy appeared in a London classroom for the first time and the teacher asked his name. He told her it was Van Ratarataam Narasimha Rattaiah. 'How do you spell it? asked the teacher. 'My mother helps me,' said the little boy.

Featley (Eng) A corrupted form of FAIRCLOUGH via FAIRCLEY, FATELEY.

Feffer *see* FABER.

Feild, Feilden, Feilding *see* FIELD.

Felhouse *see* **Fellow.**

Fell, Feller, Fellman (Eng) There are two distinct meanings of 'fell' which could lie behind these names. The reference could be to someone who lived on a 'fell,' ie an upland tract of moorland. They could also be occupational names for someone who dealt in 'fells,' animal skins or hides. There was formerly a surname *Fellmonger*, who would have been someone who prepared fells for the tanner.

Gideon Fell is the private detective, created by the American writer John Dickson Carr, who specializes in solving locked-room murder mysteries. Fell has been described as a 'Chestertonian figure' in himself, and is said to recall that writer's detective-priest, Father Brown.

Fellow, Fellowes, Fellows, Fellowship (Eng) Nickname of a comrade, co-worker, partner, fellow-member of a trade guild. Fellowes, Fellows could also be corrupt forms of FIELDHOUSE via FELHOUSE.

Feltham (Eng) Someone who originally came from one of the places so-named because it was a 'homestead in open country.'

Fenn, Avann, Fann, Fanning, Fenning, Van, Vance, Vann, Vanne, Vanns, Venn, Venning (Eng) Descendant of someone who lived near a fen or marsh.

Fenner *see* VENNER.

Fenning *see* FENN.

Fenton (Eng) Someone who came from one of the several places so-named because it was a 'settlement by a fen.'

Fereday *see* FARADAY.

Fergus, Farris, Ferguson, Fergusson, Fergyson, Ferris, MacFergus, MacFerries, MacKerras, O'Farris, O'Fearguise, O'Fergus, O'Ferris (Scot, Irish) Descendant of *Fearghus*, a Gaelic personal name which Irish authorities explain as 'man strength,' though Scottish writers seem to prefer 'super choice.'

In *The Innocents Abroad*, Mark Twain decides that a French guide must be renamed. 'I expected to have a guide named Henri *de Montmorency*, or Armand *de la Chartreuse*, or some thing that would sound grand in letters to the villagers at home; but to think of a Frenchman by the name of *Billfinger*! Oh, this is absurd. We can't say Billfinger; it is nauseating. Name him over again.' 'Call him *Ferguson*,' says one of the party. It is agreed that Ferguson is a name that is 'practical, unromantic good sense'

Fermor (Eng) A variant of FARMER.

Fernie, Farny, Ferney, Ferny (Scot) Descendant of someone who came from Fernie in the parish of Monimail, Fife.

In *The Stone Angel* the Canadian novelist Margaret Laurence writes: 'Murray F. Lees . . . The F stands for Ferney. Murray Ferney Lees. My mother thought I'd be a poet, I guess, with a name like that. Ferney was mother's maiden name. She loved the name and hated to part with it when she married Dad. Rose Ferney, that was her. A delicate name, she used to say.'

Ferrey, Ferri, Ferrie, Ferrier, Ferriman, Ferrior see FERRY.

Ferris *see* FERGUS.

Ferry, Farriman, Ferrey, Ferri, Ferrie, Ferrier, Ferriman, Ferrior, Ferryman (Eng) Occupational name of a ferryman. In some instances a 'farrier' may be indicated.

Fever, Fevre (Fre) Occupational name of a smith, worker in iron.

Fiddy, Fido, Fidoe (Fre) A name used for an illegitimate child, especially the son of a priest. The French words which lie behind the name literally mean 'son of God.'

Field, Atfield, Byfield, De la Feld, Delafield, Feild, Feilden, Feilding, Fielden, Fielder, Fieldhouse, Fielding, Fields, Fieldsend, Velden (Eng) Descendant of someone who lived on cleared land, a cultivated field. See also CALDWELL, STANSFIELD.

The standard work *English Field Names* is by John Field, who has said that he was attracted to the subject partly because of his name. Field names often preserve earlier meanings of words which can help with the interpretation of surnames. *See* BALL.

Fieldhouse *see* FELLOW.

Fieldsmith *see* SMITH.

Fill *see* PHILIP.

Fillingham (Eng) Someone who originally came from the Lincolnshire place so-named because it was the 'homestead of *Fygla's* people'. *See* STAMP.

Fills, Filson *see* PHILIP.

Finch, Finching (Eng) A reference to the bird, which formerly had a reputation for stupidity. The surname may therefore have been given as a nickname which commented on that quality. Finches were also kept as pets or eaten as a delicacy; the name may therefore indicate someone who caught and traded in them. Fincham 'homestead where there are finches' also occurs, referring to someone who came from the place of that name in Norfolk.

Atticus Finch is the lawyer who defends a black man accused of rape in Harper Lee's best-seller *To Kill A Mockingbird*.

P.G. Wodehouse, in *A Slice of Life,* has a character who spells his name ffinch-ffarowmere, the doubling of the initial letter being a medieval alternative to a capital letter. At one point Wodehouse writes: '"Sir Jasper Finch-Farrowmere?" said Wilfred. "ffinch-ffarowmere," corrected the visitor, his sensitive ear detecting the capital letters.' There are later jokes along the lines of: '"Give me that key, you Fiend." "ffiend," corrected Sir Jasper, automatically.' Mrs Gaskell had earlier made fun of such spellings in Cranford: 'There was a deal in a name – she had had a cousin who spelt his name with two little ffs – ffoulkes – and he always looked down upon capital letters and said they belonged to lately-invented families. When he met a Mrs ffaringdon, at a watering place, he took to her immediately. Mr ffoulkes married her; and it was all owing to her two little ffs.' *See* GRAY.

In *Little Dorrit* Dickens has: '"Is that your married name?" asked Arthur. "Finching?" "Finching oh yes isn't it a dreadful name but as Mr F said when he proposed to me he wasn't answerable for it and couldn't help it could he?'

Finn, Finne, Fynn, O'Finn, O'Finne, O'Fionn (Irish) A nickname based on Gaelic *fionn* 'fair,' a reference to someone's complexion or hair. The diminutive form of *fionn* leads to **Kennan, Kinnan, MacKennan, MacKynnan** via Gaelic *Mac Fhionnáin*.

Huckleberry Finn is the magnificent literary creation of Mark

Twain, described by T.S. Eliot as 'one of the permanent symbolic figures of fiction not unworthy to take a place with *Ulysses, Faust, Don Quixote, Don Juan, Hamlet* and other discoveries which man has made about himself.' *Huckleberry Finn* was published as a sequel to *Tom Sawyer* in 1884.

Firth, Firk, Firks, Freak, Freake, Freaker, Freed, Freeder, Freeth, Freke, Frid, Fridd, Frift, Fright, Frith, Fryd, Thrift, Vreede (Eng) The name originally indicated that someone lived on or near scrubland. For the complex linguistic explanation of how these various names developed from the same original Old English word, see *A Dictionary of British Surnames* by P.H.Reaney. The change of *-ir-* to *-ri-* is well attested and is known as metathesis. The other changes were due to dialectal variations.

Modern bearers of these names report that they continue to be changed because of carelessness, mis-hearing or whatever. A Mrs Frith who wrote to *Woman* magazine in 1970 reported that she had received letters addressed to Smith, Froth, Flitch and Filth.

Fish, Fishe, Fisher, Fisk, Fiske, Fysh (Eng) Occupational name for a fishmonger or professional fisherman.

Collectors of surnames who are fond of compiling lists of names by theme have established a 'fish' group containing such names as *Bass, Bream, Brill, Bullhead, Carp, Chubb, Cockle, Codde, Codling, Conger, Crabbe, Cuttell, Dabb, Dace, Dory, Grayling, Gudgeon, Haddock, Hake, Herring, Keeling, Lamprey, Ling, Loach, Mackrell, Mullett, Mussell, Parr, Perch, Pickerell, Pike, Pilchard, Place, Pollock, Pope, Powter, Ray, Roache, Salmon, Shadd, Shark, Skeate, Smelt, Sole, Spratt, Sturgeon, Tench, Thrasher, Tope, Trout, Tunney, Turbett, Weaver, Welk, Whiting, Winkle*. These may be 'fishy' names by their modern appearance, but in most cases this is merely coincidence. BASS, for example, along with its diminutive BASSETT, was a nickname for a short man. BREAM is from a Middle English word meaning 'fierce, energetic.' BRILL contains an Old Welsh element meaning 'hill,' to which the English word 'hill' was added.

The most ardent surname collector of all time was probably C.L. Lordan, who eventually published a book entitled *Of Certain English Surnames and their Occasional Odd Phases when seen in Groups*. Lordan established over forty groups of names, perhaps the most ingenious being that of 'Imperative Verbs' – *Bang, Crouch, Dance, Dodge, Dye, Fidget, Gotobed, Hide, Hunt, Jingle, Ogle, Pickup, Rattle, Read, Revere, Sitwell, Swallow, Tarry, Tickle, Waddle, Worship*, and the like. In an Introduction he made it quite clear that the names had 'been assorted and grouped, not by the rules of etymology, but from their having a kindred signification or an apparent relationship, though the legitimacy of such relationship etymology would frequently disown.'

An epitaph on a Mr Fish reported by Bardsley in his *Romance of the London Directory*:

Worm's bait for fish, But here's a sudden change,

Fish's bait for worms, – Is not that passing strange?

Fitzadam, Fitzalan, Fitzgerald, Fitzgilbert, Fitzhenry, Fitzhugh (Fitzhugues), Fitzjohn, Fitzmaurice, Fitzneal, Fitzpatrick, Fitzpayn, Fitzralf, Fitzrandolph, Fitzsimon (Fitzsimmons), Fitzwalter (Fitzwater), Fitzwilliam (Eng) The first element in names of this kind is ultimately from French *fils* 'son' in its Anglo-Norman form *fis* (pronouced fits). Some families then retain a capital letter for the name that follows. Names beginning with *Fitz-* at one time had a decidedly aristocratic flavour about them, though Professor Reaney long ago pointed out that there was never any guarantee that they were a sign of noble birth. Presumably the social value of such names came about because Charles II used to name his illegitimate sons Fitzroy, 'son of the king.' As it happens, this particular name had long been in existence, probably with reference to a man who had played the part of a king in a medieval pageant. *See* CHOMONDELEY.

Fitz- surnames were also amongst those that appealed to Elizabeth Gaskell's quiet sense of humour (see Finch). In *Cranford* she writes: 'She had always supposed that Fitz meant something aristocratic. Fitz-Adam! – it was a pretty name, and she thought it very probably meant 'child of Adam.' No one, who had not some good blood in their veins, would dare to be called Fitz.'

Dickens is similarly light-hearted in 'Horatio Sparkins,' one of his Sketches by Boz: 'Teresa's heart beat high. Could he be the Honourable Augustus Fitz-Edward Fitz-John Fitz-Osborne? What a name to be elegantly engraved upon two glazed cards, tied together with a piece of white satin ribbon! 'The Honourable Mrs

Augustus Fitz-Edward Fitz-John Fitz-Osborne. The thought was transport.'

Flamank, Flament, Flanders *see* FLEMING.

Flash, Flasher, Flashman (Eng) Dweller near swampy grassland.

    Flashman is the school bully in *Tom Brown's Schooldays*, by Thomas Hughes. He was turned into the hero (albeit a disreputable one) of a series of witty historical novels by George MacDonald Fraser.

Flather (Eng) Occupational name for a maker of *flathes* earlier *flathons,* 'flat cakes, pancakes.' These cakes were also called *flawns,* giving rise to FLAWN as a surname.

There was formerly a proverbial saying: 'as flat as a flawn'.

Flaxman (Eng) Occupational name for a dealer in flax.

Flecher, Flecker *see* FLETCHER.

Fleeman, Fleeming *see* FLEMING.

Flello, Flellow *see* LEWIS.

Fleming, Flamank, Flament, Flanders, Fleeman, Fleeming, Flemming, Flemons, Flemyng, Flinders (Eng) Descendant of someone who came from *Flanders*, a Fleming. Many Flemish weavers and dyers settled in England in the Middle Ages.

Flesher (Eng) Occupational name for a butcher. *Flesher* was the native English word that was later replaced by Old French *bouchier* 'butcher.'

Fletcher, Flecher, Flecker, Flicker (Eng) Occupational name for an arrow maker, from the Old French *flechier*. See also MACINLESTER. Some Fletcher families may have borne the name Flesher in former times.

    Norman Stanley Fletcher was the central character of the highly successful BBC television series, *Porridge*. Ronnie Barker brilliantly portrayed the old lag of that name who was determined not to let the system beat him down.

Flewellen, Flewelling, Flewellyn *see* LEWIS.

Flewett, Flewitt *see* LLOYD.

Flicker *see* FLETCHER.

Flock, Fluck (Eng) These names probably indicate an ancestor who came from Flocques, Seine-Maritime, France, though 'descendant of *Floki*,' an Old Norse personal name meaning 'out-spoken' which gave rise to **Flook**, is another possibility for Fluck.

These explanations mean little in a day-to-day context. Diana Mary Fluck explained in her autobiography that 'to be born with the name of Fluck, particularly if one is a girl, can be nothing less than disastrous. When I was cast in my first film the director tried gently to explain that the second part of my name would have to be altered. I was only fourteen and did not quite understand his well meant reasoning then, but as I wished to call myself something more exotic anyway, I agreed willingly. But my father was incensed that the family name was not to be used. Finally my mother in a moment of brilliance decided that I would stick to a family name after all, and because my grandmother's maiden name had been Dors, she felt it sounded good to have two names with the same initial.' (Diana Dors, *Behind Closed Dors*).

Bowditch, in his *Sussex Surnames*, records the equally embarrassing *Flucker*, a Scottish name which according to Black (*The Surnames of Scotland*) developed into *Flockhart*. Black saw both names as variants of 'Frisian *Folker* or *Folcker*.'

Flood, Flowitt, Floyd, Floyde, Flude *see* LLOYD.

Fluellen *see* LEWIS.

Flynn, O'Flinn, O'Flynn (Irish) Descendant of a man who bore the Gaelic personal name *Flann* 'red-haired' or 'of ruddy complexion.'

Folster *see* FULLER.

Ford, Foard, Foord, Forde, Forder, Forth (Eng) From residence near a ford. In an Irish context Ford is an Anglicization of various Gaelic names.

In a churchyard at Potterne, Wiltshire, is a gravestone with the following epitaph:

Here lies Mary, the wife of John Ford,
We hope her soul is gone to the Lord;
But if for Hell she has chang'd this life
She had better be there than be John Ford's wife.

Fordham (Eng) Someone who originally came from one of the many places so-named because it was a 'homestead near a ford.'

Forest, Forester *see* FORREST.

Foresyth, Foresight, Foresyte, Foresythe (Scot) Black derives this name from two sources: a place of some such name which he is unable to trace or a personal name *Fearsithe* 'man of peace.' Weekley reports on the *Foresight* variant in his *Surnames,* and it was presumably some such variant that suggested *Foresyte* to John Galsworthy for *The Forsyte Saga.*

There are some interesting comments on attitudes to one's own surname in *In Chancery*: 'All bearers of the Forsyte name would feel the bloom was off the rose. He had no illusions like Shakespeare that roses by any other name would smell as sweet. The name was a possession, a concrete, unstained piece of property, the value of which would be reduced by some twenty per cent at least. There had never been a distinguished Forsyte. But that very lack of distinction was the name's greatest asset. It was a private name, intensely individual, and his own property; it had never been exploited for good or evil by intrusive report. He and each member of his family owned it wholly, sanely, secretly.'

Forrest, Forest, Forester, Forrester (Eng) Occupational name for a forest worker or official, or descendant of someone who lived near a forest. In the Middle Ages a 'forest' was not just a 'wood,' it would have been associated with royal hunting.

Forth *see* FORD.

Foster (Eng) A reference to a foster-parent, or a variant of FORESTER. *See* FORREST.

Fotheringham, Fotheringay (Scot) Someone who originally came from the Scottish place of this name, which was derived in turn from Fotheringhay ' grazing island' in Northamptonshire.

H.G.Wells writes in *The Man Who Could Work Miracles*: 'His name was George MacWhirter Fotheringay – not the sort of name by any means to lead to any expectation of miracles.'

Foulerton *see* FULLERTON.

Foulweather, Foweather, Fowweather (Eng) A nickname for someone whose temperament was being compared to a wet and stormy day. ROWEDDER 'rough weather' is a similar name. Those who had a sunnier disposition were likely to be nicknamed FAIRWEATHER, FAREWEATHER, FAYERWEATHER, FEARWEATHER, MERRYWEATHER, MERRYWETHER, MERIWEATHER. ALLWEATHER and MANYWEATHERS were people whose mood was unpredictable. Professor Reaney states in his *Origin of English Surnames* that the names *Coldweather, Illweather* and *Starkweather,* which occur in medieval records, have not survived, but an American bearer of the name *Starkweather* 'rough weather' is listed by Bowditch in his *Sussex Surnames.*

Fowle, Fowell, Fowells, Fowles, Fowls, Fuggle, Fuggles, Vowell, Vowells, Vowels, Vowles (Eng) The name is based on Old English *fugol* 'fowl, bird,' and could be a nickname for someone who was thought to be bird-like. The forms in V- show normal West Country pronunciation.

Fowler, Fugler, Vowler (Eng) Occupational name of a bird-catcher, fowler. *See* CALDWELL.

Fowles, Fowls *see* FOWLE.

Fowweather *see* FOULWEATHER.

Fox, Foxe (Eng) Descendant of someone who received this animal nickname because he was 'cunning,' had red hair, or reminded his neighbours of a fox for some other obscure reason. Place names containing the element 'fox' that have led to surnames include FOXALL 'fox hollow,' FOXLEY 'fox wood,' FOXTON 'fox valley,' FOXWELL 'fox stream.'

Francis, Frances, Francey, Francie, Francies (Eng) Descendant of *Francis,* from a Latin name meaning 'Frenchman.' The name was well used in the Middle Ages because of St Francis of Assisi, who lived in the 12th century.

Franklin, Francklin, Francklyn, Franklen, Frankling, Franklyn (Eng) A freeman, a gentleman ranking below a knight but otherwise of considerable social status.

Fraser, Frazer, Frazier (Scot) This name is thought to be Norman, but no satisfactory origin of the name can be found. Legend has long associated it with French *fraises* 'strawberries,' saying that the name was bestowed by a king of France on the man who presented him with a dish of strawberries.

Freak, Freake, Freaker, Freed, Freeder *see* FIRTH.

Frear, Frearson *see* FRIAR.

Freeman, Freebody, Freedman (Eng) Descendant of someone who was not a serf. The latter was a modified slave, his duties to his master being limited by law and custom, but his position was probably not a happy one.

Freer *see* FRIAR.

Freeth, Freke *see* FIRTH.

Freud (Ger) Nickname for soomeone who was cheerful, from German *Freude* 'joy.'

Frewen, Frewin, Frewing, Frowen, Fruen, Fruin (Eng) Descendant of *Freowine,* an Old English personal name composed of elements meaning 'free-friend.'

Frewer (Eng) Descendant of *Freowaru*, an Old English personal name composed of elements meaning 'free-shelter.'

Frewin, Frewing *see* FREWEN.

Friar, Frear, Frearson, Freer, Frier, Frierson, Fryer (Eng) Nickname for someone who acted as piously as a friar, or monk, or occuptional name for an employee at a friary.

Frid, Fridd, Frift, Fright *see* FIRTH.

Frisby (Eng) Someone who came from a place so-named because it was a 'settlement of the *Frisians.*'

Frith *see* FIRTH.

Frowen, Fruen, Fruin *see* FREWEN.

Fryd *see* FIRTH.

Fryer *see* FRIAR.

Fuggle, Fuggles *see* FOWLE.

Fugler *see* FOWLER.

Fuller, Folster, Fullen, Fulloon, Voller (Eng) Occupational name for a fuller of cloth. This involved treading or beating it to cleanse it and make it thicker. Folster indicates a woman who pursued this trade. Fullen is from Old French *fulun* 'fuller.' WALKER and TUCKER refer to the same occupation.

Fullerton, Foulerton, Fullarton (Eng) Someone who came from a place so-named because it was a 'settlement of bird-catchers.'

Fulloon *see* FULLER.

Fylan *see* WHELAN.

Fynn *see* FINN.

Fysh *see* FISH.

Gail *see* GALE.

Gailer *see* GALLANT.

Gaiter (Fre) Occupational name of a watchman, guard.

Galasby *see* GILLESPIE.

Gale, Gail, Gayle (Eng) Nickname for a cheerful person, or descendant of a man bearing a Germanic personal name which also meant 'cheerful.'

In *The Wizard of Oz* it is Dorothy Gale who is carried away to Oz. Perhaps L. Frank Baum, who wrote the original story, was thinking of 'gale' in its weather sense and wanted her name to link with the 'cyclone' that was to transport her.

Galeaspe *see* GILLESPIE.

Galer *see* JAILER.

Gall, Gaul, Gaule, Gault, Gaw, Gell, Gill, Killea, Killey, Killie, Killy, Magill, MacAgill, MacGill, MacEgill, MacIngill (Gaelic) Forms of Gaelic *Mac an Ghaill* 'son of the foreigner.' Gill can also be from *Giles* or *Julian*.

Gallagher, Gallacher, Gallaher, Galliher, Gallogher, O'Gallagher, O'Galleghure (Irish) Descendant of *Gallchobhar,* a Gaelic personal name meaning 'foreign help, support.'

Gallant, Gaillard, Galand, Galant, Galland, Gallard, Galliard, Gay, Gaye, Gaylard, Gaylord, Gillard (Fre) Nickname for a cheerful person.

Galliford, Galliver *see* GULLIVER.

Galliher, Gallogher *see* GALLAGHER.

Galsworthy (Eng) From a Devonshire place name, indicating a 'slope with bog myrtle.' There is also a Cornish surname GOLDSWORTHY, from a Cornish place name possibly indicating a 'field where fairs took place.'

Galton (Eng) Someone who came from a place so-named because it was a 'settlement subject to tax.'

Gamut A name apparently invented by James Fenimore Cooper for a character in *The Last of the Mohicans*. It is difficult to see how the name could derive from the word gamut, which originally had a technical sense in music before it came to mean 'the complete range' in more general terms. Cooper makes use of the name to launch into the subject of Indian naming: '"How do you name yourself?" "Gamut - David Gamut." "A very good name, and, I dare say, handed down from honest forefathers. I'm an admirator of names, though the Christian fashions fall far below savage customs in this particular. The biggest coward I ever knew was called Lyon; and his wife, Patience, would scold you out of hearing in less time than a hunted deer would run a rod. With an Indian 'tis a matter of conscience, what he calls himself, he generally is – not that Chingachgook, which signifies Big Serpent, is really a snake, big or little, but that he understands the windings and turnings of human natur', and is silent, and strikes his enemies when they least expect him".'

Ganson *see* GAVIN.

Gant, Gaunt, Gaunter (Eng) Gaunt is in some cases a form of *Ghent*. It then indicates an ancestor who came from the place in Flanders of that name, as did many skilled workmen in the early Middle Ages. The name can also derive from a nickname, describing a man who had a gaunt appearance. Another possibility is that it comes from French *gant* 'glove,' making it an occupational name for a glove-maker. Professor Weekley noted that most bearers of this name live in Lincolnshire, where the crested grebe is called the *gannet* or *gant*. Since he also believed that the fen country was 'one of the great centres of bird nicknames,' he concluded that this was a nickname based on the bird, presumably indicating the stupidity or greediness with which it has traditionally been associated.

In *Richard II*, when the king asks: 'How is't with aged Gaunt?' Shakespeare makes John of Gaunt comment on his own name: 'O, how that name befits my composition! Old Gaunt, indeed; and gaunt in being old. Within me grief has kept a tedious fast; And who abstains from meat who is not gaunt? For sleeping

England long time have I watch'd; Watching breeds leanness, leanness is all gaunt.'

Garbo (Ital) Nickname for someone with 'pleasing manners, grace.'

Joseph G. Fucilla adds a note, in *Our Italian Surnames*, that 'the Florentine del Garbo is related to *lana del Garbo*, 'garbo wool,' ie 'wool from *Algarvia* (the Algarve) in Portugal.' The textile gave the name to a street in Florence. It was then assumed as a surname by the famous doctors, Dino and Tommaso, who lived in it.'

The Swedish actress Greta Lovisa Gustaffson was later to make the name far more famous when she adopted it in 1923 and became Greta Garbo. A dozen different explanations have been offered in various Garbo biographies as to why she chose this name; they are summarized by Adrian Room in his *Naming Names*. In her later search for anonymity, Garbo used various other names, including Harriet Brown, Gussie Berger, Mary Holmquist, Jean Clerk, Karin Lund, Emily Clark, Jane Emerson and Alice Smith.

Gardner, Garden, Gardener, Gardiner, Gardyne, Jardin, Jardine (Eng, Scot) Occupational name of a gardener, who was concerned with producing food rather than ornamental flowers. French *jardin 'g*arden' gives rise to the Scottish forms of this name.

Garrett, Garrad, Garratt, Garred, Garrets, Garretson, Garrettson, Garrison, Gerald, Geratt, Gerold, Gerrett, Gerrod, Jarad, Jared, Jarratt, Jarred, Jarrett, Jarritt, Jarrold, Jerratt, Jerred, Jerrold (Eng) Descendant of a man named *Gerard* 'spear brave' or *Gerald* 'spear rule'. The forms with *l* in them are from the latter name only. These two names were both popular amongst the Normans and were quickly adopted in Britain.

Gascoigne, Gascon, Gascoyne, Gaskin, Gasking (Eng) Descendant of someone who came from *Gascony*, the former French province in the south west of the country. In the 6th century the place name was *Vasconia*, reflecting its occupation by the *Vascones*, the Spanish tribe now known as *Basques*.

Gaston (Fre) Descendant of *Gaston*, a Germanic personal name meaning 'guest.' The name was introduced to Britain by the Normans.

Gaul, Gaule, Gault *see* GALL.

Gavin, Ganson, Gaunson, Gauvain, Gauvin, Gaven, Gawen,

Gawenson, Gawne, Wane (Eng) From an Old French name *Gauvin* which became *Gawayne, Gawain* in Middle English. Made known by the tales of King Arthur and his knights, one of whom was Sir Gawain, nephew of the king. Possibly an Old Welsh name with a meaning something like 'hawk of the plain' or 'white hawk.'

Names sometimes come into their own when juxtaposed with others. A newspaper correspondent reported some time ago that three of his colleagues were named, respectively, *Beane* and *Gawne* and *Dunnett*.

Gaw *see* GALL.

Gay, Gaye, Gaylard *see* GALLANT.

Gayle *see* GALE.

Gayler *see* JAILER.

Gaylord *see* GALLANT.

Gazard *see* GOOSE.

Geffen, Geffers *see* GEOFFREY.

Gell *see* GALL.

Gellion *see* JULIAN.

Gemson *see* JAMES.

Genner, Genower *see* JENNER.

Genyns *see* EVAN.

Geoffrey, Geffen, Geffers, Geoffroy, Gepson, Giffen, Giffin, Jaffray, Jaffrey, Jaffry, Jeafferson, Jeaffreson, Jebbs, Jebson, Jefcoat, Jefcoate, Jefcott, Jeff, Jeffares, Jeffcoat, Jeffcoate, Jeffcock, Jeffcote, Jeffcott, Jeffe, Jefferds, Jefferey, Jefferies, Jefferis, Jeffers, Jefferson, Jeffery, Jefferyes, Jefferys, Jeffes, Jeffkins, Jeffkyns, Jeffray, Jeffree, Jeffress, Jeffrey, Jeffreys, Jeffries, Jeffry, Jeffryes, Jeffs, Jefts, Jeoffroy, Jephcot, Jephcott, Jephson, Jeppeson, Jepps, Jepson, Jibson, Jiffin (Eng) Son or servant of *Geoffrey*, the original meaning of which is uncertain. This was a popular name in the Middle Ages at all levels of society.

George, Georgeson (Eng) Descendant of a man named *George*, Greek 'farmer.' The name was surprisingly little used in medieval times, in spite of the fact that St George was patron saint of England.

Gepson *see* GEOFFREY.

Gerald, Geratt, Gerold, Gerrett, Gerrod *see* GARRETT.

Gibb, Gibben, Gibbens, Gibbes, Gibbeson, Gibbin, Gibbings, Gibbins, Gibbon, Gibbons, Gibbs, Giblet, Gibling, Gibson *see* GILBERT.

Giffen, Giffin *see* GEOFFREY.

Giggle *see* JEKYLL.

Gilbert, Fitzgilbert, Gibb, Gibben, Gibbens, Gibbes, Gibbeson, Gibbin, Gibbings, Gibbins, Gibbon, Gibbons, Gibbs, Giblet, Gibling, Gibson, Gilbard, Gilbart, Gilbeart, Gilbertson, Gilburt, Gillbard, Gipson, Guilbert, Gypson (Eng) Descendant of *Gilbert*, a Germanic name composed of the elements 'pledge – bright.' The name was introduced to Britain by the Normans and was much used in the Middle Ages. In the 12th century there was a St Gilbert, born in Lincolnshire. He joined the order of monks which he had himself founded and lived a life of penance until his death at the age of 106.

Gilbride *see* KILBRIDE.

Giles, Giliat, Giliot, Gill, Gillatt, Gillet, Gillett, Gillette, Gilliot, Gillot, Gillott, Gillyat, Gilson, Gillson, Gilyot, Gilyott, Gyles, Jellett, Jellis, Jellis, Jiles, Jillet, Jillitt (Eng) Son of *Giles*, a corrupt form of a Latin name which meant 'young goat.' An 8th century saint who bore this name was responsible for its popularity in the Middle Ages.

Gilhaspy, Gilispie *see* GILLESPIE.

Giliot *see* GILES.

Gill (Eng) A pet form of *Giles* or *Julian*.
An 18th century epitaph in an English churchyard comments unkindly:

> Beneath this smooth stone,
> By the bone of his bone,
> Sleeps Mr Jonathan Gill.
> By lies when alive
> This attorney did thrive
> And now that he's dead he lies still.

Gillanders *see* ANDREW.

Gillard *see* GALLANT.

Gillaspik, Gillaspy, Gilhespy *see* GILLESPIE.

Gillatt *see* GILES.

Gillbard *see* GILBERT.

Gillbride *see* KILBRIDE.

Gillespie, Aspig, Aspol, Galasby, Galeaspe, Gilaspy, Gilhaspy, Gilispie, Gillaskie, Gillaspik, Gillaspy, Gilhespy, Gillespey, Gillespy, MacGillaspick (Gaelic) Forms of Gaelic *Mac Gille Easbuig* servant of the bishop.

Gillet, Gillett, Gillette *see* GILES.

Gillian, Gillings, Gillion, Gillions *see* JULIAN.

Gilliot, Gillot, Gillott, Gillyat *see* GILES.

Gilliver *see* GULLIVER.

Gillson *see* JULIAN.

Gilman (Eng) Descendant of someone who was a servant of a Norman called *Guillaume*, the French form of *William*.

Gilson, Gillson, Gilyot, Gilyott *see* GILES.

Gimson *see* JAMES.

Ginner *see* JENNER.

Gipson *see* GILBERT.

Gittins, Gittings, Gittoes, Gittus *see* GRIFFITH.

Givons, Givvons *see* EVAN.

Glubb (Eng) This seems to be a Cornish name, possibly a form of *glyb* 'damp.' The name is rare, but it had certainly reached America by the 1860s. A John Glubb is mentioned by Nathaniel Bowditch in his *Suffolk Surnames*.

Dickens was also familiar with the name. In *Dombey and Son* occurs: 'I wish you'd tell old Glubb to come and see me, if you please.' 'What a dreadful low name!' said Mrs Blimber. 'Unclassical to a degree. Who is the monster, child?'

Goadby (Eng) Someone who came from one of the several places so-named because it was '*Gouti's* village.'

Godbeer, Godber *see* GOODBY.

Godsal (Eng) Nickname for a 'good soul,' an honest person.

Godsafe, Godsave, Godsalve, Godseff, Godsiff (Eng) From a man's frequent use of the common medieval oath 'God's (be)half,' meaning 'for God's sake.'

Godwin *see* GOODWIN.

Goldie, Goldney *see* BIRDSEYE.

Goldrich, Goldwright (Eng) Descendant of *Goldric*, an Old English personal name composed of elements meaning 'gold-ruler.'

Goldsworthy *see* GALSWORTHY.
Goldwright *see* GOLDRICH.
Gollins *see* JEKYLL.
Goodale, Goodall, Goodayle, Goodhale, Goodhall (Eng) A man who made and sold good ale. A connection with one of the Northern English places called Goodhall is also possible.
Goodanew *see* GOODENOUGH.
Goodayle *see* GOODALE.
Goodbairn, Goodband, Goodbun, Goodchild, Goodson (Eng) A good child.
Goodbody, Goodboddy, Goodbaudy, Goodfellow, Goodfriend, Goodhart, Goodheart, Goodwill (Eng) Complimentary nicknames for a good person.

These would seem to be harmless enough as names, but a Miss Goodbody who wrote to a newspaper some years ago remarked: 'you can imagine the way I get ragged about my name by some thin-witted boys.'
Goodbun *see* GOODBAIRN.
Goodby, Godbeer, Godber, Goodchap, Goodday, Gooden, Goodenday, Goodier, Goodspeed, Goodyear, Goodyer, Goudier (Eng) These appear to be nicknames derived from a person's frequent use of a standard phrase. 'God be with you,' which became 'God b'ye' then 'Goodbye,' would lead to Goodby. Godbeer and Godber appear to be from 'May God be here (in this house). 'Good cheap' would have been uttered by a trader offering bargains and would have given rise to Goodchap. 'Goodenday' is a variant of Goodday. 'God give you good even' led to Gooden, while a similar wish for a good year gave Goodyear, Goodier, Goodyer and Goudier. Goodspeed is from 'God give you speed.'
Goodchild *see* GOODBAIRN.
Goodday, Gooden, Goodenday *see* GOODBY.
Goodenough, Goodanew, Goodenow, Goodner, Goodnow (Eng) Possibly a phrase 'good enough, all right' often used by the person to whom it was given as a name. Reaney thinks it was a nickname that damned with faint praise, like a schoolmaster's comment in an end-of-term report.

A Dr Goodenough once preached a sermon to the House of

Lords. An anonymous wit wrote:

'Tis well enough, that Goodenough,
Before the Lords should preach;
For, sure enough, they're bad enough
He undertakes to teach.

Goodfellow, Goodfriend *see* GOODBODY.

Goodhale, Goodhall *see* GOODALE.

Goodhart, Goodheart *see* GOODBODY.

Goodier *see* GOODBY.

Goodjohn *see* JOHN.

Goodlad, Goodlatt, Goodlet, Goodlett (Scottish) Nickname for a good servant.

Goodner, Goodnow *see* GOODENOUGH.

Goodrich, Goodwright (Eng) Descendant of *Godric*, a Germanic personal name composed of elements meaning 'good' and 'power.'

Goodson *see* GOODBAIRN.

Goodsmith *see* SMITH.

Goodspeed *see* GOODBY.

Goodwill *see* GOODBODY.

Goodwin (Eng) Nickname of a good friend or descendant of a man named *Godwin*, a given name of the same meaning.

Goodwright *see* GOODRICH.

Goodyear, Goodyer *see* GOODBY.

Goodyear tyres owe their name to Charles Goodyear (1800-60) who invented a vulcanization process which allowed rubber to be used commercially.

Goose, Gazard, Gooseman, Gosman, Gozzard (Eng) Occupational name for a keeper of geese, a goose-herd, or in some instances a nickname for a foolish person. *See* NEGUS.

The goose's reputation for stupidity still exists, though Lower quotes Robert Ferguson's eloquent defence of the bird: 'The nobility of the goose is not so obvious as that of the swan. Yet it was in ancient and honourable use as a man's name. *Genseric*, the name of the great Vandal chief, is referred by Grimm to *gänserich*, a gander. But it was no doubt the wild goose that gave the name; and if we consider, we shall see that this bird has some qualities calculated to command the respect of those early roving tribes. A powerful bird, strong on the wing, taking long flights to distant lands, marshalled with the most beautiful discipline of instinct, it formed no inapt emblem of those migratory plunderers who renewed their unwelcome visitations with each succeeding spring.'

Goosey *see* BIRDSEYE.

Gooseman *see* GOOSE.

Gordon, Gourdon, Gurdon (Scot) Descendant of someone who came from the Scottish place of this name in the Borders region, or from Gourdon in France.

'A correspondent in a recent issue (1943) of the London *Times*,' says George F. Black, in his *Surnames of Scotland*, 'has made the absurd suggestion that the name is derived from *Gordium* in Phrygia and was introduced into Britain by a returned Crusader.'

Gosman, Gozzard *see* GOOSE.

Gourdon *see* GORDON.

Gow *see* FABER.

Graeme *see* GRAHAM.

Grafton (Eng) Someone who came from one of the several places so-named because it was a 'settlement by a grove.'

Graham, Graeme, Grahame, Grayham, Greim (Scot) From residence in the Scottish place of this name, which derived it in turn from the Lincolnshire *Grantham*, possibly '*Granta's* homestead.'

Granger, Grainger (Eng) One in charge of a grange or outlying farm, a farm-bailiff.

Grant, Grand, Graunt, Legrand (Eng, Scot) A use of the Norman French *graund, graunt* as a nickname for a tall person.

In *The Jewel in the Crown*, Paul Scott writes of 'the senior chaplain. His name was Grant, which caused restrained smiles during services when he intoned prayers that began 'Grant, O Lord, we beseech Thee.'

Grason *see* GRAVE.

Gratton (Eng) Someone who came from a place so-named because it was near a 'great hill.'

Graunt *see* GRANT.

Grave, Grason, Graveling, Graves Graveson, Graveston, Grayshon, Grayson, Grayston (Eng) *Grave* could equally well be a form of *grove*, indicating someone who lived near one, or *gravel*, for residence on gravelly ground, or *greyve*, a Middle English word for a farm-bailiff, steward. The last of these is the most likely source, as it is also of GREAVE, GREAVES, GREAVISON, GREEF, GREESON, GREEVES, GRESON, GREVE, GRIEF, GRIEVE, GRIEVES, GRIEVESON, though in some of these names the 'grove' meaning might apply.

Gray, Graye, Grey (Eng) Nickname for a man with gray hair, although de Gray indicates ancestors who came from Graye, in Calvados.

Rumer Godden writes, in *The Greengage Summer*: 'Our surname was Grey: I wished it had been Shelmerdine, or de Courcy, ffrench with two small 'ff's, or double-barrelled like Stuyvesant-Knox, but it was, simply, Grey. "Better than Bullock," said Joss. We had not quite escaped that; Uncle William was a Bullock, William John Bullock.'

Graygoose *see* NEGUS.

Grayham *see* GRAHAM.

Grayshon, Grayson, Grayston *see* GRAVE.

Greathead (Eng) Descendant of someone who bore this descriptive nickname.

Greave, Greaves, Greavison, Greef *see* GRAVE.

Green, Greene, Greening, Greenman (Eng) Usually this indicates that someone lived near a village green. Weekley thought that a reference to a preferred colour of clothing was very unlikely, though there are French (*Levert*) and German (*Grün*) family names which have that meaning. 'The Green Man' was as important to Mayday celebrations as the May Queen. The name may therefore refer on occasion to someone who played that role. A nickname is also possible, based on the 'immature, gullible' sense of 'green.'

Greenacre (Eng) Descendant of someone who lived on fertile land. Similar names with Green as a first element, all indicating where someone lived, include GREENAWAY 'near a grassy path', GREENFIELD, GREENGRASS, GREENHALGH 'green hollow', GREENHAM 'green homestead', GREENHILL, GREENHORN 'green corner' from Old English *hyrne*, GREENHOUGH 'green hollow', GREENHOUSE 'house near the village green', GREENLAND, GREENSLADE 'green valley', GREENWELL 'spring in green field', GREENWOOD.

Black mentions in the Introduction to his *Surnames of Scotland* that one of the absurd derivations that has seriously been put forward is that *Greenhorn* refers to 'a man who used a green drinking cup.'

Greene *see* GREEN.

Greenfield *see* GREENACRE.

Greengrass, Greenhalgh, Greenham, Greenhill, Greenhorn, Greenhough, Greenhouse *see* GREENACRE.

Greening *see* GREEN.

Greenland *see* GREENACRE.

Greenman *see* GREEN.

Greenslade, Greenwell, Greenwood *see* GREENACRE.

Greeson, Greeves *see* GRAVE.

Greg, Gregs, Gregg, Greggs, Gregor, Gregson, Greig *see* GREGORY.

Gregory, Greg, Gregs, Gregg, Greggs, Gregor, Gregson, Greig, Grieg, Grigg, Grigor, Grigson (Eng) Descendant of a man named *Gregory*, from Greek 'to be watchful.' The name was borne by sixteen popes before the surname formation period. *See* MACGREGOR.

Greim *see* GRAHAM.

Gresham (Eng) From residence in a place so-named because it was a 'homestead on grassland.'

Greson, Greve *see* GRAVE

Grewcock, Grocott, Groocock, Groucutt, Growcock, Growcott, Grucock (Eng) Nickname based on French *grue*, 'crane.' Crane itself occurs as a surname, presumably commenting on a man's long legs.

Grey *see* GRAY.

Grief *see* GRAVE.

Grieg *see* GREGORY.

Grieve, Grieves, Grieveson *see* GRAVE.

Griffith, Gittins, Gittings, Gittoes, Gittus, Griffee, Griffen, Griffett, Griffetts, Griffey, Griffice, Griffin, Griffies, Griffis, Griffiths, Griffri, Griffyn, Gruffudd, Gruffydd, Guto (Welsh) Descendant of a man who bore an Old Welsh name (or one of its diminutives) with a basic meaning of 'lord.' The various spellings represent attempts to reproduce Welsh sounds in English, or in

Latin as written by an English-speaking cleric. Griffin, for example, was better suited to take case-endings in Latin than Griffith. The main pet forms of the name in the Middle Ages were *Guto* (*Gitto* in South Wales) and *Gutyn,* the latter becoming *Getyn, Gitton* in the Border area. There is a full treatment of the name in *Welsh Surnames,* by T.J. and Prys Morgan.

Clyde Griffiths is the young man in *An American Tragedy*, by Theodore Dreiser, whose ambition leads him to disaster.

Grigg, Grigor, Grigson *see* GREGORY.

Grubb, Grub, Grubbe (Eng) Nickname for a small person. Burke's *Landed Gentry* reports that a 'family of Grubbe, spelt in the old registers Grube or Groube, migrated from Germany about the year 1430, after the Hussite persecutions, and subsequently settled in Wiltshire.' In this instance the surname would link with German *Grube* 'hollow, pit.'

Margaret Forster's *Georgy Girl* has a woman asking the man she is considering marrying: 'What's your awful surname? It isn't Grubb, is it?'

Gruffudd, Gruffydd *see* GRIFFITH.

Gudgeon (Eng) a spelling variant of 'good John.'

Guilbert *see* GILBERT.

Gulliver, Galliford, Galliver, Gullifer, Gulliford (Eng) This name has understandably been associated with the place name Guildford, but Reaney referred it convincingly to French *goulafre* 'glutton.'

It has been suggested that Jonathan Swift made use of the name for his *Gulliver's Travels* because he was in dispute with Lawton Gilliver, a bookseller. The latter name also has a 'food' connection, since it probably refers to someone who grew 'gilofers' or 'clove gillyflowers,' used as a spice in soups, etc.

Gun, Gunn, Gunns, Gunson (Eng) Descendant of someone who bore the Old Norse name *Gunnr.*

Charles Bardsley writes, in *The Romance of the London Directory*: 'There is a slang phrase about being the "son of a gun." The fact is, "Gun" was a baptismal name, and the surnames Gun, Gunn and Gunson are but sprung from it. It is not many years since Mr. Gunson preached the assize sermon at Cambridge before Mr. Baron *Alderson* and Mr. Justice *Patteson*. The following rhyme got abroad:

> A Baron, a Justice, a Preacher, – sons three:
> The Preacher, the son of a Gun is he;
> The Baron, he is the son of a tree;
> Whose son is the Justice I can't well see,
> But read him Paterson, and all will agree
> That the son of his father the Justice must be.'

(Patteson is in fact 'son of Patrick).

The origin of the phrase 'son of a gun' was explained some what differently in a *Sailor's Word Book* of 1867: 'Applied to boys born afloat, when women were permitted to accompany their husbands to sea.' Some writers claim that this is a euphemistic version of the tale, that the women allowed on board during the 18th century were not necessarily wives. When a child was born it was not always clear who had fathered it. The birth would be entered in the log-book as 'son of a gun', a canvas having been stretched between guns to provide a makeshift lying-in room. This explanation would carry more weight if log-books containing such entries were available for inspection.

Gunsmith *see* SMITH.

Gurdon *see* GORDON.

Guto *see* GRIFFITH.

Guyat, Guyatt, Gyatt *see* WYATT.

Gyles *see* GILES.

Gypson *see* GILBERT.

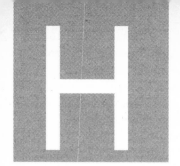

Habbeshaw, Habberjam, Habbijam, Habbishaw, Habergham, Habersham, Habershon, Habeshaw, Habishaw, Haversham, Havisham (Eng) Occupational name of a maker of *hauberks* (military tunics made of chain or ring mail) or the slightly smaller tunics known as *habergeons*.

In Dickens's *Great Expectations,* Miss Havisham is a woman abandoned by her husband-to-be on her wedding day, an event which unhinges her mind. She shuts herself away in Satis House from that day onward, but raises an orphan girl, Estella, and teaches her to hate men. Dickens nevertheless makes his 'happy ending' the marriage of Pip, the hero of the story, and Estella, but only when the latter is older and wiser.

Hachewolf *see* CATCHLOVE.

Hack *see* HAKE.

Hacker (Eng) Occupational name of a cutter of wood (or meat). Hackwood is another name for a wood-cutter. Bardsley also mentions the surname *Hacklittle,* which he thinks was applied to a lazy wood-cutter.

Hackett, Hacking, Hackleman, Hackling, Hackman, Haclin *see* HAKE.

Hadaway *see* HATHAWAY.

Hadgkiss *see* ROGER.

Hafter, Haft (Eng) Occupational name for a maker of tool handles.

Hagan *see* HIGGINS.

Haggard, Agard, Hagard, Haggar, Haggart, Haggatt, Hagger (Eng) Occupational name of a keeper of falcons, or a nickname for a wild and untamed person.

Haggett *see* HAKE.

Haggis, Haggas, Hagges, Haggish (Eng, Scot) Forms of haghouse, thought to be either a place in which firewood was stored or the dwelling of a wood-cutter. In some instances, however, these names may be variants of *Aggis*. As a Scottish surname, the reference is to someone who originally came from any of the places named because they were once a 'clearing in a wood.'

Haggitt *see* HAKE.

Haimes *see* HAMMOND.

Haiselden *see* HAZELWOOD.

Haisell *see* HAZEL.

Haizelden *see* HAZELWOOD.

Hake, Acket, Acketts, Ackling, Hack, Hackett, Hacking, Hackleman, Hackling, Hackman, Haclin, Haggett, Haggitt, Hakes (Eng) Descendant or servant of *Hake* (or a diminutive form of this name). Hake in turn was a form of *Haki,* an Old Norse nickname for someone who had a hook nose or a crooked body.

Halfpenny, Halfpeny, Halpenny, Hapenny (Eng) The reference is to the coin, perhaps to someone who paid a halfpenny rent. It has also been suggested that this could have been a nickname for a small man. *See* PENNY.

Haliburton *see* HAMILTON.

Halison *see* ALLEN.

Halkett *see* ELLIS.

Hall, Halls (Eng) Occupational name for someone who worked at or lived near a manor house.

The famous hour bell 'Big Ben' is thought to have been named after Sir Benjamin Hall, who was Minister of Works when the bell was cast.

Halliwell, Hallawell, Hallewell, Hallowell, Helliwell, Holliwell, Hollowell (Eng) Descendant of someone who lived near a holy spring, or in one of the English places named for its holy well. Bardsley suggests that the reference may sometimes be to *wholesome* rather than *holy* water.

Halpenny *see* HALFPENNY.

Ham (Eng) Descendant of someone who lived on flat low-lying pasture, near a river or stream. *Ham* is also a common element in surnames that derive from place names. Its meaning can be as above or 'farm, estate,' 'enclosed fold.' The modern spelling of a surname, however, may disguise what was once a different word. In **Hambrook,** for example, the first element was originally Old English *han* 'rock,' so that the name meant 'stream with rocks.' *Ham-* may also be part of a longer word, as in **Hamer**, a form of Old English *hamor* 'craggy rock.' Names like **Hambly** and HAMMOND refer to a Germanic personal name *Haimo*. In MAUGHAM what is now *-ham* was originally *-han,* MAUGHAN deriving from a Scottish place name Machan. The *-ham* of Durham was originally a *holm* 'island.' Nevertheless, *-ham* as an element in a surname remains a useful indicator of a place-name origin. Typical names of this type include ALTHAM, ASHAM, BARHAM, BELLINGHAM, BENTHAM, BINGHAM, BRIGHAM, BUCKINGHAM, BURNHAM, CHATHAM, CLAPHAM, COBHAM, CUNNINGHAM, DENHAM, FARNHAM, FELTHAM, GRESHAM, HEXHAM, HIGHAM, INGHAM, LANGHAM, LATHAM, MARKHAM, MASSINGHAM, NEEDHAM, OLDHAM, OXENHAM, PAKENHAM, PEACHAM, PELHAM, SHOREHAM, SMEATHAM, SOUTHAM, STATHAM, TOPHAM, WALSINGHAM, WALTHAM, WENHAM, WHITTINGHAM, WINDHAM, WYNDHAM, YELDHAM.

Hamerton, Hammerton (Eng) Someone who came from one of the several places so-named because it was a 'settlement near a crag.'

Hames *see* HAMMOND.

Hamilton (Eng, Scot) According to George F. Black, in *The Surnames of Scotland,* the Scottish Hamiltons do not derive their name from Hamilton in Lanarkshire, but from one of the English places named *Hambledon* or *Hambleton*. These place names usually denote a 'settlement on a bare hill.' In more general terms, the ending -ton usually indicates a transferred place name, indicating where the family bearing the surname was living between the 12th and 14th centuries. *Ton* was *tun* in Old English, and originally meant an 'enclosed piece of ground.' Later it came to mean 'enclosed land with dwellings, estate, village,' and finally 'town.'

English surnames of this type are very common. When the Mayflower sailed to America in 1620, for instance, there were passengers on board named *Alderton, Allerton, Billington, Button, Chilton, Crackston* and *Eaton*. Similar surnames, which usually mean simply 'family who originally came from one of the places so named' include ACTON, ALDINGTON, APPLETON, ARLINGTON, ASHTON, ASTON, BARRINGTON, BARTON, BEATON, BEETON, BLANTON, BLESSINGTON, BOLTON, BRAMPTON, BRENTON, BRITON, BRITTON, BROUGHTON, BURTON, CARLETON, CARLTON, CARRINGTON, CAXTON, CHARLTON, CHATTERTON,CHESTERTON, CLAYTON, CLIFTON, COMPTON, COVINGTON, CREIGHTON, CROMPTON, DENTON, DRAYTON, DUNTON, EASTON, EDGERTON, ELLINGTON, FARRINGTON, FENTON, FULLERTON, GALTON, GRAFTON, HALIBURTON, HAMERTON, HAMPTON, HARRINGTON, HATTON, HELTON, HILTON, HORTON, HOTTON, HUTTON, KINGTON, KIRTON, LANGTON, LAUGHTON, LAYTON, LEIGHTON, LEYTON, LYTTELTON, LYTTON, MELTON, MERTON, MIDDLETON, MILTON, MINTON, MONCKTON, MORTON, NEWTON, NORTON, OVERTON, PAXTON, PAYTON, PENDLETON, PILKINGTON, PINKERTON, PLUMPTON, PRESTON, QUINTON, REMINGTON, SCRUTTON, SEATON, SEFTON, SHACKLETON, SHIPTON, SINGLETON, SKELTON, SMEATON, STAPLETON, STRATTON, SUTTON, SWANTON, SWINTON, TEMPLETON, THORNTON, THURSTON, TIPTON, UPTON, WADDINGTON, WALTON, WARBURTON, WARRINGTON, WASHINGTON, WATERTON, WESTON, WHARTON, WHITTINGTON, WILTON, WOLTON, YELVERTON. Not all names ending in *-ton* can be interpreted in this way. *Gratton,* for example, is from Old English *greate dun* 'great hill.' *Gaston* is a Germanic personal name.

Hammersmith *see* SMITH.

Hammerton *see* HAMERTON.

Hammond, Haimes, Hames, Hampson, Hamson, Haymes (Eng) Descendant of a man who bore a Norman personal name beginning with the element *Hamo* 'home.'

Hamper, Hanaper (Eng) Occupational name of a maker of *hanapers*, wicker-work baskets, in which valuables were kept.

Hampson *see* HAMMOND.

Hampton (Eng) Descendant of someone who came from one of the several places so-named because it was a 'village settlement,' or 'settlement in a meadow near a stream,' or a 'high settlement.'

Hamson *see* HAMMOND.

Hanaper *see* HAMPER.

Hancock, Hancocks *see* HANKS, JOHN.

Hancox *see* JOHN.

Hand (Eng) Probably a nickname for a man with a deformed hand.

Handcock, Handcocks, Hankin *see* JOHN.

Hanks (Eng) Comments on this surname by various experts in the field reveal the problems of surname interpretation. Patrick Hanks, one of the editors of *A Dictionary of Surnames,* published by Oxford University Press, links his surname to the names *John, Henry* or *Randolph* via *Hankin* and *Hann.* P. H Reaney, in his *Origin of English Surnames,* is convinced that Hanks indicates an ancestor who bore the Old Norse name *Anki.* Basil Cottle, in the *Penguin Dictionary of Surnames,* says it is either a reduced form of HANKINS or comes from an Old Norse name containing the element *arn* 'eagle.' Ernest Weekley, in *Surnames*, remarks that HANN, HANCOCK, HANKIN, HANSON are 'rightly connected by Bardsley (author of *A Dictionary of English and Welsh Surnames*) with Flemish forms of *John.*' He then adds that Camden is equally correct to say that Hann links with *Rann* and *Randolph* (compare HOB from *Robert,* HICK from *Richard.*) A 14th century source also equates Hanne with *Henry.* Weekley comments: 'the harrassed reader will be tempted to conclude that any name can come from anything, nor will he be far wrong.'

Hannibal, Hanniball *see* ANNABLE.

Hanrott *see* HENRY.

Hansard (Eng) Occupational name of a maker/seller of cutlasses or daggers.

Hansom, Hanson *see* HANKS, JOHN.

Hapenny *see* HALFPENNY.

Harber, Arber, Harbage, Harberer, Harbidge, Harbisher, Harbour, Harbur, Herbage (Eng) Occupational name of someone who was responsible for guests in a lodging house. The names derive from the same Old English word that gave rise to harbour in its sense of 'shelter for ships,' the original meaning of *herebeorg* being 'army shelter.'

The *Cambridge Evening News* reported on January 1, 1971 that twin girls had been born to a local *Harber* family over Christmas. One of them had been named Pearl.

Hard *see* HARDY.

Hardacre, Hardaker *see* HARDY.

Hardcastle (Eng) Descendant of someone who came from the Yorkshire place, so-named because of its 'impregnable castle.'

Hardy, Hard, Hardeman, Harder, Hardey, Hardie, Hardiman, Harding (Eng) Nicknames for a brave man, a 'tough guy.' Hard had also become a name in its own right by the surname formation period, so 'descendant of *Hard*' is a possible meaning. In some instances the name may be the same as HARDACRE, HARDAKER, indicating residence on 'stony ground.'

Harenc *see* HERRING.

Hares *see* HENRY.

Harle *see* EARL.

Harliss *see* Airrless.

Harlock, Horlick, Horlock (Eng) Nickname for a man with 'hoary (grey) hair.'

Harp, Harper, Harpin, Harpour, Harpur (Eng) Occupational name of a harp-player employed by a nobleman.

Harreys, Harrie, Harries, Harriman *see* HENRY.

Harrington (Eng) Someone who came from one of the several places so-named because it was a 'settlement on stony ground' or 'settlement on heath land.'

Harriot, Harris, Harrison, Harriss, Harrisson *see* HENRY.

Harrow (Eng) Descendant of someone who came from Harrow in London, named originally for its pagan temple.

Harrowsmith *see* SMITH.

Harry, Harryman *see* HENRY.

Hart, Harte, O Hairt, O'Hart (Irish) Descendant of someone who bore a Gaelic personal name meaning either 'noble' or 'bear, hero.'

Hart, Harte, etc., can also be English, presumably nicknames based in some way on the animal. The hart, a mature male deer, was also the heraldic symbol of Richard II and was widely displayed as a sign during his reign. *The White Hart* has existed as an inn sign, for example, since the early years of his rule in the 14th century.

Hartrick, Hartwright *see* ARKWRIGHT.

Harvey, Harvie, Hervey (Eng, Scot) Descendant of a man named *Hervé*, itself a form of a Breton name meaning 'battle worthy.'

The US military programme to develop a stealth aircraft was unofficially known as 'Project Harvey.' The reference was to the six-foot invisible rabbit who is the friend of Elwood P. Dowd in *Harvey* (1944), the play by Mary C. Chase. This was later filmed with James Stewart as Dowd.

Harys *see* HENRY.

Hasard, Hasardoue *see* HAZARD.

Hasel, Haselar *see* HAZEL.

Haselden, Haseldene, Haseldine *see* HAZELWOOD.

Haseler, Hasell, Haseltine, Haselton, Haselwood *see* HAZELWOOD.

Hasler, Haslet, Haslett *see* HAZEL.

Haslewood, Hastleton *see* HAZELWOOD.

Hathaway, Hadaway, Hathway (Eng) Descendant of someone who originally lived near a heathway, a path across heathland.

There is a long poem *To the Idol of my Eye, and Delight of my Heart, Ann Hathaway*. Since Ann Hathaway was the maiden name of Shakespeare's wife, there are those who have claimed that the poem is his early work. That theory can be discounted, but the verses are of reasonable quality. The last verse runs as follows:

But were it to my fancy given
To rate her charms, I'd call her heaven;
For though a mortal made of clay,
Angels must love Ann Hathaway;
She hath a way so to control,
To rapture the imprisoned soul,
And sweetest heaven on earth display,
That to be heaven Ann hath a way;
She hath a way, Ann Hathaway;
To be heaven's self, Ann hath a way!

Hathorn *see* HAWTHORN.

Hatt, Hatmaker, Hatter (Eng) Occupational name of a hat-maker. *Hatt* may occasionally have been the nickname of someone who wore a distinctive hat.

Hatton (Eng) Someone who came from a place so-named because it was a 'settlement on heath land.'

Hattrick *see* ARKWRIGHT.

Haversham, Havisham *see* HABBESHAW

Hawken *see* HAWKIN.

Hawkesford, Hawkinge, Hawkley, Hawkeswood, Hawkshaw,

Hawkworth, Hawkyard (Eng) Descendant of someone who originally lived in one of the places so named, which refer variously to a (hawk) ford, wood, enclosure, etc.

Hawkey *see* BIRDSEYE.

Hawkin, Hawken, Hawking, Hawkings, Hawkins, Hawkyns (Eng) Descendant of a man called *Hawkin*, a name based on 'hawk' and presumably referring to a man's hawk-like appearance or behaviour. **Hawk, Hawke, Hawkes, Hawks** as surnames can have the same meaning or, like **Hawker,** be the occupational name of a man who trained hawks.

Magnolia Hawks is a main character in Edna Ferber's *Showboat*.

Jim Hawkins is the narrator of Robert Louis Stevenson's *Treasure Island*.

Hawkinge *see* HAWKESFORD.

Hawkings, Hawkins *see* HAWKIN.

Hawkley, Hawkeswood, Hawkshaw, Hawkworth, Hawkyard see **Hawkesford.**

Hawkyns *see* HAWKIN.

Hawthorn, Hathorne, Hawthorne (Eng) Descendant of someone who lived near hawthorns, much used to form hedges.

Hayes, Hays, Heyes, Heys (Eng) Descendant of someone who came from any of the places so-named because they were 'enclosures' or surrounded by 'brushwood.'

Hayman, Heaman, Heyman (Eng) Occupational name of a hay-seller.

Haymes *see* HAMMOND.

Hays *see* HAYES.

Hayselden, Hayzelden, Hayzeldene, Hayzeldeane *see* HAZELWOOD.

Hazard, Hasard, Hasardour, Hazzard (Eng) Nickname for a gambler. CHANCE could have the same meaning.

Hazel, Haisell, Hasel, Haselar, Haseler, Hasell, Hasler, Haslet, Haslett, Hazelman, Hazell, Hazleman, Hazlet, Hazlett, Hazlitt, Heasler, Heaslett, Heazel, Heazell, Hessel, Hessels, Hezlet, Hezlett (Eng) Descendant of someone who lived near hazel trees.

Hazelwood, Aizlewood, Haiselden, Haizelden, Haselden, Haseldene, Haseldine, Haseltine, Haselton, Haselwood, Haslewood,

Hastleton, Hayselden, Hayzelden, Hayzeldene, Hayzeldeane, Hazeldene, Hazeldine, Hazeldon, Hazelhurst, Hazeltine, Hazelton, Hazleden, Hazlegrove, Hazlehurst, Hazlewood, Hazzeldine, Hazzledine, Heaselen, Heselden, Heseldin, Heselton, Heselwood, Heseltine, Hesleden, Hesselden, Hesseltine, Hesselwood, Hesslegrave (Eng) Descendant of a dweller near a thicket of hazel trees, or someone from a place originally named for its hazels.

Hazleman, Hazlet, Hazlett *see* HAZEL.

Hazlewood *see* HAZELWOOD.

Hazlitt *see* HAZEL.

Hazzard *see* HAZARD.

Hazzeldine, Hazzledine *see* HAZELWOOD.

Heaman *see* HAYMAN.

Heams, Hemes *see* EAME.

Heard, Hearder *see* HERDSMAN.

Hearl, Hearle *see* EARL.

Heaselen *see* **Hazelwood.**

Heasler, Heaslett, Heazel, Heazell *see* Hazel.

Heath, Heather, Heathman (Eng) Descendant of someone who lived on a heath or where heather grew. *Heath* is also a common element in place names and the surname can indicate someone who originally lived in such a place.

Heavan, Heavans, Heaven, Heavens *see* EVAN.

Heckingbottom *see* HIGGINBOTTOM.

Heckler (Eng) Occupational name for a dresser of hemp or flax.

This is one of those rare instances where the modern meaning of a word, in this case 'interrupt a speaker with questions and comments,' is justifiably linked with the surname. To heckle was suggested by the idea of 'teasing' in its technical sense of separating fibres.

Hedgcock *see* RICHARD.

Hedge, Hedgeman, Hedger, Hedges, Hedgman (Eng) Dweller by a hedge or occupational name for a man who maintained hedges.

Hedgecock, Hedgecoe *see* RICHARD.

Hedgeman, Hedger, Hedges, Hedgman *see* HEDGE

Heegan *see* HIGGINS.

Heelis *see* ELLIS.

Heffer, Hefferman, Hepher (Eng) Occupational name of a cowherd.

Hegan *see* HIGGINS.

Heginbotham, Heginbottom *see* HIGGINBOTTOM.

Height, Hight, Hite (Eng) Descendant of someone who dwelt on a height, summit of a hill.

Helis *see* ELLIS.

Hell *see* HILL.

Hellcat *see* ELLIS.

Heller (German, Jewish) This could be a money name similar to PENNY, a *heller* being a small medieval German coin, originally silver but later copper. The name survives as Czech *Haler*. As a Jewish name, probably based on German *hell* 'light, bright,' with reference to someone of light complexion.

The American author Joseph Heller amuses himself with surnames in his novel *Something Happened*: 'I am currently occupied (as one of my private projects) with trying to organize a self-sufficient community out of people in the company whose names are the same as occupations, tools, or natural resources, for we have many Millers, Bakers, Taylors, Carpenters, Fields, Farmers, Hammers, Nichols (puns are permitted in my Utopia, else how could we get by?), and Butchers listed in the internal telephone directory.'

Hellhouse, Hellis, Hellison *see* ELLIS.

Helliwell *see* HALLIWELL.

Helton (Eng) Someone who came from one of the several places so-named because it was a 'settlement on a slope.'

Helwys *see* ELLIS.

Hemson *see* EMSON.

Henderson, Hendrey, Hendrick, Hendricks, Hendrie, Heneries, Henery, Henkin, Henn, Henkin *see* HENRY.

Henn (Eng) Ususally a pet form of *Henry,* but a nickname from the fowl is possible, commenting on some aspect of a person's behaviour thought to be hen-like. Several bird names were terms of endearment in the Middle Ages, and Henn could also derive from this source.

Henry, Fitzhenry, Hanrott, Hares, Harreys, Harrhy, Harrie, Harries, Harriman, Harriot, Harris, Harrison, Harriss, Harrisson, Harry, Harryman, Harys, Henderson, Hendrey,

Hendrick, Hendricks, Hendrie, Hendry, Heneries, Henery, Henkin, Henn, Henkin, Henson, Henrey, Henriot, Heriot, Herriott, Hinkins, MacHenry, Parries, Parry, Penry (Eng, Welsh, Scot, Irish) Descendant of a son or servant of *Henry, Harry*. Harry represents English-speakers efforts to pronounce French *Henri*. The name is Germanic, composed of elements which mean 'home' and 'ruler.' The Normans introduced the name to Britain, where it was subsequently bestowed on eight kings. It had already named six kings of France. The *P-* forms represent reductions of Welsh *ap* (son of) *Harries*, etc.

In his novel *Travelling People*, by B.S. Johnson, the hero is named Henry Henry. After he has introduced himself to someone we are told that 'he paused at this perpetual social hurdle to see if he had to explain his parents' Shandean fixation with economy in nomenclature.' The 'Shandean fixation,' however, as described by Laurence Sterne in *Tristram Shandy*, has nothing to do with economy in naming. Walter Shandy believes that there is 'a strange kind of magic bias, which good or bad names, as he called them, irresistibly impressed upon our characters and conduct.' In other words, it is important to choose the right first name.

Johnson's Henry Henry would have been eligible to join the 'My Name is a Poem Club,' founded by an American journalist. Members include Heather Feather, Nancy Clancy, Jane Cane and Hugh Blue.

Hepher *see* HEFFER.

Herbage *see* HARBER.

Herdsman, Heard, Hearder, Herd, Herder, Herdson, Hird, Hord, Horder, Hurd, Hurdman (Eng) Occupational name of a herder of cattle or a shepherd.

Hering *see* HERRING.

Heriot *see* HENRY.

Herrero *see* FABER.

Herring, Harenc, Hering, Herrin (Eng) Occupational name of a fishmonger, seller of herrings.

Herriott *see* HENRY.

Hervey *see* HARVEY.

Heselden, Heseldin, Heselton, Heselwood, Heseltine *see*

HAZELWOOD.

Hesleden *see* HAZELWOOD.

Hessel *see* HAZEL.

Hesselden *see* HAZELWOOD.

Hessels *see* HAZEL.

Hesseltine, Hesselwood, Hesslegrave *see* HAZELWOOD.

Hewat, Hewes, Hewet, Hewetson, Hewett *see* HUGH.

Hewin, Hewins *see* EWAN.

Hewison, Hewit, Hewitson, Hewitt, Hewkin, Hewlet, Hewlett, Hewlings, Hewlins, Hewlitt, Hews, Hewson *see* HUGH.

Hexham (Eng) Descendant of someone who originally came from the place so-named because it was the 'homestead near the warrior's stream.'

Heyes *see* HAYES.

Heyman *see* HAYMAN.

Heys *see* HAYES.

Hezlet, Hezlett *see* HAZEL.

Hick *see* RICHARD.

Hickenbotham *see* HIGGINBOTTOM.

Hickes, Hickeson, Hickin *see* RICHARD.

Hickinbottom *see* HIGGINBOTTOM.

Hickish, Hicklin, Hickling, Hickman, Hickmer, Hickmet, Hickmore, Hickmott, Hicks, Hickson *see* RICHARD.

Hie *see* HIGH.

Higenbotham, Higenbottam, Higgenbottom *see* HIGGINBOTTOM.

Higgens, Higget *see* RICHARD.

Higginbottom, Heckingbottom, Heginbotham, Heginbottom, Hickenbotham, Hickinbottom, Higenbotham, Higenbottam, Higgenbottom, Higginbotham, Higginbottam, Higinbothom (Eng) Descendant of someone who lived at the bottom of a valley where oak trees grew. *See* LONGBOTTOM.

Matthew Arnold thought the name Higginbottom unpoetic. He says in his essay on the *Function of Criticism at the Present Time*: 'What a touch of grossness in our race, what an original shortcoming in the more delicate spiritual perceptions, is shown by the natural growth amongst us of such hideous names – Higginbottom, Stiggins, Bugg!'

Higgins, Higginson, Higgit, Higgons, Higgot, Higgs see RICHARD. In an Irish context Higgins is 'descendant of *Aodhagän,* 'fire.' Other Irish forms of this Gaelic personal name include **Eagan, Eakin, Egan, Hagan, Heegan, Hegan, O'Heagane, O'Heaken, O'Hegane, O'Higane, O'Higgins, O'Huggin.**

Higinbotham *see* HIGGINBOTTOM.

High, Hie, Highe, Highman, Hightman, Hightsman, Hyman (Eng) Nickname for a tall man, or same meaning as **Height.**

Higham, Hyam (Eng) Descendant of someone who originally came from one of the places so-named because it was a 'high homestead.'

Highman *see* HIGH.

Highsmith *see* SMITH.

Hight *see* HEIGHT.

Hightman, Hightsman *see* HIGH.

Higman, Higson *see* RICHARD.

Hill, Hell, Hillam, Hiller, Hillman, Hills, Hull (Eng) Normally an indication of residence on or near a hill, though Hull can also be 'descendant of *Hugh.*' Since there are several Germanic personal names, such as *Hilary,* which begin with *Hil-,* that could also (on very rare occasions) be a source. The first element in such names means 'battle.'

Fanny Hill is a well-known literary bearer of this name. She is the heroine of John Cleland's *Memoirs of a Woman of Pleasure.*

Hillcoat *see* ELLIS.

Hiller, Hillman, Hills *see* HILL.

Hillhouse *see* ELLIS.

Hilton (Eng) Someone who came from one of the several places so-named because it was a 'settlement on a hill.'

Hinkins *see* HENRY.

Hird *see* HERDSMAN.

Hiscock, Hiscocks, Hiscoke, Hiscott, Hiscox, Hiscutt, Hiskett, Hitch, Hitchcock, Hitchcoe, Hitchcott, Hitchcox, Hitchen, Hitchens, Hitcheon, Hitches, Hitchin, Hitching, Hitchings, Hitchins, Hitchisson, Hitchman, Hitchmough, Hitchon, Hix, Hixon, Hixson *see* RICHARD.

Hite *see* HEIGHT.

Hoar, Hore (Eng) Nickname for a man with 'hoary (grey) hair.'
Hob, Hobb, Hobbes, Hobbin, Hobbins, Hobbis, Hobbiss, Hobbs, Hobkin, Hobkins, Hoblin, Hobling, Hoblyn, Hobson *see* ROBERT.

The phrase 'Hobson's choice' has been in use for several centuries. T. Stenhouse explained its meaning and origin in his little book *Lives Enshrined in Language*: 'Tobias Hobson had a stable of forty horses at Cambridge in the 17th century; when a customer came to hire a horse he was not allowed to choose, but was obliged to take the animal standing in the stall near the door. Whence it became a proverb when what ought to be your election was forced upon you, to say "Hobson's choice".'

Hochkins *see* ROGER.
Hodd, Hodde, Hoddes *see* HOOD.
Hodge, Hodgen, Hodgens, Hodgeon, Hodges, Hodgeskinson, Hodgess, Hodgett, Hodgetts, Hodgin, Hodgins, Hodgkiess, Hodgkin, Hodgkins, Hodgkinson, Hodgekinson, Hodgkiss, Hodgkisson, Hodgeon, Hodgshon, Hodgskins, Hodgson, Hodkin, Hodshon, Hodskin, Hodkinson, Hodskins, Hodgson, Hodson *see* ROGER.
Hogg, Hogarth, Hoggard, Hoggart, Hoggarth, Hogge, Hogger, Hoggett (Eng) Occupational name for a swine-herd. A hog in the Middle Ages could also refer to a young sheep that had not been shorn, so these names could refer to a shepherd. Hogg(e) could also have been a nickname, likening the person concerned to a pig.

One of the most publicized 'funny names' in the English-speaking world is that of Ima Hogg, and one of the legends it is most difficult to dismiss is that she had a sister, Ura Hogg. An obituary in *Newsweek*, September 1, 1975, read: 'Ima Hogg, 93, philanthropist who helped found the Houston Symphony in 1913 and served as a mainstay of the orchestra and other Texas cultural institutions, while recuperating from a broken leg, on a visit to London, Aug, 19. Her father, a Texas governor in the 1890s, named Ima after the heroine of a poem written by his brother. Contrary to legend, she did not have a sister Ura.' This lady, usually known as Miss Ima, was very much respected in her home state. It has been said that every Texan has to refute, at one time or another, the story of her non-existent sister.

Hoggins *see* ROGER.

Elizabeth Gaskell, in *Cranford*, has: 'The name of these good people was *Hoggins*. Mr Hoggins was the Cranford doctor now; we disliked the name and considered it coarse; but, as Miss Jenkyns said, if he changed it to Piggins it would not be much better. We had hoped to discover a relationship between him and the Marchioness of Exeter whose name was Molly Hoggins; but the man, careless of his own interests, utterly ignored and denied any such relationship.'

Hogsbotham *see* LONGBOTTOM.

Holdefeld *see* OLDFIELD.

Hollens, Holles, Holley, Hollies, Hollings, Hollins, Hollis, Holly *see* HOLME.

Holliwell, Hollowell *see* HALLIWELL.

Holme, Holmes, Home, Hulme, Hume (Eng) The Middle English word *holm* meant 'holly tree.' Someone who lived near holly trees can therefore be indicated, as with the surnames HOLLENS, HOLLES, HOLLEY, HOLLIES, HOLLINGS, HOLLINS, HOLLIS, HOLLY. Another word *holm* meant 'island' or 'raised land in a fen.' This can also indicate where ancestors were originally living, either in general terms or with reference to one of the places named because it was an island.

Conan Doyle became disenchanted with Sherlock Holmes, the violin-playing, opium-addicted detective he had created in 1887, and tried to have him killed off by Moriarty in 1891. The public insisted on his return and in 1905 he reappeared, having spent the intervening years, said Conan Doyle, in Tibet. He must certainly be one of the world's best-known literary characters.

Holt, Holter, Hoult (Eng) Ancestor of someone who lived near a holt, a small wood or copse, or one who came originally from one of the many places named for such a wood.

Home *see* HOLME.

Honey, Honeyman, Honneyman (Eng) Occupational name of a gatherer and seller of honey.

Honeyball, Honeybell *see* ANNABLE.

Honeybunn, Honeybone, Honeyborne, Honeybum, Hunnybun (Eng) Descendant of someone who originally came from the

Gloucestershire place so-named because of a 'honey stream.' Presumably honey could be collected on its banks.

Honiball, Honneybell *see* ANNABLE.

Honneyman *see* HONEY.

Honniball *see* ANNABLE.

Hood, Hodd, Hodde, Hoddes, Hoods (Eng) Occupational name of a maker of hoods.

Hook, Hooke, Hooker (Eng) Occupational name of a hook-maker, or nickname for someone with a hooked nose, or someone who lived near a river bend.

One explanation of the American slang term *hooker* 'prostitute' derives it from the surname, as borne by a General Hooker in the Civil War. He supposedly encouraged his men to frequent brothels. Robert L. Chapman, in his *Dictionary of American Slang*, prefers a different explanation, relating it to Corlear's Hook, in New York City. This was a red-light district in the 19th century.

Hookins *see* HUGH.

Hoopersmith *see* SMITH.

Hooson, Hoosun *see* HUGH.

Hoover (Eng) An Anglicized form of German *Huber, Hübner* referring to the owner or tenant of a measure of land, a *Hube*. This word occurs also as an element in compound German surnames such as *Mitterhuber* 'middle Hube,' *Halbhuber* 'half Hube.'

Hoover is one of those rare surnames that has become a normal verb in English. People might still speak of 'hoovering' a carpet even if they were using a machine made by another company. The company was founded by William Hoover of North Canton, Ohio, who saw the potential of an 'electric suction sweeper' invented by Murray Spangler.

Hopkin, Hopkins, Hopkinson, Hopp, Hopson *see* ROBERT.

Hord, Horder *see* HERDSMAN.

Hore *see* HOAR.

Horlick, Horlock *see* HARLOCK.

The malted milk drink known as *Horlicks* takes its name from James Horlick, an English pharmacist, and his brother William, who established the Horlicks Milk Company in 1885.

Horn, Horne, Horner, Hornor (Eng) In some instances this name is the same as HORNBLOWER. In other cases it refers to someone who made articles from horn or who lived near a horn-shaped bend in a river.

Hornblower, Hornblow, Horniblow, Orneblow (Eng) Basil Cottle, in his *Penguin Dictionary of Surnames,* compares the official hornblower with the modern factory hooter, since one of his tasks was to summon the workers. A horn was also used as a warning signal.

Hornby (Eng) Someone who came from one of the several places so-named because it was '*Horni's* village.'

Horne, Horner, Hornor *see* HORN.

Horniblow *see* HORN.

Horsewreath, Horsewright (Eng) Reaney suggests that this may be 'descendant of *Osric,*' via forms such as **Ostridge, Ostrick**, though the latter name also means 'keeper of goshawks, falconer.' *Osric* is a Germanic personal name composed of elements meaning 'divine' and 'rule.'

Horsler *see* OSTLER.

Horton (Eng) Someone who came from one of the several places so-named because it was a 'settlement on muddy land.' In one instance the place name refers to a 'hill frequented by stags.'

Hose, Hosier (Eng) An occupational name for a maker of 'hose,' leggings, stockings and socks. This is the obvious explanation, since 'hose' was the normal word in medieval times for what was worn on the legs, but Reaney points out that Old French *heuse, hose* meant 'boot.' The name may therefore occasionally indicate a shoemaker.

Hoselur *see* OSTLER.

Hoskin, Hosken, Hosking, Hoskings, Hoskins, Hoskison, Hoskisson, Hoskyn, Hoskyns, Hoskys, Huskinson, Huskisson (Eng) Descendant of someone called *Oskin*, itself a diminutive form of a name such as OSBORN, OSGOOD where the *Os-* means 'god.'

These names are familiar in Devonshire, but seem to cause confusion elsewhere. Bearers of the name Hosking, for example, claim to be addressed as *Soskins, Oskings, Hisking* and the like, but rarely as Hosking.

Hosteler, Hosteller, Hostler *see* OSTLER.

Hotchen, Hotchin *see* HUGH.

Hotchkin, Hotchkins, Hotchkiss *see* ROGER.

Hotton (Eng) Someone who came from one of the several places so-named because it was a 'settlement on the spur of a hill.'

Houchen, Houchin *see* HUGH.

Hoult *see* HOLT.

How *see* HUGH.

Howard (Eng) Of several possible origins; eg descendant of a man who bore a personal name such as *Huard (Hugihard)* or *Haward*. The former is a Germanic name composed of elements meaning 'heart, mind' and 'hardy, brave.' Haward is ultimately from Old Norse and means 'high guardian.' But some Howards have an ancestor who was a 'ewe-herd' or shepherd, others a 'hayward,' the officer who had charge of fences and enclosures. *See* BUGG.

Howat, Howatt, Howchin, Howe, Howes, Howett, Howitt, Howkins, Howlett, Howlin, Howling, Howlings, Howson, Huckin, Hudd, Hudden, Huddle, Hudman *see* HUGH.

Huber, Hübner *see* HOOVER.

Hudsmith *see* SMITH.

Hugh, Fitzhugh, Fitzhugues, Hewat, Hewes, Hewet, Hewetson, Hewett, Hewison, Hewit, Hewitson, Hewitt, Hewkin, Hewlet, Hewlett, Hewlings, Hewlins, Hewlitt, Hews, Hewson, Hookins, Hooson, Hoosun, Hotchen, Hotchin, Houchen, Houchin, How, Howat, Howatt, Howchin, Howe, Howes, Howett, Howitt, Howkins, Howlett, Howlin, Howling, Howlings, Howson, Huckin, Hudd, Hudden, Huddle, Hudman, Hudsmith, Hudson, Huelin, Huet, Huetson, Huett, Huget, Hugget, Huggett, Huggin, Huggins, Huggon, Huggons, Huggonson, Hughes, Hughlin, Hughson, Huglin, Hugo, Hugon, Huison, Huitson, Huitt, Hukin, Hukins, Hulance, Hulatt, Huleatt, Hulin, Hulles, Hullet, Hullin, Hullins, Hullot, Hulson, Huot, Huson, Hutchence, Hutchens, Hutcheon, Hutcherson, Hutchin, Hutchings, Hutchins, Hutchingson, Hutchinson, Hutchison, Hutchons, Hutson, Huws, Pugh, Pughe, Ugo (Eng, Welsh) Descendant of *Hugh* (or *Hugo* in its Latin form) 'heart, mind, spirit,' a name introduced to Britain by the Normans. It then became immensely popular. Several medieval saints bore the name, including Hugh of Lincoln, described by John Ruskin as 'the most beautiful sacerdotal figure known to me in history.' Hugh was a fearless man who did not hesitate to defend ordinary people against unjust treatment by the king. He was famous, amongst other things, for having a pet swan which became his emblem. The name Hugh was used with a wide range of diminutive endings. In Wales it seems to have become associated with *Hywel*. *Ab* or *ap Hugh* 'son of Hugh' led to Pugh, Pughe. In an Irish context **Hueson**, Hughes etc are likely to represent Anglicizations of the Gaelic *Aodh* 'fire.' *See* MacKay.

In *Abbie*, by Dane Chandos, there is the comment: 'His opponent was a Welsh ex-Sunday-school teacher who calls himself ap Hugh (affectation, a Pugh is a Pugh the world over).' *See* Jones.

Hull *see* Hill.

Hulles, Hullet, Hullin, Hullins, Hullot, Hulson *see* Hugh.

Hulme *see* Holme.

Human (Eng) Occupational name of '*Hugh's* servant.'

Hume *see* Holme.

Humphrey, Bumphrey, Bumphries, Humfrey, Humphery, Humphreys, Humphries, Humphrys (Eng) *Humphrey* is an Old French personal name composed of elements meaning 'bear cub' and 'peace.' The Normans introduced it to Britain. The Welsh *ab Humphrey* 'son of Humphrey' led to **Bumphrey.**

Hunnable, Hunneyball, Hunneybell, Hunnibal, Hunnibell *see* Annable.

Hunnybun *see* Honeybunn.

Hunt, Hunte, Hunter (Eng) Occupational name of a hunter. He was more likely to hunt from necessity than for sport.

Laura Hunt is the heroine of Vera Caspary's novel *Laura*. The film version of this, in which Gene Tierney played the lead, had a very successful song also called 'Laura.' Both film and song have had a great impact on the use of Laura as a first name in Britain since the 1940s.

Huntington, Huntingdon, Huntinton (Eng) Descendant of some-one who originally came from one of the places so-named because it was a 'hunters' enclosure or hill.'

The religious controversialist who was born William *Hunt* in 1744 thought his surname would not impress his congregations. To abandon his name completely might have attracted criticism; by merely adding to it he could claim to have retained it. He therefore became William Huntington, S.S. The letters after his name were his version of the more usual D.D. (Doctor of Divinity). They stood for 'Sinner Saved.'

Hunwin *see* UNWIN.

Huot *see* HUGH.

Hurd, Hurdman *see* HERDSMAN.

Hurle, Hurles, Hurll *see* EARL.

Hurran, Hurrell, Hurren (Eng) Nickname for a man with shaggy hair.

Huskinson, Huskisson *see* HOSKIN.

Huson *see* HUGH.

Hustler *see* OSTLER.

Hutchence, Hutchens, Hutcheon, Hutcherson, Hutchin, Hutchings, Hutchins, Hutchingson, Hutchinson, Hutchison, Hutchons, Hutson *see* HUGH.

Hutton (Eng) Someone who came from one of the several places so-named because it was a 'settlement on the spur of a hill.'

Huws *see* HUGH.

Hyam *see* HIGHAM.

Hyman *see* HIGH.

Hytch *see* RICHARD.

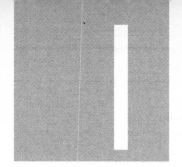

Idle, Idel, Idell, Idler (Eng) This can be what it looks like, a nickname for an idle person, but it can also indicate someone who originally lived in the Yorkshire place, so-named perhaps because it was once 'idle, unused ground.' *Idle* was also the Anglo-Norman form of Old French *isle* 'island.' It could therefore refer to someone who came from a French place named for its island.

Illingsworth (Eng) Descendant of someone who came from the Yorkshire place of this name, '*Illa's* enclosure.'

Ince (Eng) Descendant of someone who lived on an 'island' or came from a place named because it was an island, or land between two rivers.

Inchbald (Eng) Descendant of *Ingebald*, a Germanic personal name composed of elements meaning '*Angle* (tribal name)' and 'bold.'

Ingham (Eng) Descendant of someone who originally came from one of the places so-named because it was '*Inga's* homestead.'

Inglis, Inglish *see* ENGLISH.

Ingoldsby (Eng) Someone who came from the Lincolnshire place of this name, which was '*Ingjaldr's* settlement.'

The Ingoldsby Legends by 'Thomas Ingoldsby,' who was actually Richard Harris Barham (1785-1845), consist mainly of a comic interpretation of medieval legends. There is usually a 'Moral' attached to each of the poems: a sample from 'A Lay of St Romwold' will show Barham's typical style:

> To persons about to be married, I'd say,
> Don't exhibit ill-humour, at least on The Day!
> And should there perchance be a trifling delay
> On the part of officials, extend them your pardon,
> And don't snub the parson, the clerk or churchwarden.

127

> To married men this – For the rest of your lives,
> Think how your misconduct may act on your wives,
> Don't swear then before them, lest haply they faint,
> Or what sometimes occurs – run away with a Saint!

Ingram, Ingraham, Ingrams, Ingrem, Ingrum (Eng) Descendant of a man who bore a Germanic personal name meaning '*Ing's* raven,' Ing being the name of a Norse god of fertility. The personal name might also have meant '*Angle* raven,' with a reference to the tribe of the Angles.

William Faulkner is not quite correct when he speaks, in *Intruder in the Dust*, of 'people named Gowrie and MacCallum and Fraser and Ingrum that used to be Ingraham and Workitt that used to be Urquhart, only the one that brought it to America and then Mississippi couldn't spell it.' Ingraham certainly exists as a modern surname, but like Ingrum, it is a variant of the original name. *See* URQUART.

Inman (Eng) Occupational name of an inn-keeper.

Innes, Inness, Innis, Inniss (Scot) Descendant of someone who came from the Scottish place of this name in the Grampian region. The name is based on Gaelic *inis* 'island.' But Innes etc., can also be a variant of ANGUS, *see* MAC-.

Innocent (Eng) Descendant of a man called *Innocent,* probably because he was born on Holy Innocents' Day, or Childermas. This is one of those surnames which immediately attracts journalistic attention if the bearer commits a mild misdemeanour.

Ireland, Irish (Eng) Names indicating where the name-bearers originally lived.

Ironmonger (Eng) Occupational name of an ironmonger.

Irvine, Irvin, Irving (Scot) Descendant of someone who came from Irvine or Irving in Scotland, both of which reflect ancient river names, possibly meaning 'green water.'

Isherwood, Usherwood (Eng) A Lancashire surname, evidently a place name but the location cannot be found.

Izard, Izzard (Eng) Descendant of *Iseult* or *Isolde,* A Germanic female name composed of elements meaning 'ice' and 'battle.' The medieval romance about Tristram (or Tristan) and Isolde, part of the Arthurian cycle, was well-known and admired.

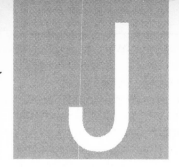

Jack, Jackaman, Jackes, Jackett, Jacklin, Jackling, Jackman, Jacks, Jackson, Jacot *see* JOHN.

Jaffray, Jaffrey, Jaffry *see* GEOFFREY.

Jagg, Jaggs *see* JOHN.

Jago (Cornish) The Cornish form of *James*.

Jagson *see* JOHN.

Jailer, Gailer, Galer, Gayler, Jailler (Eng) Occupational name of a prison officer. John *Hangman* is mentioned in a 14th century document, but that particular surname does not seem to have survived.

Jakes, Janes, Janks, Jannings *see* JOHN.

James, Gemson, Gimson, Jameson, Jamieson, Jamison, Jemison, Jimson, Jimpson, MacJames, MacKeamish (Eng, Scot) Descendant of a man called *James*. This name and *Jacob* are from the same Hebrew source. The meaning is 'let God protect,' though in Genesis the connection is made with the Hebrew word for 'heel' as well as another word which means to 'supplant, deceive.' As the name of two of Christ's disciples James has always had an appeal in Christian countries. In Scotland it was also a well-established royal name.

Jarad *see* GARRETT.

Jardin, Jardine *see* GARDNER.

Sir Walter Scott adds a note to his novel *Guy Mannering* to the effect that: 'a beggar woman, repulsed from door to door as she solicited quarters through a village of Annandale, asked in her despair if there were no Christians in the place. To which the hearers, concluding that she inquired for some persons so surnamed, answered: 'Na, na, there are nae Christians here; we are a' Johnstones and Jardines.'

Jared *see* GARRETT.

Jarmay, Jarmey, Jarmy *see* JEREMY.

Jarratt, Jarred, Jarrett, Jarritt, Jarrold *see* GARRETT.

Jay, Jaye, Jayes, Jays, Jaze, Jeayes, Jeays, Jeyes (Eng) Nickname for someone with the qualities of a *jay*, a bird known as a great chatterer and for being highly acquisitive.

Jayne, Jaynes, Javens *see* EVAN.

Jays, Jaze *see* JAY.

Jeacock, Jeacocke *see* JOHN.

Jeafferson, Jeaffreson *see* GEOFFREY.

Jeanes, Jeavon, Jeavons *see* EVAN.

Jeayes, Jeays, Jeyes *see* JAY.

Jebbs, Jebson *see* GEOFFREY.

Jeeves, Geaves, Geves, Jeves (Eng) Descendant of *Geva*, itself a short form of *Genevieve*, a Germanic name usually explained as composed of elements meaning 'people' and 'woman.'

Jeeves is one of the most famous modern literary names, evoking immediately the intelligent and dignified manservant of the weak-minded Bertie Wooster in a number of books by P.G. Wodehouse. Jeeves is constantly rescuing Wooster from the embarrassing situations in which he inevitably finds himself. As a manservant, Jeeves is never normally addressed by his first name. It is probably only the most avid readers of Wodehouse who are aware that he is actually *Reginald* Jeeves.

Jefcoat, Jefcoate, Jefcott, Jeff, Jeffares, Jeffcoat, Jeffcoate, Jeffcock, Jeffcote, Jeffcott, Jeffe, Jefferds, Jefferey, Jefferies, Jefferis, Jeffers, Jefferson, Jeffery, Jefferyes, Jefferys, Jeffes, Jeffkins, Jeffkyns, Jeffray, Jeffree, Jeffress, Jeffrey, Jeffreys, Jeffries, Jeffry, Jeffryes, Jeffs, Jefts *see* GEOFFREY.

Jekyll, Giggle, Gollins, Jeckell, Jeckells, Jeggons, Jewell, Jewels, Jewkes, Jickells, Jickles, Jiggins, Jiggle, Jockel, Jockelson, Jockle, Joell, Joels, Joelson, Jollands, Jolson, Joule, Jowle, Juell, Juggins, Juggons, Jukes (Eng) Descendant of *Iudicael* or *Judicael,* a Celtic personal name meaning 'bountiful lord.' The name was borne by a 7th century Breton saint, a king who abdicated his throne to spend the last twenty years of his life in a monastery.

Jellett *see* GILES.

Jellings *see* JULIAN.

Jellis *see* GILES.

Jellison *see* JULIAN.

Jemison *see* JAMES.

Jencks *see* JOHN.

Jenifer *see* JENNIFER.

Jenings *see* EVAN.

Jenkerson, Jenkin, Jenking, Jenkins, Jenkinson, Jenks, Jenkyns, Jenn, Jennens *see* EVAN, JOHN.

In *The Every-Day Book*, there is an article by William Hone about Henry Jenkins, who died in December 1670, aged 169. His age cannot be verified by documentary evidence, but he satisfied all contemporary enquiries and investigations and was accepted as genuinely the age he claimed to be. His epitaph in the church at Bolton, near Catterick and Richmond, reads:

'Blush not, Marble! to rescue from oblivion the memory of Henry Jenkins; a person obscure in birth, but of a life truly memorable: for, he was enriched with the goods of Nature if not of Fortune; and happy in theduration, if not variety, of his enjoyments: And, though the partial world despised and disregarded his humble state, the equal eye of Providence beheld and blessed it, with a patriarch's health, and length of days: to teach mistaken man, these blessings were intail'd on temperance, a life of labour, and a mind at ease. He lived to the amazing age of 169, was interr'd here December 6th, 1670; and had this justice done to his memory 1743.'

Jenner, Genner, Genower, Ginner, Jenoure (Eng) Occupational name for an 'engineer,' who was originally mostly concerned with building military machines. By the 12th century an *ingeniator* was also a military architect.

Jennett, Jennette, Jenney *see* JOHN.

Jennifer, Jenifer, Juniper, Junifer, Junifor, Junipher (Eng) Descendant of *Jennifer*, exclusively a Cornish name in early times. It is a form of *Guinevere,* Welsh 'white, blessed' and 'smooth, soft.' In some instances, a dweller near juniper shrubs may be indicated.

Jennings, Jennins, Jennison, Jenno, Jenns, Jennyns *see* EVAN, JOHN.

For a great many readers, the name Jennings immediately calls to mind a certain John Christopher Timothy Jennings, of Linbury Court preparatory school. Some twenty books by Anthony Buckeridge detailed the scrapes into which he managed to get himself. His best friend Darbishire, in the words of David Pringle, in *Imaginary People*, is 'a staid bespectacled foil for Jennings's hilarious antics.'

Jenoure *see* JENNER.

Jeoffroy, Jephcot, Jephcott, Jephson, Jeppeson, Jepps, Jepson *see* GEOFFREY.

Jeremy, Jarmay, Jarmey, Jarmy, Jermey, Jermy (Eng) Descendant of *Jeremy,* English form of the Hebrew *Jeremiah* 'Yah raises up' or 'Yah opens (the womb'). Jeremiah, son of Hilkiah, is one of the great prophets of Israel. Seven other men bearing this name are mentioned in the Bible.

Jerratt, Jerred, Jerrold *see* GARRETT.

Jessep, Jessop, Jessopp, Jessope, Jessup, Jesup *see* JOSEPH.

Jestice *see* JUST.

Jevan, Jevans see EVAN.

Jeves *see* JEEVES.

Jevon, Jevons *see* EVAN.

Jewell, Jewels *see* JEKYLL.

Jewesson, Jewett, Jewison, Jewitson, Jewitt *see* JULIAN.

Jewkes *see* JEKYLL.

Jewry, Jurey, Jury (Eng) Descendant of someone who lived in the Jewish quarter of a town.

Jewson *see* JULIAN.

Jewster *see* JUSTER.

Jeyn, Jeynes *see* EVAN.

Jibson *see* GEOFFREY.

Jickells, Jickles *see* JEKYLL.

Jiffin *see* GEOFFREY.

In *East Lynne*, a novel by Mrs Henry Wood, a character remarks: 'It wouldn't be so bad a catch. The worst is the name. Jiffin. Joe Jiffin! How could I even bear to be called Mrs Joe Jiffin?'

Jiggins, Jiggle *see* JEKYLL.

Jiles, Jillet *see* GILES.

Jillings, Jillions *see* JULIAN.

Jillitt *see* GILES.

Jillson, Jilson *see* JULIAN.

Jimson, Jimpson *see* JAMES.

Jinkin, Jinks, Joans *see* JOHN.

Jockel, Jockelson, Jockle, Joell, Joels, Joelson *see* JEKYLL.

Joester *see* JUSTER.

John, Brownjohn, Goodjohn, Gudgeon, Hancock, Hancocks, Handcock, Handcocks, Hancox, Hankin, Hanks, Hansom, Hanson, Jack, Jackaman, Jackes, Jackett, Jacklin, Jackling, Jackman, Jacks, Jackson, Jacot, Jagg, Jaggs, Jagson, Jakes, Janes, Janks, Jannings, Jeacock, Jeacocke, Jencks, Jenkerson, Jenkin, Jenking, Jenkins, Jenkinson, Jenks, Jenkyns, Jennens, Jennett, Jennette, Jenney, Jennings, Jennins, Jennison, Jinkin, Jinks, Joans, Johncock, Johncook, Johnigan, Johnikin, Johns, Johnson, Johnston, Johnstone, Joinson, Joncock, Joncook, Jones, Joneson, Jonet, Jonetson, Jonigan, Jonikin, Jonson, Joynson, Junkin, Junkins, Junkinson, Littlejohn, Upjohn (Eng) These names all have to do with an ancestor who bore the name *John* or one of its medieval forms, *Jan, Jen, Johan, Jon.* These names in turn had their diminutives, *Jankin, Jenkin, Han, Jonkin,* to which could be added other diminutive endings such as *-et* and *-cock.* Jack probably came about by a modification of *Jankin,* the ending being dropped and the *n* being lost. Gudgeon is from Goodjohn, early clerks often devising their own spelling systems. John is ultimately from a Hebrew name meaning 'Yah has shown favour.' As the name of John the Baptist it has always been much used in all Christian countries.

Dr Samuel Johnson's famous *Dictionary* was not concerned with surnames, but he was keenly aware of them. Boswell says, in his *Life of Samuel Johnson*: 'Nothing is more common than to mistake surnames, when we hear them carelessly uttered for the first time. To prevent this, he used not only to pronounce them slowly and distinctly, but to take the trouble of spelling them; a practice which I have often followed, and which I wish were general.'

Joie *see* JOY.

Joiner, Joyn, Joyner, Joynt (Eng) Occupational name of a joiner, carpenter.

Joinson *see* JOHN.
Jollands *see* JEKYLL.
Jolles *see* JULIAN.
Jolly, Jolley, Jollie, Jolliff, Jolliffe, Jollye, Joly, Juliffe (Eng)
Nickname for a man of a happy nature.
Jolson *see* JEKYLL.
Joly *see* JOLLY.
Joncock, Joncook *see* JOHN.
Jones *see* JOHN.

The frequency of this name in Wales has often made it ineffective as a means of identification, a 'perpetual incognito' as it has been called. Traditionally this has made the use of an additional nickname necessary. In his *Welsh Nicknames*, D. Leslie Chamberlain discusses names like *Jones the Bread* (who became *Jones the Rolls* when his business prospered, until finally he was *Jones Upper Crust*). *Two Foot Jones* was a South Wales miner who habitually worked a seam that was two feet high. *Jones Popbottle* was a tee-totaller; *Jones the Spy* was known for peeking at passers-by from behind his curtains. *Jones Balloon* was a foreman who once exhorted his men: 'Now don't let me down, boys.'

In the 16th century the Bishop of Litchfield commented on Welsh names as follows:

'Take ten,' he said, 'and call them *Rice*,
Another ten, and call them *Price*,
Take fifty others, call them *Pughs*,
A hundred more, I'll dub them *Hughes*.
Now *Roberts* name a hundred score;
And *Williams* name a a legion more:
And call,' he moaned in languid tones,
'Call all the other thousands – *Jones*.'

Thomas Hood composed the following epitaph:
Here lies the body of William Jones,
Who all his life collected bones,
Till Death, that grim and boney spectre,
That universal bone collector,
Boned old Jones, so neat and tidy,

And here he lies, all bona fide.

Another epitaph runs:

> Here lie the bones of Joseph Jones,
> Who ate while he was able:
> But, once o'er fed,
> He dropped down dead,
> And fell beneath the table.
> When from this tomb,
> To meet his doom,
> He rises amidst sinners,
> Since he must dwell In Heaven or Hell,
> Take him, which gives best dinners.

In spite of its being such an ordinary name, writers have managed to make characters named Jones individual enough. Henry Fielding did so with the hero of his novel *Tom Jones*. Eugene O'Neill created Brutus Jones, the former railway worker and convict who becomes dictator of a West Indian island in *The Emperor Jones*. In the cinema the adventures of Indiana Jones have pleased huge audiences and the television series Barnaby Jones has had some success. Grave Digger Jones is the black New York detective who features in the novels of Chester Himes.

Jonet, Jonetson, Jonigan, Jonikin, Jonson *see* JOHN.

Jordan, Judd, Judson, Jutson (Eng) Descendant of *Jordan*. Ultimately this is the name of the largest river in Palestine which flows into the Dead Sea, its name in Hebrew meaning 'the Descender.' It was in the Jordan that John baptized the crowds who came to him, and Jesus in particular. In medieval times flasks of Jordan water were brought back to England to be used for baptisms. It was then natural that Jordan itself should often become the name given to a child. *Judd*, etc., represent pet forms of the name.

Lower, in his *Patronymica Britannica*, says of this name: 'Not, as has been fancifully conjectured, from the river Jordan, in Crusading times, but from Jourdain, an early Norman baptismal name.' He then goes on to derive Jourdain from Latin *Hodiernus*, obviously believing that *Jour-* had something to do with 'day.' But Jourdain is merely the French name of the Jordan. It was bestowed in baptism on French children for the same reason as in England

and all other Christian countries. In France its use led to surnames such as Jourdain itself and the variants *Jordain, Jordanet, Jordaney, Joudain, Joudan, Jourda, Jourdaine, Jourde, Jourdin, Jourdon.*

Jory (Cornish) Descendant of a man named George.

Joseph, Jessep, Jessop, Jessopp, Jessope, Jessup, Jesup, Josephs, Josephson (Eng) Descendant of a man named *Joseph* or the servant of such a man. Joseph is a Hebrew name meaning 'May (God) add (other children to those already born). Several men in the bible bear this name, including the Patriarch, first son of Jacob and Rachel, and the Joseph who was the husband of Mary, regarded as the father of Jesus. This Joseph, the carpenter, makes no appearance during the public life of Jesus. Some of the surname forms indicate early pronunciation of the name in England (compare Italian *Giuseppe*).

Joudain, Joudan *see* JORDAN.

Joule *see* JEKYLL.

Jourda, Jourdaine, Jourde, Jourdin, Jourdon *see* JORDAN.

Jowetson, Jowett, Jowitt *see* JULIAN.

Jowle *see* JEKYLL.

Joy, Joie, Joye, Joyes (Eng) Nickname for someone with a happy disposition.

Joyn, Joyner *see* JOINER.

Joynson *see* JOHN.

Joynt *see* JOINER.

Judd, Judson *see* JORDAN.

Judge, Judges (Eng) A judge, or judicial officer such as a constable. Sometimes a nickname for a man who behaved in a solemn way. JUSTICE may also belong here in some instances, but *see* JUST.

Juell, Juggins *see* JEKYLL.

Juggler, Jugler (Eng) Occupational name of a professional juggler.

Juggons *see* JEKYLL.

Jugler *see* JUGGLER.

Jukes *see* JEKYLL.

Julian, Gellion, Gillian, Gillings, Gillion, Gillions, Gillson, Jellings, Jellison, Jewesson, Jewett, Jewison, Jewitson, Jewitt, Jewson, Jillings, Jillions, Jillson, Jilson, Jolles, Jowetson,

Jowett, Jowitt, Juet, Jules, Julians, Julien, Jullens, Jullings, Jullion, Julyian, Juson (Eng) Descendant of *Julian,* originally the English form of both Julianus and Juliana, though the much used feminine form soon became *Gillian.* The names with a *t* in them mostly derive from *Juliet,* a pet form of Juliana. Behind all these names lies Julius, a Roman family name of unknown meaning.

Juliffe *see* JOLLY.

Jullens, Jullings, Jullion, Julyian *see* JULIAN.

Juniper, Junifer, Junifor, Junipher *see* JENNIFER.

Junkin, Junkins, Junkinson *see* JOHN.

Jurey, Jury *see* JEWRY.

Juson *see* JULIAN.

Just, Justice, Jestice, Justicer, Justis, Justus (Eng) Nickname of a man whose decisions were accepted in matters of dispute; or someone who had played the part of *Justice* in a medieval religious play. *See* VERITY.

Juster, Jewster, Joester, Justerer (Fre) A *jouster*, one who took part in jousting tournaments. In their early form these were contests between groups, with the winners gaining the horses and arms of the losers.

Justice, Justicer *see* JUST.

Justin (Eng) Descendant of a man who bore this given name, a form of *Justus.* Its Russian equivalent is USTINOV.

Justis, Justus *see* JUST.

Jutson *see* JORDAN.

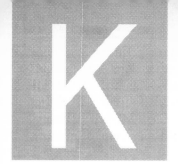

Kalvis *see* FABER.

Kare, Karr *see* KERR.

Kean, Keane, Keen, Keene (Eng) Nickname for a brave, proud man. When an Anglicized form of an Irish name, the meaning is descendant of a man who bore the Gaelic personal name *Cathán* (battle).

Kear, Care, Keer (Eng) Occupational name of a key-maker.

Keat, Keate, Keates, Keats *see* KITE.

Kedge, Ketch (Eng) Nickname for a lively person, though *Ketch* notoriously became almost a synonym for a 'hangman' or 'the gallows' because of Jack Ketch, the barbarous executioner who died in 1686.

Mrs Henry Wood writes, in *The Channings*: 'He bore an unfortunate name – Ketch – and the boys, you may be sure, did not fail to take advantage of it, joining to it sundry embellishments, more pointed than polite.'

Keel, Keeler (Eng) Occupational name of a bargeman or barge-builder.

Keen, Keene *see* KEAN.

Keer *see* KEAR.

Keet, Keight, Keighte, Keit *see* KITE.

Keith (Scot) Descendant of someone who came from the Scottish place of this name in Aberdeenshire. The name is possibly from *cet* 'wood.'

Kell, Kells *see* KETTLE.

Kelly, Kelley, Kelloch, Kellog, O'Kelly (Irish, Scot, Eng) The Irish name is an Anglicization of *O Ceallaigh*, itself indicating a descendant of someone bearing the Gaelic personal *Ceallach*. The meaning of the name is disputed, though the traditional explanation 'frequenter of churches' can be discounted. In his *Irish Family Names,* Patrick Kelly glosses it as 'troublesome' or 'contentious,' an explanation which wins recent scholarly support. Others prefer 'bright-headed.' As the name of several Irish saints it gained great popularity. It is also frequently found in Scotland, where it denotes an ancestor who came from the lands of Kelly, near Arbroath, or a place similarly named for its *coille* 'wood, copse.' A Cornish form of *coille* occurs in several local place names (*Treskellow, Kellow,* etc.) and accounts for Cornish families of the name.

Kendall, Kendal, Kendell, Kendle, Kindall, Kindell, Kindle (Eng) Descendant of someone who came from one of the northern places Kendale 'spring in a valley' or Kendal 'valley of the river Kent.'

Kendrew *see* ANDREW.

Kendrick, Kenrick, Kenwrick, Kerrick, Kindrick (Eng, Welsh) Descendant of someone bearing a form of the Old English name *Cyneric* 'royal power,' or Welsh *Cynrig* 'chief man.' In a Scottish context the name could be a reduction of MACKENDRICK 'son of *Henry.*'

Kennan *see* FINN.

Kennedy, O'Kennedy (Irish) Descendant of someone who bore the Gaelic personal name Cinnéidigh, 'head armoured, helmeted.' This was also used metaphorically to describe someone who had an 'ugly head.'

Kenrick, Kenwrick *see* KENDRICK.

Kenyon (Eng) Descendant of someone who came from the Lancashire place of this name, the meaning of which is uncertain.

Keogh, Keoghoe, Keough, MacEoghoe, MacGeogh, MacKehoe, MacKeo, MacKeogh, MacKeough, MacKough (Irish) Descendant of a man who bore the Gaelic personal name *Eochaidh*, from *eocach* 'possession of horses.' Hanks and Hodges, in *A Dictionary of Surnames*, say that **Quaggin** is a Manx form of this name, though Kneen, in *Manx Personal Names*, links it with Dubhagán, making it a form of DUGGAN.

Keown *see* EWAN.

Ker *see* KERR.

Kerbey, Kerby *see* KIRBY.

Kercher, Kerchey, Kurcher (Eng) Occupational name of a maker of kerchiefs.

Kerk *see* KIRK.

Kerkham *see* KIRKHAM.

Kermode *see* DERMOTT.

Kerr, Care, Carr, Kare, Karr, Ker (Scot) Descendant of someone who came from a place named for its 'brushwood' (Old Norse *kjarr*). A traditional explanation of the name derives it from Gaelic *cearr* 'awkward, left-handed.'

Some years ago the journal of the Royal College of General Practitioners asked its members to check on the Kerrs and Carrs to see whether they were indeed left-handed. The actress Deborah Kerr came into this category, but the (right-handed) former Labour MP and founder member of the Royal College, Dr David Kerr, was outraged at the journal's survey. 'Anyone would think it was April 1,' was his comment.

Kerrick *see* KENDRICK.

Kerswell, Kerswill *see* CRESWELL.

Ket *see* KITE.

Ketch *see* KEDGE.

Ketchen *see* KITCHEN.

Ketcher *see* CATCHPOLE.

Ketchin *see* KITCHEN.

Ketill, Ketless *see* KETTLE.

Kett *see* KITE.

Kettel, Kettell, Kettelson *see* KETTLE.

Ketting *see* KITE.

Kettle, Kell, Kells, Ketill, Kettel, Kettell, Kettelson, Kettles, Ketless, Kitell, Kittle (Eng) Descendant of someone called *Ketill*. This was an element in several Old Norse personal names and meant 'cauldron.'

In modern times Kettle has become associated with hillbillies, thanks to the films and television programmes devoted to the adventures of Ma and Pa Kettle and their numerous offspring. There is also Captain Owen Kettle, whose adventures around the globe were chronicled by C.J.Cutliffe Hyne.

Ketts, Keyt, Keyte *see* KITE.

Khaddad *see* FABER.

Kid, Kidd, Kidde, Kidder, Kidman, Kyd, Kydd, Kydds (Eng) Occupational name of a goatherd, or nickname for a person thought to be as frisky as a young goat, or a seller of faggots – bundles of twigs used for firewood. The Middle English word *kidde* meant 'faggot.'

Kiddle, Kidall, Kiddall, Kiddell, Kidwell (Eng) Dweller near a weir fitted with nets to catch fish; or forms of the Welsh name *Cadwal.*

Kidman *see* KID.

Kidson (Scot) Descendant of *Kit (Christopher).*

Kidwell *see* KIDDLE.

Kight, Kighte, Keit *see* KITE.

Kilbride, Bridson, Brigetson, Brydson, Gilbride, Gillbride, MacBride, MacBryde, MacGilbride, MacGillbride, MacKillbride (Irish, Scot) Descendant of someone who bore a Gaelic name meaning 'devotee of *St Brigid,* a name usually explained as 'exalted.' Kilbride in a Scottish context can also indicate someone who lived in a place of the same name which had a church of St Brigit.

Killea, Killey, Killie, Killy *see* GALL.

Kilpatrick (Scot, Irish) As a Scottish name this is linked with one of the places so-called because it had a church dedicated to St Patrick. In Ireland the name means 'descendant of a devotee of St Patrick.'

In *The American Language* H.L.Mencken relates the tale of a Dr *Levy* who officially changed his name to *Sullivan.* A month later he applied to the court for permission to change this to *Kilpatrick.* He explained that his patients kept asking him what his name was before. He wanted to be able to tell that it was Sullivan. Mencken goes on to remark that Jewish families change their surnames more easily than most, usually having been compelled to adopt them in the first place.

Kindall, Kindell, Kindle *see* KENDALL.

Kindon *see* KINGSLEY.

Kindrick *see* KENDRICK.

King, Kinge, Kingman, Kings, Kingson (Eng) Nickname for someone who acted in a royal manner, or had played the part of a king in one of the medieval pageants or had been appointed king of a local tournament. In some cases the reference is to someone who declared his allegiance to the king rather than a local baron.

Kingdon *see* KINGSLEY.

Kingman, Kings *see* KING.

Kingsley (Eng) Descendant of someone who came from any of the English places so-named, all of which were the 'king's wood or clearing.' Similar place names which led to surnames include KINGDON, KINDON, 'king's hill' **Kingsbury** 'king's stronghold' **Kingscote, Kingscott,** 'king's cottage, shelter' **Kingwell** 'king's stream.'

Kingson *see* KING.

Kingston, Kington (Eng) Descendant of someone who came from one of the several places so-named because it was a 'royal manor.'

Kingwell *see* KINGSLEY.

Kinman, Kynman (Eng) Occupational name of a man in charge of *kine* 'cows'.

Kinnan *see* FINN.

Kirby, Kerbey, Kerby, Kirkby, Kirkebye (Eng) Descendant of someone who came from any of the places so-named as a 'settlement with a church.'

Kirk, Kerk, Kirke, Kirckman, Kirkman, Kyrke (Eng, Scot) Descendant of someone who lived near a church, or an occupational name for someone who worked in one.

For millions of *Trekkies*, Kirk can only refer to James T. Kirk, captain of the Starship Enterprise, as played by William Shatner in *Star Trek*.

Many, however, will associate the name with Howard Kirk, the hero of Malcolm Bradbury's *The History Man*, who single-handedly managed to give sociology a bad name.

Kirkam *see* KIRKHAM.

Kirkby, Kirkebye *see* KIRBY.

Kirkham, Kerkham, Kirkam (Eng) Someone who originally came from Kirkham (church-homestead) in Lancashire or Yorkshire.

Kirkman *see* KIRK.

Kirkpatrick (Scot) Descendant of someone who came from the place of this name, which had a 'church dedicated to St Patrick.'

Marie Eugenie, wife of Napoleon III, was the granddaughter of a Kirkpatrick, which perhaps accounts for the attitude of Molly

Gibson's stepmother, in Elizabeth Gaskell's *Wives and Daughters*. The new Mrs Gibson complains to her husband that 'you jump at invitations without ever consulting me, or thinking of how awkward it would be for me to go stumping into a drawing room all by myself; following my new name, too, which always makes me feel uncomfortable, it is such a sad come-down after Kirkpatrick!'

Kirton (Eng) Someone who came from one of the several places so-named because it was a 'settlement with a church.'

Kitchen, Ketchen, Ketchin, Kitcheman, Kitchener, Kitchenman, Kitchin, Kitching, Kitchingman, Kitchman (Eng) Occupational name for a cook, man who worked in the kitchen of a large house.

Kite, Keat, Keate, Keates, Keats, Keet, Keight, Keighte, Keit, Ket, Kett, Ketting, Ketts, Keyt, Keyte, Kight, Kighte, Kites, Kitte, Kyte (Eng) Nickname for a greedy or rapacious person, likening him to a kite. There was also an Old English personal name *Cyting*, based on *cyta* 'kite.' Keating may derive from someone who bore that name.

This bird of prey was formerly more commonly found in Britain than it is today. It had the reputation of swooping down to steal food from a child's hand. It would also steal items of linen hung out to dry when it was building its nest. The 'kite' flown by children and some adult enthusiasts takes its name from the bird.

Kitell *see* KETTLE.

Kitson, Kidson (Eng) Descendant of a man named *Christopher*, a Greek name meaning 'Christ bearer.'

Kitte *see* KITE.

Kittle *see* KETTLE.

Kittler (Eng) Occupational name for a 'kettle-maker.'

Knape (Eng) Occupational name of a young servant.

Knatchbull (Eng) Nickname for a butcher, slaughterer of bulls.

Kneale (Manx) Descendant of someone called *Neil,* an Irish name meaning 'champion.'

Knee *see* NEVILLE.

Kneebone (Eng) Possibly a corrupt form of *Carnebone*, Cornwall, since the surname is mainly found in that county.

In his *Genealogy and Surnames*, William Anderson quotes a letter written to the Times newspaper in which the correspondent (a Mr

Buggey) listed names which he considered to be like his own – in need of changing. *Kneebone* was one of the names mentioned, some of the others were *Asse, Bones, Bub, Clodd, Cripple, Cheese, Demon, Dunce, Fat, Fiend, Goose, Hagg; Holdwater, Jelly, Idle, Kidney, Lazy, Leakey, Milksop, Mudd, Pighead, Poopy, Quicklove, Rumpe, Sheartlifte, Stiffe, Swine, Spittle, Teate, Vile*. All had been extracted from wills in the Prerogative Court, in Doctor's Commons.

Kneler, Knell, Kneller *see* KNOLL.

Knevet, Knevett, Knevit *see* KNIGHT.

Knifesmith *see* SMITH.

Knight, Knevet, Knevett, Knevit, Knights, Knightson, Knivett, Knyvett, Nevet, Nevett, Nevitt (Eng) A mounted soldier, especially one of noble birth; or a servant in a knight's establishment. The spellings which include a *v* reflect Norman pronunciation of an English word.

Knoll, Kneler, Knell, Kneller, Knill, Knolles, Knollys, Knowlder, Knowler, Knowles, Knowling, Knowlman, Knull, Knyll, Nowles (Eng) Descendant of someone who lived on a knoll, summit of a hill, or someone from any of the places named for its prominent hill.

Knott, Knotts, Knottson (Eng) Descendant of *Knutr* or *Knut,* a Scandinavian personal name more familiar in the form *Canute* and meaning a 'knot.' This would originally have been a nickname for a thickset person, or would have indicated residence near the kind of hillock called a knot. In some instances the surname may have become confused with NOTT.

There is said to be a gravestone inscription in an English cemetery which reads:

> Here lies a man who was Knott born
> He did Knott live
> He did Knott die
> And is Knott buried here.

Knowler, Knowles, Knowling, Knowlman *see* KNOLL.

Knox (Scot) Descendant of someone who lived on a round hill. Old English *cnocc* 'hillock' also occurs in several English place names as *Knock*.

Fort Knox is the US Army camp in Kentucky which has bomb-proof vaults containing American gold reserves worth millions of dollars. The fort is in Knox County, named in honour of General Henry Knox (1760-1806), first US Secretary of War (1785-1794) under Washington. Auric Goldfinger's plan to raid Fort Knox was, needless to say, thwarted by James Bond.

Knudssen *see* NUTT.

Knull, Knyll *see* KNOLL.

Knyvett *see* KNIGHT.

Kortwright (Eng) Occupational name for a maker of carts.

Kovac, Kovar, Kowal *see* FABER.

Kreutznaer *see* CRUSO.

Kurcher *see* KERCHER.

Kuznetzov *see* FABER.

Kyd, Kydd, Kydds *see* KID.

Kynman *see* KINMAN.

Kyrke *see* KIRK.

Kyte *see* KITE.

Labourer, Labbree, Laber, Labor, Laborier, Laborre, Labree, Labrey, Labrie (Eng, Fre) Occupational name of a farm worker, ploughman.

Lachlan, Lacklinson, Laghlan, Laughlan, Laughland, Laughlin, Loghlan, Loghlin, Loughlan, Loughlen, Loughlin, MacGloughlin, MacLachlan, MacLachlane, MacLauchlan, MacLauchlane, MacLauchlin, MacLaughlan, MacLaughlane, MacLaughlin, MacLochlin, MacLoghlin (Irish, Scot) Descendant of *Lochlainn, Lochlann* 'stranger, Viking, person who came from *lake-land*, ie Scandinavia.'

Lack *see* LAKE.

Ladd, Ladds, Laddy, Lads, Ladson (Eng) Descendant of someone who was a 'young servant.

Ladyman (Eng) Descendant of someone who was a 'lady's servant.'

Laghlan *see* LACHLAN.

Lain *see* LANE.

Lake, Lack, Lakeman, Laker, Lakes (Eng) Descendant of someone who lived near a stream or lake. Laker may in some instances refer to a player, or actor, or as Weekley thought, a man who 'is fond of fun.'

The actress known as Veronica Lake was born Constance Ockleman. She relates in *Veronica* that her stage name was suggested by film-producer Arthur Hornblow. He told her: 'It isn't just a matter, though, of creating a name that can be remembered. If that were all it took, we'd just name you Maude Mudpie or Tilly Tits or something. The name has to be the person. I believe that when people look into those navy blue eyes of yours, they'll see the calm coolness of a lake.'

Lalor, Lawler (Irish) Nickname of a 'sick person.'

Lamb, Lambe, Lambie, Lambin, Lambkin, Lambking, Lambson, Lamby, Lamin, Laming, Lamkin, Lammey, Lammie, Lammin, Lamming, Lampen, Lampin, Lamping, Lampkin, Lampson, Lamson (Eng) These names probably indicate a shepherd who looked after lambs, but nicknames based on animals were common and the original reference may have been to a mild person who was of a lamb-like nature. In some cases LAMBERT may belong here.

Lambert, Lambard, Lambarde, Lambart, Lambarth, Lambelet, Lamberson, Lamberts, Lambertson, Lambrick, Lammert, Lampard, Lampart, Lampel, Lamperd, Lampert (Eng) Descendant of a man named *Lambert*, a Germanic personal name composed of the elements 'land' and 'bright, famous.' There was a similar Old English name but it had been relatively little used. The Normans made greater use of this name in honour of three saints who bore it. Most of the surnames given above relate to the name Lambert, but a derivation from 'lamb-herd, shepherd' is also possible.

Lambie, Lambin, Lambkin, Lambking, Lambson, Lamby, Lamin, Laming, Lamkin, Lammey, Lammie, Lammin, Lamming *see* LAMB.

Lammert *see* LAMBERT.

Lammond, Lamond, Lamont *see* LAWMAN.

Lampard, Lampart, Lampel, Lamperd, Lampert *see* LAMBERT.

Lampen *see* LAMB.

Lampet, Lampitt, Lamputt (Eng) Occupational name of a worker in a loam-pit, loam being the kind of clay that was mixed with sand and straw to form a paste, used for building. Someone living near a loam-pit might also have borne this name.

Lampin, Lamping, Lampkin, Lampson, Lamson *see* LAMB.

Lampitt, Lamputt *see* LAMPET.

Lancaster, Lancastle, Lanckister, Langcaster, Langcastle, Lankester, Loncaster, Longcaster (Eng) Someone who came from Lancaster, county town of Lancashire.

Lance (Eng) Descendant of *Lance* or *Lancelot*. An American correspondent mentions that when his ancestors came from

Germany and pronounced their name as *Lenz* to the authorities, it was recorded as *Lance*. Lenz usually indicates an ancestor named *Lorenz (Laurence)*.

Landless (Eng) Bardsley hazarded a guess that the – less of this name was really a place-name element, perhaps from Old English *laes,* 'pasture, meadow land.' *Land* does not necessarily have its normal sense; it can refer to a forest glade. Landless could therefore indicate someone who lived in a meadow near a forest.

Dickens has a Helena Landless in *Edwin Drood*, 'an unusually handsome, little girl, very dark and rich in colour – almost of the gypsy type – with something untamed about her.' Critics have commented on Dickens's 'astonishing indiscretion' in using this name, since it comes close to Ellen Lawless Ternan, the name of the mistress whose identity he was desperate to conceal from the public.

Lane, Lain, Lanes, Layne (Eng) Descendant of someone who lived in a lane. In an Irish context these forms may represent an Anglicization of Gaelic *O Laighin* 'spear, javelin,' or *O Luain* 'warrior.' The Irish names also occur as O LANE, O LAYNE, O LEYNE, O LOYNE.

Lois Lane is the reporter on the *Daily Planet* who does not see the resemblance between Clark Kent and Superman.

Miss Memory Lane, a teacher at the Roskyn High School, New York, is one of the entries in *Remarkable Names of Real People*, a little book published in 1977 by John Train. Many of the names are accompanied by footnotes. We are told, for instance, that the actress Gisella Werberserch-Piffel, who lived in Hollywood in the 1930s, was constantly the victim of jokers who telephoned to ask whether she was the Gisella Werberserch-Piffel they had met in Monte Carlo the previous summer. On being told 'No' they would invariably say that it must have been some other Gisella Werberserch-Piffel. Train's book was successful enough to be followed in 1979 by *Even More Remarkable Names of Real People*.

Lang, Long (Eng) Nickname for a tall person.

Langcastle *see* LANCASTER.

Langdon (Eng) Descendant of someone who originally came from one of the places named for its 'long hill.' Similar names are LANGFORD, LANGLANDS, LANGLEY 'long clearing in a wood',

LANGRIDGE.

Langham (Eng) Descendant of someone who lived in one of the places so-named because it was a 'long homestead.'

Langlands, Langley, Langridge *see* LANGDON.

Langton (Eng) Someone who came from one of the several places so-named because it was a 'long village.'

Langtree (Eng) Someone who originally came from one of the places so-named for its tall tree.

Lard, Larder, Lardiner, Lardnar, Lardner (Eng) Occupational name of a steward in charge of a larder, storehouse for bacon and meat.

Lardge *see* LARGE.

Lardiner, Lardnar, Lardner *see* LARD.

Large, Lardge, Largey, Largman, Largy (Fre) Nickname for a generous man, a dispenser of largesse.

Lariot *see* LAURENCE.

Lark, Larke, Larkman, Laverack, Laveric, Laverick (Eng) A nickname associated with the lark, perhaps indicating cheerfulness, or an occupational name for someone who caught and sold larks (eaten as a delicacy).

Larkin, Larking, Larkins *see* LAURENCE.

Larman *see* LARK.

Larky *see* LAURENCE.

Larner, Lerner (Eng) Occupational name of a schoolmaster. As an Irish name it is said to be a variant of LARDNER or DELANEY.

Larrance, Larrett, Larrie, Larritt, Larry, Larson *see* LAURENCE.

Latham, Lathem, Lathom, Laytham, Leatham, Leathem, Letham (Eng) Descendant of someone who lived in one of the places so-named because it was a 'homestead with barns.'

Latimer, Latimore, Latner, Lattimer, Lattimore (Eng) Occupational name of a clerk who had a knowledge of Latin and was able to keep records in that language. Written Latin was used for most official purposes in the Middle Ages.

Latter, Latterman (Eng) Occupational name of a maker of 'laths,' the thin strips of wood which form a base for plaster, tiles, etc., in buildings.

Lattimer, Lattimore *see* LATIMER.

Laughlan, Laughland, Laughlin *see* LACHLAN.

Laughton (Eng) Someone who came from one of the several places so-named because it was a 'settlement where leeks were grown.'

Laurence, Lariot, Larkin, Larking, Larkins, Larky, Larrance, Larrett, Larrie, Larritt, Larry, Larson, Laurance, Laurens, Laurenson, Laurie, Law, Lawe, Lawes, Lawrance, Lawrence, Lawrenson, Lawrey, Lawrie, Lawry, Laws, Lawson, Lorence, Lorenz, Lorie, Lorkin, Lorking, Lorkins, Lorriman, Lorrison, Lorry, Lory, Loryman, Loury, Low, Lowe, Lowery, Lowrance, Lowrey, Lowrie, Lowry, Lowson (Eng, Scot) Descendant of *Laurence*. The name was introduced to Britain by the Normans, with whom it was popular because of St Laurence, a third century martyr. It is difficult to sort out fact from fiction in the accounts of St Laurence's life, but there is no doubt that he was widely venerated. Originally the name Laurence referred to a 'man from *Laurentum*,' a town in Italy named for the laurel trees that grew in the area. The usual pet forms of the name in English were LAWE, LOWE and **Lar,** which with diminutive endings became Lariot and Larkin.

Laverack, Laveric, Laverick *see* LARK.

Law, Lawe, Lawes *see* LAURENCE.

Lawless (Eng) Nickname for a man with no respect for the law. Outlaw is a similar name.

Lawley (Eng) Descendant of someone who lived in the Shropshire place, so-named because it was *'Lafa's* clearing.'

Lawman (Eng) Descendant of *Lagman*, a Scandinavian personal name which meant 'lawman,' or a use of the noun to describe an officer of the law. In Scotland the Old Norse form of the personal name developed into LAMOND, LAMMOND, LAMONT and thence into MACCLEMENT, MACCLEMENTS, MACCLEMONT, MACCLIMENTS, MACCLYMOND, MACCLYMONT, MACCLYMOUNT, MACLAMOND, MACLAMONT, MACLEMAN, MACLEMON, MACLIMONT. 'Servant of *Laurence*' is also a possible explanation of Lawman.

Lawrance, Lawrence, Lawrenson, Lawrey, Lawrie, Lawry, Laws, Lawson *see* LAURENCE.

Layne *see* LANE.

Laytham *see* LATHAM.

Layton, Leighton (Eng) Someone who came from one of the several places so-named because it was a 'settlement where leeks were grown.' Layton can also mean a 'settlement near a stream.'

Lea *see* LEE.

Learnard, Learned *see* LEONARD.

Leatham, Leathem *see* LATHAM.

Leather, Leatherman, Leathers (Eng) Occupational name for a leather-worker, or dealer in leather goods.

Ledster *see* LISTER.

Lee, Atherlee, Atlee, Attlee, Atley, Attle, Lea, Leigh (Eng) Old English *leah* at first denoted woodland, then a clearing in a wood. Eventually its meaning was little more than 'open country,' including heathland, pasture and cultivated land. It is commonly found as an element in English place names, especially in the counties which were once thickly wooded. Bearers of these surnames usually came originally from a place with *lee*, in one form or another, as the whole or part of its name, but it would be difficult to pinpoint the exact place.

Lefevre *see* FABER.

Leighton *see* LAYTON.

Lello, Leoline *see* LEWIS.

Lenard, Lennard *see* LEONARD.

Leon *see* LYON.

Leonard, Learnard, Learned, Lenard, Lennard (Eng) Descendant of a man who bore the Norman personal name *Leonard*, 'lion-brave.' Its use in the Middle Ages was influenced by its being the name of three early saints.

Lerner *see* LARNER.

Lester, Lestor *see* LISTER.

Lestrange *see* STRANGE.

Letham *see* LATHAM.

Letsom, Letsome, Letson, Lett, Lettey, Letts, Lettsom, Letty (Eng) Descendant of a woman called *Laetitia*, 'happiness', usually *Lettice* in its English form.

Dr Isaac Lettsom was a friend of Dr Samuel Johnson who signed his prescriptions 'I. Lettsom.' An anonymous wag was responsible for:

'If any folk applies to I, I physics, bleeds and sweats 'em;

If after that they choose to die,
Why, what cares I? I Lettsom.'

Levi, Levin, Levinson, Levis, Levison, Levit, Levitt, Levy, Lewit, Lewitt (Jewish) Descendant of *Levi,* a Hebrew name meaning 'united to, joined to.' It is the name of the third son of Jacob and Leah, from whom the Levites take their name.

Lewis, Louis (Eng, Welsh, Scot, Irish) English families of this name will probably have had an ancestor called *Lowis* or *Lodowicus*, a Norman personal name meaning 'fame warrior.' In Wales, where the name is most frequently found, it is the name that was deliberately substituted by the medieval clerks for LLYWELYN. It was standard policy to use Anglo-Norman names for Welsh names. Lewis would have been an obvious choice because Llywelyn had usually become LLEWELYN or LLEWELLYN, pronounced with an initial *Lew-* sound. The change to *Llew-* had probably occurred because it was wrongly thought that Llywelyn was derived from Welsh *llew* 'lion.' This fact also caused the name on occasions to become *Leoline* in its English form. In fact Llywelyn is more likely to mean something like 'leader likeness.' The Welsh name occurs in registers in many different forms, including FLELLO, FLELLOW, FLEWELLEN, FLEWELLING, FLEWELLYN, FLUELLEN, LELLO, LLEWELLEN, LLEWHELLIN, LLEWHELYN, WELLEN, WELLIN, WELLING, WELLINGS, WELLON. The names in *F-* show the difficulty English-speakers had with the Welsh pronunciation of *Ll-*. For a full discussion of these and many other forms, see *Welsh Surnames,* by T.J. and Prys Morgan. In a Scottish context some scholars believe that Lewis indicates someone who came from the Hebridean island of the same name, though David Dorward, in *Scottish Surnames*, does not support this theory. In both Scotland and Ireland it can also be an Anglicization of Gaelic *Mac Lughaid*, a personal name based on *lugh* 'brightness.' The latter name, according to Black in his *Surnames of Scotland*, is also found as MACCLOY.

Lewit, Lewitt *see* LEVI.

Leyton (Eng) Someone who came from a place so-named because it was a 'settlement on the river Lea.'

Libby (Eng) Descendant of *Libby,* a pet form of *Elizabeth*, a Hebrew name probably meaning 'my God is plenitude, fullness, perfection.'

Lidster *see* LISTER.

Lightfoot (Eng) Nickname for someone able to run fast. *See* PUDDY.

Linch, Linchey, Linchy *see* LYNCH.

Lincoln (Eng) Descendant of someone who came from the English city of this name, which was originally a 'lake settlement.'

Linney (Eng) Descendant of *Lindgeofu*, an Old English personal name composed of elements meaning 'shield-gift.'

Lion *see* LYON.

Lister, Ledster, Lester, Lestor, Lidster, Litstar, Litster, Lyster (Eng) Occupational name of a dyer. A lister would originally have been a woman, but the word was later used for both sexes.

Litten *see* LYTTON.

Little (Eng) Nickname for a small person, or the younger of two people bearing the same first name.

Littleboy, Littleboys (Fre) Anglicization of a French name indicating someone who lived in a small wood.

Littlejohn *see* JOHN.

Littleproud (Eng) Nickname for someone of 'little worth,' the second element being French *prud* 'value, worth.'

A 14th century Henry Littleproud had a wife who was known as *Crist a pes*, presumably because she was constantly saying 'Christ have peace!' Reaney remarks: 'this suggests her husband deserved his nickname.'

Littleton, Lyttelton (Eng) Someone who came from one of the several places so-named because it was a 'small settlement.'

Littley *see* BIRDSEYE.

Litton *see* LYTTON.

Llewellen, Llewellyn, Llewelyn, Llewhellin, Llewhelyn, Llywelyn *see* LEWIS.

Lloyd, Flewett, Flewitt, Flood, Flowitt, Floyd, Floyde, Flude, Loyd, Loydd (Welsh) A reference to the colour of an ancestor's hair, either 'grey' or 'brown.' The forms beginning with *F*- represent attempts by English clerks to cope with the Welsh pronunciation of '*Ll*.'

Lock, Locke (Eng) A nickname for someone with curly hair.

Lockless denoted someone whose hair was straight. **Blacklock, Blakelock,** also occurs for someone with black curly hair. Lock can also at times be a form of *Luke*.

Locksmith *see* SMITH.

Loggerheads (Eng) Descendant of someone who lived in one of the places bearing this name, eg in Denbighshire and Staffordshire.

In *Why the Clock Stopped*, a short story by Arnold Bennett, there is the comment: 'I ought to explain that it was not the peculiarity of Mr Loggerhead's name that produced the odd effect. Loggerheads is a local term for a harmless plant called the knapweed, and it is also the appellation of a place and quite excellent people, and no-one regards it as even the least bit odd.'

Loghlan, Loghlin *see* LACHLAN.

Loncaster *see* LANCASTER.

Long, Longfellow, Longman (Eng) Nickname of a tall man. *See* CALDWELL.

Thomas Longfellow was at one time landlord of the *Golden Lion* inn at Brecon. A dissatisfied customer was responsible for the following:

Tom Longfellow's name is most justly his due:
Long his neck, long his bill, which is very long, too;
Long the time ere your horse to the stable is led;
Long before he's rubbed down, and much longer till fed;
Long indeed may you sit in a comfortless room
Till from kitchen long dirty your dinner shall come;
Long the oft-told tale that your host will relate;
Long his face while complaining how long people eat;
Long may Longfellow long ere he see me again;
Long 'twill be ere I long for Tom Longfellow's inn.

Longbotham, Longbottom (Eng) Descendant of someone who lived at the bottom of a long valley, or in a place named for this feature. In its 'valley bottom' sense, BOTTOM or BOTTOMS occurs as a surname on its own, though often disguised as BOTHAM, BOTTAMS, or in combinations such as HIGGINBOTTOM, HIGGINBOTHAM, SHUFFLEBOTTOM, SIDEBOTTOM, WINTERBOTTOM.

The name *Hogsbotham*, cited by Leslie Charteris in *Follow the Saint*, is almost certainly his own invention. Charteris writes of 'a guy whose name, believe it or not, is Ebenezer Hogsbotham. Comrade Hogsbotham, having been born with a name like that and a face to match it, has never had a chance in his life to misbehave. Mr Hogsbotham had to be a bachelor, because it was not plausible that any woman, unless moved by a passion which a man of Mr Hogsbotham's desiccated sanctity could never hope to inspire, would consent to adopt a name like Mrs Hogsbotham.' It has in fact been seriously suggested that surnames of this kind might die out for the reason Charteris gives. The theory is that women will refuse to marry men so-named, and that there will therefore be no male dscendants to carry on the names. Further problems are mentioned at RAMSBOTTOM.

There is no real evidence to support the claim that an epitaph for a Mr Longbottom, who died young, was *Arse longa, vita brevis*.

Longcaster *see* LANCASTER.

Longfellow *see* LONG.

Longfoot *see* PUDDY.

Longman *see* LONG.

Look *see* LUKE.

Lorence, Lorenz, Lorie, Lorkin, Lorking, Lorkins, Lorriman, Lorrison, Lorry, Lory, Loryman, Loury *see* LAURENCE.

Loughlan, Loughlen, Loughlin *see* LACHLAN.

Louis *see* LEWIS.

Love, Lovekin, Lovetot, Luff (Eng) The English word *love* had become a given name by the Middle Ages, perhaps from use of the word as a term of address. It was then able to take diminutive endings. Ewen mentions a *Lovecock* as well as *Lovekin* in an early record, but the former name does not seem to have survived. Anglo-French *love* was a different word meaning 'female wolf' which was used as a nickname. This could be another source of the surname, in its simple form or as a diminutive such as LOVEL, LOVELL, LOWELL. It is this 'wolf' sense of love which occurs in compound names like CATCHLOVE, CHASSELOVE 'hunt wolf' SPENDLOVE, SPENDLOW, SPENLOW, SPINDELOW 'disembowel wolf' PRITLOVE 'prick the wolf' CUTLOVE, MARKLOVE 'aim at the wolf' TRUSLOVE 'bind the wolf' WILDLOVE, LOVEGROVE, LOVELAND.

Loveday (Eng) In the Middle Ages a 'loveday' was one set aside for disputes to be settled. The word became a given name, probably to commemorate birth on such a day. The surname can mean "descendant of someone who bore the name *Loveday*,' or of someone connected in any special way with the day itself.

Lovegrove *see* LOVE.

Lovejoy (Eng) Nickname for a happy person.

For many readers Lovejoy is the only name by which they know an antiques dealer who often engages in detective work. His adventures are related in the novels of Jonathan Gash, some of which have been adapted for television.

Lovekin *see* LOVE.

Lovelace, Lovelas, Loveles, Loveless, Lowles, Lowless (Eng) Nickname for a man who was 'loveless' in some sense. In some instances Lovelass may be the original form, with a meaning similar to Lovelady. 'Lover of lace,' ie a dandy, is not possible. In the surname formation period 'lace' referred only to cord, as in shoe-lace.

Lovelady (Eng) Nickname for a womaniser. Weekley mentions 'cruder' forms of the name, including TIPLADY, TOPLADY, TOPLASS, TOPLEY, TOPLISS. SHACKLADY and SHAKELADY also refer to a lecherous man, especially one reputed to have been sexually involved with a woman of higher social rank.

Loveland *see* LOVE.

Lovelas, Lovelass, Loveles, Loveless *see* LOVELACE.

Lovelock (Eng) Nickname for a dandy, noted for his long locks of hair.

Lovetot *see* LOVE.

Low, Lowe, Lowery see **Laurence**. *Low, Lowe* can also be a nickname for a short person, or indicate someone who lived near a hill.

Lowles, Lowless *see* LOVELACE.

Lowrance, Lowrey, Lowrie, Lowry, Lowson *see* LAURENCE.

Lucas, Luck, Luckman *see* LUKE.

Luff *see* LOVE.

Luke, Lock, Look, Lucas, Luck, Luckman, Lugg, Lukeman, MacLucas, MacLuckie, MacLucky, MacLukie, MacLugash, MacLugish (Eng) Descendant of a man named *Luke*, derived from the Greek form of Latin *Lucius* 'man from Lucania,' a region of

Italy. Traditionally Luke is the author of the third gospel and of the Acts of the Apostles.

Lynch, Linchey, Linchy, Lynchahan, Lynchahaun, Lynchehan, O'Lensie, O'Lynche, O'Lynchey, O'Lynchy, O'Lynseghane (Irish) Descendant of someone who bore the Gaelic personal name *Loingseach*, or someone named *Linseach*, apparently a Gaelic form of a French place name that has not been traced. *Loingseach* means 'mariner.' English families named Linch or Lynch descend from someone who originally came from places of those names, where the reference is to Old English *hlinc* 'hill.'

Cecil Hunt writes, in his *Dictionary of Word Makers*: 'Lynching, or the practice of inflicting summary punishment without trial by a properly constituted court, is credited with several derivations. The name is generally attributed to Charles Lynch, Judge of Virginia, who, in 1782, was indemnified by the act of the Virginian Assembly for hanging certain Tories illegally fined and imprisoned two years previously. Another tradition associates the name with Lynch Creek, in North Carolina, where a form of court martial and execution was carried out on the corpse of a Tory who had already been hanged to prevent rescue.' There is no proof that such a judge existed, and Mr Hunt has missed the most likely explanation. Henry Howe, in *Historical Collections of Virginia* (1845) says: 'Colonel Charles Lynch, a brother of the founder of Lynchburg, was an officer of the American Revolution. The country was thinly settled and infested by bands of lawlessbands of Tories and desperadoes. Colonel Lynch, then a leading Whig, apprehended them and had them punished without any superfluous legal ceremony.'

Lyon, Leon, Lion, Lyons (Eng) Nickname for a man who was 'lion-like,' or descendant of a man named *Leo* or *Leon,* both of which mean 'lion.' In a few cases the surname may indicate someone who came from the French town of Lyon.

Lyster *see* LISTER.

Lyttelton *see* LITTLETON.

Lytton, Litten, Litton (Eng) Someone who came from one of the several places so-named because it was a 'settlement near a torrent.'

Mac- (Scot) George F. Black, in The Surnames of Scotland, says: '*Mac* (wrongly contracted to M', Mc) is a Gaelic prefix occurring in Scottish names of Gaelic origin, as MACDONALD, MACLEAN, MACPHIE, and the like, meaning "son".' All such names have therefore been spelt with *Mac-* in this dictionary, though many families prefer the forms condemned by Black. (These names are dealt with more fully in the companion to the present work, *Scottish Surnames,* by David Dorward). In passing it is worth remarking that the Welsh equivalent of *mac* was originally *map,* though this was shortened to *ap* or *p* at an early date (*mac* is also regularly shortened to *ac* in some parts of Scotland.) Before certain consonants Welsh *map* was also changed to *mab, ab, b.* In Irish Gaelic *map* often becomes *mag.* Thus Scottish MacAngus, Macansh, MacInnes, Mackinnes, Mackiness, all of which mean 'son of *Angus,*' occur in Ireland as MACGINNIS, MACGUINNESS, MAGUINNESS, MACGENIS, MAGENNIS, MAGUINESS, MAGINNISS.

In *Waverley* Sir Walter Scott says of a man who dislikes the Scots: 'in the excellent Colonel, the Mac at the beginning of a name would have made a devil out of an angel; and indeed he himself jocularly allowed, that he could not have endured Venus herself, if she had been announced in a drawing-room by the name of Miss Mac-Jupiter.'

MacAbee *see* MACBETH.

MacAgill *see* GALL.

MacAlaster, MacAlester, MacAlister *see* ALEXANDER.

Macall *see* ALMACK.

MacAllaster, MacAllister *see* ALEXANDER.

MacAndrew *see* ANDREW.

MacAngus, Macansh *see* MAC-.

MacArtan, MacArtane *see* MACCARTNEY.

MacArthy, MacArty *see* MACCARTHY.

MacArtney *see* MACCARTNEY.

MacArty *see* MACCARTHY.

MacAveigh, MacAvey *see* MACBETH.

MacBain *see* BEAN.

MacBay *see* MACBETH.

MacBayne, MacBean *see* BEAN.

MacBeth, MacAbee, MacAveigh, MacAvey, MacBay, MacBeath, MacBeith, MacBey, MacEvaghe, MacEveighe, MacIvagh, MacIveagh, MacVaghe, MacVay, MacVeagh, MacVeigh, MacVey, MacVie, Vahy, Veigh. (Scot, Irish) Descendant of someone who bore the Gaelic personal name *Beatha* 'life,' and by extension 'religious person.'

Shakespeare took the plot of *Macbeth* from the *Chronicles of Raphael Holinshed*, though he adapted the original with some freedom. The various accidents that have occurred during productions of the play brought about the superstition amongst actors that it should always be referred to as 'the Scottish play,' and never by its actual title.

MacBride *see* KILBRIDE.

MacBrien *see* BRIAN.

MacBryde *see* KILBRIDE.

MacCalister *see* ALEXANDER.

MacCall *see* ALMACK.

MacCarha, MacCarhie, MacCarhig *see* MACCARTHY.

MacCartan *see* MACCARTNEY.

MacCarten *see* MACCARTNEY.

MacCarthy, MacArthy, MacArty, MacCarha, MacCarhie, MacCarhig, MacCartie, MacCarty (Irish) Descendant of Carthách, a Gaelic personal name which means 'friendly, loving.' The American author Mary McCarthy notes in her *Memories of a Catholic Girlhood*: 'Names had a great importance for us in the convent, and foreign names, French, German, or plain English (which, to us, were foreign, because of their Protestant sound), bloomed like prize roses among a collection of spuds. Irish names were too common in the school to have any prestige either as surname (Gallagher,

Finn, Sullivan, McCarthy) or as Christian names.'

MacCarroll *see* CARROLL.

MacCartie, MacCarty *see* MACCARTHY.

MacCartney, Carton, MacArtan, MacArtane, MacArtney, MacCartan, MacCartane, MacCarten, MacCartin, MacCarton (Irish, Scot) Descendant of someone who bore the Gaelic personal name *Art* 'bear, hero,' which is possibly also present in ARTHUR.

MacCaull *see* ALMACK.

MacCay *see* MACKAY.

MacChruiter *see* CROWTHER.

MacClean, MacCleane *see* MACLEAN.

MacClement, MacClements, MacClemont, MacCliments *see* LAWMAN.

MacCloud *see* MACLEOD.

MacCloy *see* LEWIS.

MacClymond, MacClymont, MacClymount *see* LAWMAN.

MacCone *see* EWAN.

MacConnal, MacConnel, MacConnell *see* DONALD.

MacCown *see* EWAN.

MacCoy, MacCue *see* MACKAY.

MacCuill *see* QUILL.

MacCune *see* EWAN.

MacDaid *see* DAVID.

MacDairmond, MacDarmid *see* DERMOTT.

MacDavid, MacDavie, MacDavitt, MacDavy *see* DAVID.

MacDearmid, MacDermaid, MacDermid, MacDerment, MacDermont, MacDermot, MacDermott *see* DERMOTT.

MacDevitt *see* DAVID.

MacDiarmid *see* DERMOTT.

MacDonald, MacDonell, MacDonnell *see* DONALD.

MacDougal, MacDougall, MacDowall, MacDowell, MacDuall, MacDugald *see* DOUGAL.

MacEgill *see* GALL.

MacEoghoe *see* KEOGH.

MacEvaghe, MacEveighe *see* MACBETH.

MacEwan, MacEwen, MacEwing *see* EWAN.

MacFergus, MacFerries *see* FERGUS.

MacGee *see* MACKAY.

MacGenis *see* MAC-.

MacGeogh *see* KEOGH.

MacGeown *see* EWAN.

MacGhee *see* MACKAY.

MacGilbride *see* KILBRIDE.

MacGillaspick *see* GILLESPIE.

MacGillbride *see* KILBRIDE.

MacGinnis *see* MAC-.

MacGloughlin *see* LACHLAN.

MacGregor, MacGreigor, MacGrigor (Scot) Descendant of *Gregor,* the Scottish form of *Gregory*. This Greek name, meaning 'watchful,' was borne by many early saints as well as sixteen popes. In the 17th and 18th centuries, because of the clan members' many lawless acts, use of the name MacGregor was officially forbidden in Scotland, the name-bearers being obliged to adopt another. Robert Louis Stevenson writes in *Catriona*: '"My name is not spoken. More than a hundred years it has not gone upon men's tongues, save for a blink. I am nameless like the Fold of Peace. Catriona Drummond is the one I use." Now indeed I knew where I was standing. In all broad Scotland there was but one name proscribed, and that was the name of the Macgregors.'

MacGuinness *see* MAC-.

MacHenry *see* HENRY.

MacHugh *see* MACKAY.

MacImmie *see* SIMON.

MacIngil *see* GALL.

MacInlester, MacLeister (Scot) Forms of *Mac an (Fh)leisdeir* 'son of the arrow maker.' The Gaelic words *fleisdear* and *leisdear* were borrowings from French *flechier,* which led to the name *Fletcher*. This is the Anglicized form adopted by many families who bore the Gaelic name.

MacInnes *see* MAC-.

MacIntosh, Mackintosh, MacKintosh (Scot) A form of Gaelic *Mac an toisich* 'son of the chief, leader.'

Compton Mackenzie makes the obvious joke about the name in *Whisky Galore*: ' "Ay, Macintosh is my name," said the traveller.

Mr Brown felt inclined to say that it was a very good name to have on such a morning (it was pouring with rain), but having heard that the Celts lacked humour he decided to refrain.'

It was Charles Macintosh who patented the waterproof fabric from which were raincoats were made. His name has not quite entered the language, since the item concerned is usually spelt mackintosh.

MacIvagh, MacIveagh *see* MACBETH.

MacJames *see* JAMES.

MacKall *see* ALMACK.

MacKarrill *see* CARROLL.

MacKay, MacCay, MacCoy, MacCue, MacGee, MacGhee, MacKee, MacKey, MacKie, MacKoy, Magee, Maggee (Scot, Irish) Descendant of *Aed* or *Aodh*, a Gaelic personal name meaning 'fire.' In Ireland this is traditionally Anglicized as HUGH, though the names are not etymologically connected. Thus Irish surnames such as HUESON, HUGHES, MACHUGH sometimes belong here.

The following is taken from *Collins Dictionary of Curious Phrases*, by Leslie Dunkling: 'In a letter written in 1883, Robert Louis Stevenson referred to a man named Johnstone as 'the real Mackay.' This was in the sense of 'the genuine article, something of high quality,' the meaning that we now attach to 'the real McCoy.' Stevenson probably picked up his version of the phrase from advertisements for Mackay whisky. These had claimed since 1870 that their product was 'the real Mackay.' The change to 'the real McCoy' occurred in the U.S.A., where the phrase seems to have been deliberately adapted by a welterweight boxer, Kid McCoy, and his followers. McCoy himself is said to have promoted a story concerning an incident in a bar. When someone asked him to prove who he was, McCoy allegedly obliged by knocking the man to the ground. When the man recovered he is said to have admitted that he had met 'the real McCoy.' An even more unlikely story says that during the time Kid McCoy was champion, from 1898 to 1900, another boxer called McCoy, of inferior quality, was also pursuing his career.'

MacKeamish *see* JAMES.

MacKee *see* MACKAY.

MacKehoe *see* KEOGH.

MacKennan *see* FINN.

MacKenzie, MacQuhenzie, MacWeeney, MacWhinney, MacWhinnie, MacWinney, Mawhinney, Mewhinney (Scot) Descendant of *Coinneach,* a Gaelic name meaning 'handsome.'

MacKeo, MacKeogh *see* KEOGH.

MacKeon *see* EWAN.

MacKeough *see* KEOGH.

MacKeown *see* EWAN.

MacKerras *see* FERGUS.

MacKey, MacKie *see* MACKAY.

MacKillbride *see* KILBRIDE.

MacKimmey, MacKimmie *see* SIMON.

Mackiness *see* MAC-.

Mackintosh, MacKintosh *see* MACINTOSH.

MacKough *see* KEOGH.

MacKoy *see* MACKAY.

MacKynnan *see* FINN.

MacLachlan, MacLachlane *see* LACHLAN.

MacLain, MacLaine *see* MACLEAN.

MacLamond, MacLamont *see* LAWMAN.

MacLane *see* MACLEAN.

MacLauchlan, MacLauchlane, MacLauchlin, MacLaughlan, MacLaughlane, MacLaughlin see Lachlan.

MacLean, MacClean, MacCleane, MacLain, MacLaine, MacLane, MacLoon (Scot) Descendant of *Mac Gille Eáin* or, in Ireland, *Mac Giolla Eóin* 'son of the devotee of St John.'

MacLeister *see* MACINLESTER.

MacLeman, MacLemon *see* LAWMAN.

MacLeod, MacCloud (Scot) Descendant of someone who bore the name *Leod,* itself a form of the Norse *Ljotr* or *Ljot* 'ugly.'

MacLimont *see* LAWMAN.

MacLochlin, MacLoghlin *see* LACHLAN.

MacLoon *see* MACLEAN.

MacLucas, MacLuckie, MacLucky, MacLukie, MacLugash, MacLugish *see* LUKE.

MacMartin *see* MARTIN.

MacMaurice *see* MORRIS.

MacMichael, MacMichie *see* MICHAEL.

MacMillan, MacMilland, MacMillen, MacMowlane, MacMoylan, MacMullan, MacMullen, MacMullin, MacMullon (Scot) Descendant of *Maolán* or *Maoláin,* 'bald, tonsured,' a reference to the shaven head of a monk rather than natural baldness. In Ireland the name takes such forms as MELANE, MILLAN, MILLANE, MOLLAN, MOYLAN, MULHANE, MULLAN, MULLANE, MULLEN, MULLIN, MULLINS, MULLON, O'MELANE, O'MOLLANE, O'MOYLANE, O'MULLANE.

MacMorice, MacMorris *see* MORRIS.

MacMurray *see* MURRAY.

MacNichol, MacNickle, MacNicol *see* NICHOLAS.

MacQuhenzie *see* MACKENZIE.

MacRemon, MacRedmond *see* RAYMOND.

MacVaghe *see* MACBETH.

MacVain *see* BEAN.

MacVarish, MacVarrais *see* MORRIS.

MacVay, MacVeagh, MacVeigh, MacVey, MacVie *see* MACBETH

MacWalter, MacWatters *see* WALTER.

MacWeeney, MacWhinney, MacWhinnie *see* MACKENZIE.

MacWhirter *see* CROWTHER.

MacWilliam *see* QUILLIAM.

MacWinney *see* MACKENZIE.

Madoc, Maddaux, Maddick, Maddicks, Maddix, Maddock, Maddocks, Maddox, Maddy, Madocks, Madog, Mattacks, Mattocks, Mattox, Mattuck, Matyn (Welsh) Descendant of *Madoc* 'fortunate.'

Peter Mattocks of Sussex once complained to the *Daily Mail* that his name was frequently changed to *Catlocks, Carrots* and *Buttocks*.

Magee *see* MACKAY.

Magennis *see* MAC-.

Maggee *see* MACKAY.

Magill *see* GALL.

Maginniss, Maguiness, Maguinness *see* MAC-.

Mahood, Mald, Malt *see* MAUDE

Maingaut, Maingaud, Maingot, Mainguet, Mangaud, Mangaut (French) Descendant of a man called *Magingaut*. Professor Dauzat glosses *magin* as 'strength' and *gaut* as the name of a divinity. Bowditch describes Manigault as 'a distinguished South Carolina name.'

In William Faulkner's *Requiem for a Nun* a woman pronounces her name as *Mannigoe*. Someone comments: 'Oh yes, Manigault. The old Charleston name.' Another person present adds: 'Older than that. *Maingault*. Nancy's heritage – or anyway her patronym – runs Norman blood.'

Mainwaring, Mannering, Manwaring (Eng) From an unidentified place name. Lower reports in his *English Surnames* that Sir William Dugdale found 131 different spellings of this name relating to the same Chester family. The variants included *Mainwayringe, Meinilwarin* and *Mensilwaren*.

The British actor Arthur Lowe played the part of Captain Mainwaring in the popular BBC television series *Dad's Army*.

By coincidence the hero of Sir Walter Scott's *Guy Mannering* is also an army officer.

Majoribanks *see* MARJORIBANKS.

Makepeace, Makepiece (Eng) Nickname of a man known for his skills in settling disputes.

Malaghan *see* MILLIGAN.

Maleterre *see* MALSTER.

Malloch *see* ALMACK.

Malster, Maltas, Malter, Malthouse, Malthus, Maltman, Maltus (Eng) Occupational name for someone who worked at a malt-house, or used malt for brewing. There is a French name *Maleterre* 'bad, unprofitable earth or land' which could also have led to Malter, but the occupation of brewer was a very common one and most families bearing the name derive it from this source.

Maltravers, Matravers, Mattravers (Eng) This has all the appearance of a French place name, though no obvious candidate presents itself. There are plenty of French place names which begin with *Mal-* 'bad,' and *travers* suggests a crossing of some kind, such as a ford across a river. Traverséres exists as a French place name in its own right.

Whatever its meaning, this name has an aristocratic ring to it, though it poses problems for Mrs Beste-Chetwynde in Evelyn

Waugh's *Decline and Fall*. She remarks: 'I sometimes think of marrying old Maltravers, only "Margot Maltravers" does sound a little too much, don't you think?'

Maltus *see* MALSTER.

Man, Mann, Manning (Eng) This is basically the word man used in either a complimentary sense for a 'real man, a tough guy,' as it were, or it describes someone's servant. The word had also become a name in its own right in Old English, as well as forming an element in many Germanic names (*Erdmann, Friedemann, Hartmann, Hermann, Karlmann, Liebmann, Tillmann, Trautmann, Volkmann, Waldmann,* etc). Mann could indicate an ancestor who bore such a name. MANSON sometimes belongs with this group of names.

Man usually has its obvious meaning in the wide range of compound surnames where it is a final element, though ALLMAN, ALMAN, ALEMAN, ALIMAN, for example, are from Latin Alemannia 'Germany'. What is more complex is the relationship between *-man* and what precedes it. Examples of such names, discovered in directories by C.L.Lordan, are ACREMAN, BADMAN, BANDMAN, BANNERMAN, BARLEYMAN, BEEMAN, BELLMAN, BERRYMAN, BIGMAN, BLACKMAN, BLEAKMAN, BLYTHMAN, BOGMAN, BOOTHMAN, BONNYMAN, BOWMAN, BRICKMAN, BRIGHTMAN, BUCKMAN, CARMAN, CASTLEMAN, CHAPMAN, COLEMAN, COTMAN, CROSSMAN, DAYMAN, DEARMAN, DICKMAN, DOLLMAN, DUCKMAN, EASTMAN, FAIRMAN, FERRYMAN, FOOTMAN, FOREMAN, FREEMAN, GOATMAN, GOODMAN, GUTTERMAN, HACKMAN, HARDMAN, HAYMAN, HEADMAN, HELLMAN, HENCHMAN, HILLMAN, HOLLOWMAN, HOLLYMAN, HONEYMAN, HOOFMAN, HOUSEMAN, ILLMAN, IRONMAN, JOLLYMAN, KINGSMAN, LACKMAN, LAIDMAN, LAWMAN, LONGMAN, LOVEMAN, LOWMAN, MARYMAN, MASTERMAN, MEATMAN, MERRIMAN, NEWMAN, NORMAN, OLDMAN, PENNYMAN, PIEMAN, PITMAN, POORMAN, POTMAN, PRETTYMAN, PROUDMAN, PULLMAN, REDMAN, SACKMAN, SANDMAN, SELLERMAN, SICKMAN, SILLIMAN, SLOWMAN, SLYMAN, SMALLMAN, SNOWMAN, SPADEMAN, SPEARMAN, STRANGEMAN, TRUMAN, TWENTYMAN, TWOMAN, WAGMAN, WALKMAN, WARMAN, WELLMAN, WHATMAN, WILDMAN, WINEMAN, WISEMAN, WOODMAN, WORKMAN, YEOMAN, YOUNGMAN.

Manclark *see* CLARK.

Mangaud, Mangaut, Manigault *see* MAINGAUT.

Mann, Manning *see* MAN.

An anonymous epitaph quoted in *Verse and Worse*, by Arnold Silcock:

Here lies the body of Ann Mann
Who lived an old woman
And died an old Mann.

Mannering *see* MAINWARING.

Mansfield *see* STANSFIELD.

Manson (Eng) *see* MAN, but in a Scottish context likely to mean 'son of *Magnus*' 'great.'

Manypenny *see* MONEYPENNY.

Manwaring *see* MAINWARING.

Manyweathers *see* FOULWEATHER.

Marach *see* MARHACH.

March (Eng) From residence on the borders between England and Wales or England and Scotland. In some instances there may be a connection with the month of March.

The name's literary association is with the March sisters, Jo, Meg, Beth and Amy, portrayed in Louisa M. Alcott's classic novel *Little Women*.

Marchbanks *see* MARJORIBANKS.

Marhach, Marach, Marrach, Marrage, Marriage, Marridge (Eng) Descendant of someone who came from a place named for its 'boundary gate or ridge.'

Marjoribanks, Majoribanks, Marchbanks (Scot) The surname came about by ownership of a Scottish estate named for *Marjorie*, daughter of Robert the Bruce.

Compton Mackenzie writes, in *Whisky Galore*: '"There's some devilish queer names, like that army doctor in the war that was called Major Marchbanks although to read it you would have said it was Marjory Banks." "A very queer name altogether, that," Tom agreed. "Major Marjory Banks, as if it was a lassie that was in it".'

On the general question of a name's pronunciation, Upton Sinclair says in *World's End*: 'He knew that many English names were queer, especially the fashionable ones; the owners carefully preserved this queerness as a form of distinction, as one way of showing that they didn't care a hang whether anybody agreed with them about the way to spell, or to pronounce, or to do anything else.' The comment is made after Sinclair has introduced a character named *Codwilliger*, who pronounces her name *Culliver*. *See* CHOLMONDLEY.

Markham (Eng) Descendant of someone who came from the Nottinghamshire place, so-named because it was the 'homestead near the boundary.'

Marklove *see* LOVE.

Marler, Marlor (Eng) The name refers to 'clay' in some way, probably to someone who worked in a marl-pit. *Marl* is soil which is a mixture of clay and lime. Someone who merely lived on a patch of such soil could also be indicated.

Marrach, Marrage, Marriage, Marridge *see* MARHACH.

Marrow (Eng) A reference to a working companion, or mate, originally one whose ox combined with yours to form a ploughing team.

Marshall, Marschall, Marskell, Mascall, Maskall, Maskell, Maskill (Eng) Most bearers of these names had an ancestor who was a farrier, who both shoed horses and attended to their diseases. A marshal in early times, however, could also be an official of the highest rank in the royal household.

In his novel *As Far As You Can Go*, Julian Mitchell has: 'The man's name meant nothing to him at all: Colin Marshall. He must have met a Colin Marshall somewhere at some time in his life, the name sounded like a middle class version of John Smith.'

Martin, Marten, Martens, Martins, Martinson, Martyn, Martyns, MacMartin (Eng) Descendant of *Martin,* a name made popular throughout Europe by the 4th century saint Martin of Tours. It is usually derived from *Mars,* the Roman god of war.

Mascall, Maskall, Maskell, Maskill *see* MARSHALL.

Mason (Eng) Occupational name of a stone-mason.

For some reason Mason is a legal name in literature. Erle Stanley Gardner's *Perry Mason* became especially associated with Raymond Burr, who played the part in a long-running television series.

Randolph Mason is also a lawyer in many stories by Melville Davisson Post, though unlike Perry Mason he tends to find legal loopholes which allow his criminal clients to go free.

Massingberd, Massingbird *see* WHITBREAD.

Massingham (Eng) Descendant of someone who came from the Norfolk place of this name, so-named because it was '*Maessa's* homestead.'

Mathes, Matheson, Mathew, Mathews, Mathewson, Mathias, Mathies, Mathieson, Mathis, Mathison, Mathys *see* MATTHEW.

Matravers *see* MALTRAVERS.

Matson *see* MATTHEW.

Mattacks *see* MADOC.

Matthew, Mathes, Matheson, Mathew, Mathews, Mathewson, Mathias, Mathies, Mathieson, Mathis, Mathison, Mathys, Matson, Matterson, Mattes, Matthes, Matthews, Matthewson, Matthias, Matthieson, Matthison, Matthys, Mattingson, Mattison, Mattinson, Matts, May, Mayhew (Eng) *Matthew* is a tax-collector at Capernaum who becomes one of the twelve Apostles. His name in Greek is *Matthaios,* derived from Hebrew *Mattai* or *Matya*, abbreviated forms of *Mattenai, Mattaniah* or *Mattithiah*. The former name means 'gift of God,' the latter 'gift of Yah.' MAYHEW is from the French form of *Matthew*, namely *Mathieu,* and is also found as MAYO.

Mattleson *see* MAUDE.

Mattocks, Mattox *see* MADOC.

Mattravers *see* MALTRAVERS.

Matts *see* MATTHEW.

Mattuck, Matyn *see* MADOC.

Mauclerc *see* CLARK.

Maude, Mahood, Mald, Malt, Mattleson, Maudson, Maulson, Mault, Mawhood, Mawson, Mold, Molson, Mould, Moulds, Mouldy, Moulson, Moult, Mowat, Mowles, Mowll, Till, Tille, Tillet, Tillot, Tillotson, Tills, Tilson (Eng) Descendant of *Matilda* 'might – battle.' This was one of the most popular feminine names in the surname-formation period.The wife of William I was Queen Matilda, called *Mahald* and *Mold*.

Maugham *see* HAM.

Maulson, Mault *see* MAUDE.

Maurice *see* MORRIS.

Mawhinney *see* MACKENZIE.

Mawhood, Mawson *see* MAUDE.

May, Maye, Mayes, Mays, Mayze, Mease, Mey, Meye (Eng) A pet form of *Matthew*, via *Mayhew,* or from the Middle English word *may* which meant an adolesent girl or young man. The name is unlikely to refer to the month.

Mayhew, Mayo *see* MATTHEW.

Mays, Mayze, Mease *see* MAY.

Meek, Meeke, Meeks (Eng) Nickname for a mild person.

Melane *see* MACMILLAN.

Melican *see* MILLIGAN.

Mellar, Mellard *see* MILL.

Melsop *see* MILSOP.

Melton (Eng) Someone who came from one of the several places so-named because it was a 'middle settlement.'

Mercy (Eng) Descendant of someone who played this role in a medieval mystery play. *See* VERITY.

Meriweather *see* FOULWEATHER.

Merry, Merriman, Merriment (Eng) Nickname for someone who was inclined to be merry.

Merryweather, Merrywether *see* FOULWEATHER.

Merton (Eng) Someone who came from one of the several places so-named because it was a 'settlement near a lake.'

Messerschmidt, Messersmith *see* SMITH.

Mewhinney *see* MACKENZIE.

Mey, Meye *see* MAY.

Michael, MacMichael, MacMichie, Michaels, Michaelson, Michell, Michelmore, Michelson, Micheson, Michie, Michieson, Miggles, Mitchel, Mitchell, Mitchelmore, Mitchelson, Mitchieson, Mitchison (Eng, Scot, Irish) Descendant of a man called *Michael,* a Hebrew name meaning 'who is like God?' borne by several men in the Bible. The addition of Gaelic *mor* 'big' as a suffix converts the name into a nickname distinguishing the eldest Michael from others in the family or community.

Middlemas, Middlemass, Middlemiss (Scot) Descendant of someone who came from the 'middlemost' district around Kelso. Black scoffs at 'absurd' explanations which derive the name from 'middlemast,' supposedly an early form of 'mainmast,' used as a nickname for a very tall man.

Middleton (Eng) Someone who came from one of the several places so-named because it was a 'middle settlement.'

Miggles *see* MICHAEL.

Milar, Miler *see* MILL.

Miles, Mileson, Milsom, Milson, Myles (Eng) Descendant of *Milo's* servant, Milo being a Germanic personal name of unknown origin. In some cases there may be a connection with Latin *miles*, literally 'soldier,' though the word was used in English contexts to refer to a retainer, servant.

The *London Evening Standard* reported 28 July, 1930, that an abandoned baby had been found in Yorkshire beside a milestone, nine miles from the nearest town. The authorities named her Nina Miles.

Milford (Eng) Descendant of someone who lived in one of the many English places that bears this name because of its 'mill by the ford.'

Mill, Mellar, Mellard, Milar, Miler, Milhouse, Millar, Millard, Mille, Millener, Miller, Milles, Millis, Millman, Millner, Mills, Millward, Millwood, Milman, Miln, Milne, Milner, Milnes, Milns, Milward, Mullard, Mullender, Mulliner, Mullinger (Eng) Occupational name of a miller, mill-warden, mill-worker, dweller in the mill-house.

In spite of overwhelming evidence that derives these names from a miller, Dr Brewer, of *Brewer's Dictionary of Phrase and Fable*, solemnly stated in the 13th edition of his book that 'Miller is the Old Norse melia, our mill and maul, and means a mauler or fighter.'

Millan, Millane *see* MACMILLAN.

Millar, Millard, Mille, Millener, Miller, Milles *see* MILL.

Milligan, Malaghan, Melican, Millican, Milligen, Millikin, Molohan, Mulgan, Mulligan, Mullikin, O'Milligane, O'Mollegane, O'Molleghan, O'Moylegane, O'Mullegan (Irish) Descendant of *Maolagán*, an Irish personal name based on *maol* 'bald, tonsured,' with a double diminutive ending.

Millis, Millman, Millner, Mills, Millward, Millwood, Milman, Miln, Milne, Milner, Milnes, Milns *see* MILL.

Milsop, Milsopp, Melsop (Eng) Nickname of a milksop, a man considered to be effeminate.

Milton (Eng) Someone who came from one of the several places so-named because it was either a 'middle settlement' or 'settlement with a mill.'

Milward *see* MILL.

Minchin (Eng) From an obsolete word for a 'nun,' presumably used as a nickname for a man who was as meek and demure as a nun, of for a man who was employed at a nunnery. *See* NUNN, NUNNS.

Minto *see* MINTY.

Minton (Eng) Someone who came from a place so-named because it was a 'settlement on a hill.'

Minty (Scot) Black lists this name in his *Surnames of Scotland* but offers no explanation for it. He remarks that an Andrew *Myntie* was accused of murder in 1609. There may be a connection with MINTO, another Scottish name, which indicates someone who came from the village of this name in Roxburghshire.

In *England Made Me*, Graham Greene says of a man named Minty that 'somehow he carried off the burden of his name.'

Mitchel, Mitchell, Mitchelmore, Mitchelson, Mitchieson, Mitchison see **Michael.** One of the 'tribe of ingenious etymologists,' as Professor Weekley would have called him, solemnly explained Mitchell as German *mit Schüler* 'with pupils.'

Mockler *see* CLARK.

Mold *see* MAUDE.

Mole (Eng) Nickname for a person thought to resemble a mole, or to be as short-sighted as a mole. The reference might also be to someone who had a prominent mole on his face.

Two humorous novels by Sue Townsend about the young Adrian Mole had a great success in the early 1980s.

Earlier, in the 1950s, a boy with a similar name had also enjoyed literary celebrity. Nigel *Molesworth* was the creation of writer Geoffrey Williams and artist Ronald Searle. His name indicated an ancestor who lived in Molesworth, Cambridgeshire, where the place name means '*Mul*'s enclosure.'

Mollan *see* MACMILLAN.

Molohan *see* MILLIGAN.

Molson *see* MAUDE.

Monckton, Monkton (Eng) Someone who came from one of the several places so-named because it was a 'monks' settlement.'

Monday, Mondy, Munday, Mundy (Eng) Descendant of *Mundi* 'protection,' an Old Norse personal name, or of someone especially associated with this day of the week.

George Crabbe described one possible association in his *Parish Register*:

Some hardened knaves that roved the country round,

Had left a babe within the parish bound.

But by what name th'unwelcome guest to call

Was long a question, and it 'posed' them all;

For he who lent it to a babe unknown,

Censorious men might take it for his own.

They look'd about, they gravely spoke to all,

And not one Richard answered to the call.

Next they enquired THE DAY when, passing by,

Th'unlucky peasant heard the stranger's cry.

At last, with all their words and work content,

Back to their homes the prudent vestry went,

And RICHARD MONDAY to the workhouse sent.

Moneypenny (Eng) The early variant *Manypenny* suggests that this was a nickname for a rich man.

Elizabeth Gaskell's *Cousin Phillis* has: 'I did not like pushing myself upon strangers, who perhaps had never heard of my mother's name, and, such an odd name as it was – *Moneypenny*.'

Moneysmith *see* SMITH.

Monkton *see* MONCKTON.

Montagne, Montaigne *see* MOUNTAIN.

Montgomery, Montgomerie (Eng) From a place named in Normandy. The first part of the name is French *mont* 'hill.' The second part is a Germanic pesonal name composed of elements meaning 'man' and 'power.'

In *Georgy Girl*, by Margaret Forster, we find: '"What's your awful surname?" "Jones," said Jos solemnly. "You're joking," said Meredith, aghast. "Mrs Meredith Jones. Jos, you'll have to change it. I can't give up Montgomery for Jones. You couldn't ask me to".'

Moody *see* MUDD.

Moore, Atmore, Amore, Moir, Moor, Moorcock, Moores, Moorman, Moors, More, Moreman, Morin, Moring, Morman, Morrell, Morrin, Morring, O'Moore, O'Mora (Eng) The *Atmore* type of surname provides convincing proof that Moore can derive from the topographic feature. It would refer to someone who lived on a moor, or in one of the many English places named because it was on or near a moor. However, people of the Moorish race were considered to be 'swarthy,' and Moore would often have been a nickname for someone who was dark skinned. In an Irish context, Moore represents Gaelic *O Mordha*, descendant of a man whose name meant 'proud, stately.' The other names listed above show Moore or Moor with diminutive endings, or refer to the servant of a man so-named.

These names have long been the subject of puns. When Sir Thomas More was Chancellor, his untiring efforts brought an end to all the Chancery cases then in litigation. A verse written at the time said:

When More some years had Chancellor been,
No more suits did remain;
The same shall never more be seen,
Till More be there again.

An epitaph in St Benet's Churchyard, Paul's Wharf, London, reads:

Here lies one More, and no more than he;
One More, and no more! how can that be?
Why, one More, and no more may well lie here alone,
But here lies one More, and that's more than one!

An American epitaph is quoted by Barbara Rainbow Fletcher in *Don't Blame the Stork*:

Here lies Les Moore
Stopped a slug from a 44
No Les, no Moore.

See also the punning verses about Messrs Moore, Strange and Wright under STRANGE.

Moran, O'Moraine, O'Moran, O'Morane (Irish) Descendant of *Mórán,* a Gaelic personal name based on *more* 'great.'

More, Moreman *see* MOORE.

Morgan, Morcant, Morgant, Morgin, Morgon, Morgund, Murgan (Welsh, Scot) Descendant of *Morgan*, which Black maintains is an early Celtic *mori-canto-s* 'sea bright.' Normally this is thought of as a Welsh name, but there are many Scottish Morgans in Aberdeenshire. In Ireland Morgan is said to be an Anglicized form of various Gaelic names.

Morin, Moring, Morman, Morrell, Morrin, Morring *see* MOORE.

Morphy *see* MURPHY.

Morris, FitzMaurice, MacMaurice, MacMorice, MacMorris, MacVarish, MacVarrais, Maurice, Morce, Morison, Morrice, Morrison, Morrish, Morriss, Morse (Eng, Scot, Welsh, Irish) Descendant of a man called *Maurice* 'Moorish, dark complexioned, swarthy.' The third century saint of this name was an officer in the Theban Legion, composed of mostly Christian soldiers. The Emperor Diocletian ordered his entire army to join in a sacrifice to the gods of Rome so that success in battle might be achieved. Maurice was one of the Christian soldiers who refused to attend, for which he was martyred.

Morton (Eng) Someone who came from one of the several places so-named because it was a 'settlement by a fen.'

Moss, Mosse, Mossman (Eng) Descendant of *Moses,* or of someone who lived on 'land covered with moss' or 'swampy land.'

Motzart *see* MOZART.

Mould, Moulds, Mouldy, Moulson, Moult *see* MAUDE.

Shakespeare amuses himself with the name Mouldy in *2 Henry IV*, where Falstaff asks a potential recruit: 'Is thy name Mouldy?' 'Yea, an't please you.' ''Tis the more time thou wert used.'

Mountain (Eng) From residence on or near a hill, a small mountain. French versions of this name include MONTAGNE and MONTAIGNE.

J.I.M. Stuart writes, in *Avery's Mission*: Mountain is a respectable English surname, borne by any number of distinguished persons. It would have been unremarkable in the present instance, but for the fact that Margaret Mountain was diminutive. Here, so to speak, was a mountain turning out to be a molehill. So silly a joke wouldn't, I hope, have occurred to me but for the fact that Miss Mountain was really rather mole-like. Not in figure or features, which would be ridiculous, but simply in colouration.'

Mowat, Mowles, Mowll *see* MAUDE.

Moylan *see* MACMILLAN.

Mozart (Ger) An earlier form of this famous name was *Motzart*. Hans Bahlow suggests, in his *Deutsches Namenlexikon,* that it was a nickname for a dirty, clumsy fellow, or a reference to swampy land. Other commentators have interpreted the name more kindly as a Germanic personal name composed of elements meaning 'mind, spirit' and 'hardy, brave.'

There are comments on the name in *The Soho Summer of Mr Green*, by Cyril Kersh: 'Although it would be an exaggeration to say that Arnold Green fell in love with Bessie Mozart because of her surname, he was certainly influenced by it. "After all," he told his parents, "a name like that's historic. It's an omen. It's a name with class." "Mozart, schmozart! Omens, schmomens!" his mother growled. "As for class, any name's got class when there's money in the bank. Believe me, Green would also be the classiest name in the world if we had the money of the Rothschilds. Class in a name yet"!'

Mudd (Eng) Descendant of a woman called *Maud,* itself a variant of *Mathilda*, or of a man named *Moda*. Mathilda is a Germanic name composed of elements which mean 'strength' and 'battle;' Moda means 'spirit, will-power.' The word from which it is derived led also to the surname MOODY, a nickname for someone who was 'bold, proud, passionate.' Mudd may also be from 'mud,' indicating someone who lived in a muddy area, or used mud for building purposes, using wattle and daub.

Paul Dickson, in *Names*, quotes a letter that was written to *The Economist* about the use of the expression 'one's name is mud.' The correspondent mentioned that 'there are nearly 300 heirs of Dr Mudd (the physician who was imprisoned for life for setting the broken leg of Lincoln's assassin) and they are unhappy about this sort of thing.' This implies that the phrase came into being after that incident (in 1865), but the phrase had already appeared in print by 1823. Previously, in British slang of the early 18th century, a 'mud' was a 'fool.' The meaning of the phrase has thus become weaker, since to say that 'my name will be mud' now merely means that you will be temporarily unpopular.

Mulgan *see* MILLIGAN.

Mulhane, Mullan, Mullane *see* MACMILLAN.

Mullard *see* MILL.

Mullen, Mullin, Mullins, Mullon *see* MACMILLAN.

Mulligan, Mullikin *see* MILLIGAN.

Mulrain, Mulrine, Mulroyan, Mulryan, Mulryne *see* RYAN.

Munday, Mundy *see* MONDAY.

Murdoch, Mortagh, Murdock, Murdough, Murdow, Murtha (Scot) Descendant of someone who bore the Gaelic personal name *Muireadhach* (see Murray) or *Murchadh* 'sea warrior.'

Murdoch was an unfamiliar name to the London registrar who entered it as *Murder* on a birth certificate. Murder John Smith was also given as the name of the father.

Murgan *see* MORGAN.

Murphy, Morphy, O'Morcho, O'Morphy, O'Murphy (Irish) Descendant of someone who bore the Gaelic personal name *Murchadh* 'sea warrior.' *See* DUCK.

Murray, Murrey, Murrie, Murry (Scot, Irish) In Scotland, descendant of someone who came from *Moray*. Irish bearers of the name, including those who use the form MACMURRAY, are descendants of a man who bore the Gaelic personal name *Muireadhach*. The latter is usually explained as a derivative of *muir* 'sea,' though Donnchadh ó Corrain and Fidelma Maguire, in *Gaelic Personal Names,* prefer 'lord, master.'

Murtha *see* MURDOCH

Myles *see* MILES.

Myntie *see* MINTY.

Nailer, Nailor, Nails, Nailsmith, Naismith, Nasmyth, Naylar, Nayler, Nayles, Naysmith, Neasmith (Eng) Occupational name of a nail-maker.

Nairn, Nairne (Scot) Descendant of someone who came from the Scottish town of this name. The place name is from the river Nairn, of uncertain meaning.

Naish *see* ASH.

Naismith *see* NAILER.

Nalder (Eng) Descendant of someone who lived near an alder tree.

Napier, Naper, Napper (Eng) Someone concerned with napery, or table-linen, either as a seller of such items or a household official in charge of the linen.

    The family legend concerning the origin of Napier concerns a son of the earl of Lennox who behaved bravely in battle. Afterwards the King told his men: 'Ye have all done valiantly, but there is one amongst you that hath *na pier* (no equal).'

Nappakhu *see* FABER.

Nash *see* ASH.

Nasmyth *see* NAILER.

Navin *see* NEVILLE, NIVEN.

Naybour *see* NEIGHBOUR.

Naylar, Nayler, Nayles *see* NAILER.

Nayshe *see* ASH.

Naysmith *see* NAILER.

Nead, Neade, Need, Needes, Needs (Eng) Probably a nickname for someone who was poor, needy.

Neal, Neale, Neall *see* NEIL.

Nealon *see* NEIL.

Neam, Neame *see* EAMES.

Neasmith *see* NAILER.

Neat, Neate (Eng) Occupational name for a herdsman, from Old English *neat* 'cattle.' This cannot mean 'neat' in the sense of 'neat and tidy,' a meaning derived from a separate word which only came into being long after the surname-formation period.

Neave, Neaves *see* NEVE.

Nee *see* NEVILLE.

Need, Needes *see* NEAD.

Needham (Eng) From residence in one of the places so-named because it was 'hardship homestead,' ie a home on poor land.

Needs *see* NEAD.

Neel, Neeland, Neelands, Neeld, Neele, Neels *see* NEIL.

Neeve, Neeves *see* NEVE.

Negus (Eng) Weekley noted that Negus was a Norfolk name, and that in the same county **Negoose** occurred, along with GOOSE, GOOSEMAN, GOZZARD, GAZARD, all indicating a goose-herd. Elsewhere, compound names in -*goose* are also found, including WILDGOOSE, WILLGOSS, WILDGUST, GRAYGOOSE. Another Norfolk name is EDGOOSE, which is likely to be a form of *Edgehouse* 'corner house.' Weekley therefore wondered whether Negus was from the phrase *atten-eg-house* 'at the corner house.' A simpler explanation is that the name means 'near house,' the first element being Old English *neah*.

Neighbour, Naybour (Eng) For someone who was a neighbour. The word was also commonly used as a name-substitute in direct address, as in 'Good morning, neighbour.'

Neil, Kneale, MacNeal, MacNeale, MacNeel, MacNeil, MacNeill, MacNeille, MacNiel, Neal, Neale, Neall, Nealon, Neel, Neeland, Neelands, Neeld, Neele, Neels, Neiland, Neill, Neilson, Nell, Nelson, Neylan, Neylon, Niall, Nield, Niell, Nielson, Nihell, Nihill, Nilan, Niles, Nilon, Nilson, O'Neal, O'Neil, O'Neilane, O'Neill, O'Nelane, O'Nillane (Irish, Scot, Eng) Descendant of a man who bore the Irish Gaelic name *Niall*, usually explained as 'champion.' The Norsemen borrowed the name and used it in the form *Njall*. The Normans also had the name as *Niel* or *Nihel*. This was Latinised as *Nigellus*, and became English *Nigel*, in the mistaken belief that it derived from the Latin word for 'black.' J.J.Kneen, in *The Personal Names of the Isle of*

Man, records *Kneale* as the Manx version of this name.

Nelmes, Nelms *see* ELM.

Nelson *see* NEIL.

Nelson is the most famous name in English naval history. As Robert Southey says, in *The Life of Nelson*: 'The death of Nelson was felt in England as something more than a public calamity; men started at the intelligence, and turned pale, as if they had heard of the loss of a dear friend.'

Nemo *see* NIMMO.

Ness (Scot, Eng) Descendant of someone who lived on a '*ness,*' a headland.

Nethercott (Eng) Descendant of someone who lived in the 'lower cottage,' or in one of the English places named in the same way. Similar names using *nether* 'lower' are **Netherton** 'lower settlement' and **Netherwood.**

Nettlefield, Nettlefold (Eng) Indications of an ancestor who lived in a place where nettles grew abundantly.

Neve, Neave, Neaves, Neeve, Neeves (Eng) Literally, a 'nephew,' presumably of an uncle who was of some importance for the relationship to be marked in this way.

Neville, Nevile, Nevill (Eng, Irish) Descendant of someone who came from Neuville or Neville, both places in France named because they were 'new settlements.' In Ireland Neville is used as the English form of Gaelic names such as *Niadh* 'warrior,' from a word meaning 'valiant.' The same Gaelic name leads to KNEE, NEE, O'KNEE, O'NEA, O'NEE, O'NEY. Neville is also used for 'descendant of *Cnámh* 'bone, bony,' which in turn leads to NAVIN, NEVIN, O'KNAVIN. *See* NIVEN.

Nevin, Nevins, Nevinson *see* NIVEN.

New, Newman (Eng) Indicating someone who had newly arrived in an area. Other names in *New-*, usually indicating a place of work or residence, include **Newall** 'hall' **Newberry, Newbery, Newbury, Newborough, Newburgh** 'town, fortress' **Newbald, Newbold, Newbould, Newboult** 'building' **Newby** 'farm, village' **Newham,** NEWNHAM, **Nuneham** 'homestead' NEWHOUSE NEWSAM, NEWSHOLME, NEWSOM, NEWSOME, NEWSUM 'houses' NEWSTEAD 'place'.

Newland, Newlands (Eng, Scot) The reference is to land recently cultivated for the first time. The surname indicates an ancestor who lived in any of the places named because of such a development.

Henry Barber mentions a more unusual reason for the name in his *British Surnames*: 'A child was left with a £50 note pinned to its clothes, and it was called Japhet Newland from the name of the governor of the Bank of England, Abraham Newland, on the note.'

Newman, Newnham, Newsam, Newsholme, Newsom, Newsome, Newstead, Newsum *see* NEW.

Newton (Eng) Someone who came from one of the many places so-named because it was a 'new settlement.'

Pope's well-known lines on Sir Isaac Newton, the mathematician and philosopher, are:

Nature and Nature's laws lay hid in night:

God said, Let Newton be! and all was light.

Sir John Squire added:

It did not last: the Devil, howling Ho!

Let Einstein be! restored the status quo.

Neylan, Neylon, Niall *see* NEIL.

Nice (Eng) The early meanings of this word, current when the surname came into being, were 'foolish, weak, simple,' from Latin *nescius* 'ignorant.' The nickname was not therefore as complimentary as it appears to be today.

Nicholas, Colcock, Cole, Colin, Colkin, Coll, Collard, Colle, Collens, Collerson, Collet, Collete, Collett, Collin, Collins, Collinson, Collison, Collisson, Colls, Collyns, Coule, Coules, Coull, Cowle, Cowles, MacNichol, MacNickle, MacNicol, Niccols, Nichol, Nicholass, Nicholds, Nichole, Nicholes, Nicholetts, Nicholls, Nicholson, Nickelson, Nickerson, Nickes, Nickinson, Nickisson, Nicklas, Nicklass, Nicklen, Nickless, Nicklin, Nickson, Nicol, Nicolai, Nicole, Nicolas, Nicolay, Nicoll, Nicolle, Nicolls, Nicolson, Nix, Nixon, Nixson (Eng) Descendant of *Nicholas*, a Greek name composed of elements meaning 'victory' and 'people.' Several saints bore the name, including the 4th century St Nicholas, patron saint of children, who is better known as *Santa Claus*. Many legendary tales are associated with him, including one where he saved three girls from prostitution by throwing bags of gold into their window (the gold becoming their dowries). This story is remembered in the three balls which form his emblem. In England *Nicholas* was commonly abbreviated to *Nick* or *Coll*. Diminutive endings might then be added to those forms.

Nield, Niell, Nielson, Nihell, Nihill, Nilan, Niles, Nilon, Nilson see NEIL.

Nigel *see* NEIL.

Nightingale (Eng) Nickname for someone who could sing well.
    Florence Nightingale was born in Florence, hence her name. Her older sister had been born in Naples, which presented her parents with more of a problem. They solved it by using an earlier name of that city – Parthenope. Florence would have become Florence *Shore* under normal circumstances. Her father changed the family name when he inherited a fortune from an uncle named Nightingale.

Nimmo (Scot) The fact that the name was sometimes recorded as **Nemo** led to the suggestion that the family had adopted the Latin word for 'nobody' in order to remain anonymous. It might as well be suggested that Captain Nemo, the pirate master of the submarine *Nautilus* in the novels by Jules Verne, was a family-member, though the latter is supposedly an Indian prince. Lower thought Nimmo was a Scottish place name in corrupt form and was probably right. The modern spelling certainly means little; earlier forms were *Newmoch* and *Nemoch* as well as Nemo.

Niven, MacNevin, MacNiven, Navin, Nevin, Nevins, Nevinson (Scot, Irish) Descendant of *Naoimhin,* a Gaelic personal name which is a diminutive of *naomh* 'saint.' For Irish Navin, Nevin *see* NEVILLE.

Nix, Nixon, Nixson *see* NICHOLAS.

Noack *see* OAK.

Noad, Noade, Noades *see* OADE.

Noah, Noe, Noise, Noy, Noyce, Noyes (Eng) Descendant of someone who played the part of *Noah* each year in a medieval mystery play. The performance of these plays was an important event, bringing to life events related in the bible.

Noak, Noake, Noakes, Noaks, Noaxe *see* OAK.

Noare *see* OVER.

Nobb, Nobbs, Nobes *see* ROBERT.

Noble (Eng) Nickname for a person considered to be noble-like, though the name could also be applied sarcastically to someone exactly the opposite.

Nock *see* OAK.

Nodes *see* OADE.

Noe, Noise *see* NOAH.

Noel, Nowell, Nowill (Eng) Descendant of someone born during the Christmas season. Christmas itself occurs as a surname.

Noke, Nokes *see* OAK.

Nokkins *see* ROBERT.

Nolan, O'Noland, O'Nolane, O'Nowlan (Irish) Descendant of someone who bore the Gaelic personal name *Nuallán* 'noble.'

Noon (Eng) The Oxford *Dictionary of Surnames* suggests that this was a nickname for a bright and cheerful person, one who was being compared to the sunniest part of the day. That seems rather farfetched, and Weekley's explanation that it is a form of the French place name *Noyon* is more convincing. Dauzat explains the French name as meaning 'new market.' Noon could also be a simplified form of Irish NOONE, NOONAN.

Noonan, Noone, O'Nowan, O'Nown, O'Nowne (Irish) Descendant of *Nuadhán,* from *Nuadha*, the name of several Celtic gods.

Nopps, Nops *see* ROBERT.

Norbrook, Northbrook (Eng) Descendant of someone who lived 'north of the brook.'

Norcott *see* NORTHCOTE.

Norfolk (Eng) Someone who originally came from this English county of the 'north people.'

Frank Harris, in his biography of Oscar Wilde, quotes the playwright: 'I love even historic names, Frank, as Shakespeare did. Surely everyone prefers *Norfolk, Hamilton* and *Buckingham* to *Jones* or *Smith* or *Robinson*.'

Norkett, Norkutt *see* NORTHCOTE.

Norman, Normand (Eng) Someone from *Normandy*, France. Before the Norman invasion a *Northman,* or Scandinavian, would have been meant.

Norrington *see* NORTON.

Norris, Noriss, Norrish (Eng, Scot) Descendant of someone who came from the north of the country, or from north of the village. Occasionally the reference is to French *nourrice* 'wet-nurse.'

North, Norther, Northern (Eng) Descendant of someone who lived to the north of a village or had come there from further north. *See* WEST.

Northbrook *see* NORBROOK.

Northall (Eng) Descendant of someone who lived in or worked at the 'north hall.'

Northcliffe, Norcliffe, Nortcliffe, Norclyffe (Eng) Indicating an ancestor who lived by the 'north cliff.'

Northcote, Norcott, Norkett, Norkutt, Northcott (Eng) Descendant of someone who originally came from a place named for its 'north cottage,' or one who himself lived in a 'cottage to the north.'

Northend (Eng) Descendant of someone who lived at the north end of the village.

Norther, Northern *see* NORTH.

Norton (Eng) Someone who came from one of the several places so-named because it was the 'north settlement.' **Norrington** is a name of similar meaning.

Nothard (Eng) Occupational name of a cow herdsman.

Notman *see* NUTT.

Nott, Notting, Notts (Eng) Nickname for a bald-headed man or man with closely cropped hair. Occasionally a simplified form of KNOTT.

The wife of a Rev. Dr Nott composed the following ambiguous lines when he proposed to her:

Why urge, dear sir, a bashful maid
To change her single lot,
When well you know I've often said,
In truth I love you, *Nott.*

Notton (Eng) Descendant of someone who came from one of the English places named for its 'cattle enclosure.'

Notts *see* NOTT.

Nowell, Nowill *see* NOEL.

Nowers *see* OVER.

Nowles *see* KNOLL.

Noy, Noyce, Noyes *see* NOAH.

Nugent (Eng, Irish) A form of Norman French place names meaning 'new settlement.' The name therefore indicates an ancestor who came from Normandy.

Nuneham *see* NEW.

Nunn (Eng) A nickname for a man as pious as a nun, or a servant at a convent. *See* MINCHIN.

Nunns, Nunhouse, Nunnerley, Nunnery, Nunney, Nunniss, Nunnley, Nunny (Eng) Servant at the nuns' house, or dweller near land belonging to nuns.

Nutall, Nuthal, Nuthall, Nuttal, Nuttall, Nuttell, Nuttle (Eng) From residence in a place such as *Nuthall,* Nottinghamshire, where the name refers to the nut trees that grew there.

Nutbeam, Nutbeem, Nutbeen (Eng) Dweller near a large nut tree.

Nutbrown (Eng) A descriptive nickname. It is found also as BROWNNUTT, BROWNUTT, BROWNHUT.

Nuthal, Nuthall *see* NUTALL.

Nutt, Notman, Nutman, Nuttman, Nutts, Nutze (Eng) Occupational name for a trader in nuts.

Peter Nutt, A Scunthorpe schoolmaster, changed his surname to *Knudssen* after years of comments about his being a P. Nutt. Knudssen is Danish or Norwegian 'son of *Knutr* (*Canute*)'.

Nuttal, Nuttall, Nuttell *see* NUTALL.

Nutter (Eng) Of two possible origins, indicating either a notary, scribe, writer, or a cow herdsman.

Nuttle *see* NUTALL.

Nuttman, Nutts, Nutze *see* NUTT.

Nye (Eng) Descendant of someone who lived on at island or near a river.

Nyman (Eng) A neighbour, someone living nearby. As a Swedish surname the meaning is someone new to the neighbourhood.

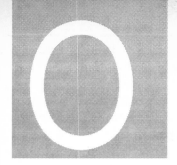

Oade, Oades, Noad, Nodes (Eng) From residence near a 'heap, pile of stones,' perhaps a funeral pile. Oade, Oades can also derive from the Germanic personal name *Otto* 'riches.'

Oak, Atack, Atoc, Attack, Attick, Attoc, Attock, Noack, Noak, Noake, Noakes, Noaks, Noaxe, Nock, Noke, Nokes, Oake, Oakeman, Oaker, Oakes, Oakland, Oke, Okes, Roak, Roakes, Roke, Rook (Eng) Dweller in or near an oak tree or oak forest.

Oakeley *see* OAKLEY.

Oakey, Okey, Okie, Oky (Eng) Dweller on an island covered with oaks.

Oakland *see* OAK.

Oakley, Oakeley, Okeley, Okely (Eng) Dweller in one of the many English places named for its 'oak clearing.'

Oastler *see* OSTLER.

Oaten, Oates, Oats, Odd, Odde, Otis, Ott, Otten, Otton (Eng) Descendant of *Odo* or *Otto*, a Germanic name meaning 'riches,' or descendant of *Oda*, *Odda*, an Old English and Old Norse personal name meaning 'point' (of a weapon).

Oatmonger, Oatman, Otemonger (Eng) Occupational name of a dealer in oats.

Oats *see* OATEN.

O'Barran, O'Barrane *see* BARNES.

O'Brian, O'Brien *see* BRIAN.

O'Brogan *see* BANKS.

O'Bryan *see* BRIAN.

Oby *see* OPIE.

O'Carroll, O'Carrowill, O'Carvill, O'Carwell *see* CARROLL.

O'Conchor, O'Conor, O'Connor, O'Connour *see* CONNOR.

Odam, Odams, Odem, Odhams, Odium, Odom (Eng) Son-in-law or brother-in-law (of a prominent man), especially one who inherited an estate from such a relationship.

Odd, Odde *see* OATEN.

Odell (Eng) From residence in the Bedfordshire place, so-named because it was a 'hill where woad grew.' The form O'DELL is from the mistaken belief that this is an Irish name.

Odem, Odhams, Odium, Odom *see* ODAM.

O'Donegaine, O'Donegan *see* DONEGAN.

O'Donovan, Donavan, Donavin, Donovan (Irish) Descendant of someone bearing a Gaelic personal name *Donndubhán* 'brown black,' presumably to be interpreted as 'dark brown, swarthy.'

O'Dungan *see* DONEGAN.

O'Dunn, O'Dunne *see* DUNN.

O'Farris, O'Fearguise *see* FERGUS.

O'Feolane *see* WHELAN.

O'Fergus, O'Ferris *see* FERGUS.

Offer, Offor, Orfaure, Orfeur (Eng) Occupational name for a 'goldsmith,' from French *orfevre*.

Officer (Eng) Occupational name for the holder of an office, especially a 'servant of the crown.' A derivation from *orphrey* 'gold embroidery' is also possible, which would relate the bearer of the surname to someone who sewed the embroidery to clothes.

Offield, Ofield *see* OLDFIELD.

Offor *see* OFFER.

O'Finn, O'Finne, O'Fionn *see* FINN.

O'Flinn, O'Flynn *see* FLYNN.

O'Folane, O'Fylan *see* WHELAN.

O'Gallagher, O'Galleghure *see* GALLAGHER.

Ogilvie, Ogilvy (Scot) Descendant of someone who came from the Scottish place of this name, possibly named because it was a 'high plain.'

O Hairt *see* HART.

O'Hara (Irish) 'Descendant of *Eaghra*,' a Gaelic personal name of uncertain meaning, though Patrick Kelly, in his *Irish Family Names,* suggests that it is from *gearthac* 'bitter.'

This name is famous in literature because of Kipling's *Kimball O'Hara*, the young hero of *Kim*, and Scarlett O'Hara, heroine of

Margaret Mitchell's *Gone With the Wind*.

O'Hart *see* HART.

O'Heagane, O'Heaken, O'Hegane, O'Higane, O'Higgins, O'Huggin *see* HIGGINS.

Oill *see* OYLER.

Oke *see* OAK.

O'Kelly *see* KELLY.

Okeley, Okely *see* OAKLEY.

O'Kennedy *see* KENNEDY.

Okes *see* OAK.

Okey, Okie *see* OAKEY.

O'Knavin, O'Knee *see* NEVILLE.

Oky *see* OAKEY.

O'Lane, O'Layne *see* LANE.

Old, Oldman, Olds, Oldson, Oldys, Olman, Ould, Oulds (Eng) The older son, or elder of two men bearing the same name. AULD, AULDSON are Scottish forms of this name.

Oldacre, Oldaker (Eng) Dweller near an old ploughed field.

Oldcastle (Eng) Someone from the place of this name in Cheshire, or from residence near an old castle.

Oldfield, Aldefeld, Allfield, Holdefeld, Offield, Ofield (Eng) Dweller near an old field or someone who came originally from one of the many English places named for such a field.

Oldham (Eng) Descendant of someone who came from the place of this name in Lancashire, named originally because it was on an old piece of dry land in a marshy area.

Oldman *see* OLD.

Oldroyd (Eng) Dweller in one of the several places of this name in northern England, where the original reference is to an 'old clearing of wooded land.'

Olds, Oldson *see* OLD.

Oldwright *see* ARKWRIGHT.

Oldys *see* OLD.

O'Lensie *see* LYNCH.

O'Leyne *see* LANE.

Olier *see* OYLER.

Olifant *see* OLIPHANT.

Oliff, Olif, Oliffe, Olliff. Olliffe, Olliph, Olyff, Olyffe (Eng) Descendant of *Olaf,* a Scandinavian personal name.

Oliphant, Olifant, Olifon, Oliphard, Olivant (Eng) The name means 'elephant'; perhaps a nickname for a large person, or the sign marking someone's house. A dealer in ivory is also a possibility.

Olive, Olivet, Ollett, Ollive, Olyet (Eng) Descendant of *Olive*.

Oliver, Oliverson, Olivier, Olliver, Olver (Eng) Descendant of *Oliver (Olivier)* Normally explained as 'olive tree,' but the original form of the name has been lost. The name figured in many medieval romances and was popular amongst the Normans, who brought it to Britain.

Olivet, Ollett *see* OLIVE.

Olivier *see* OLIVER.

Ollier *see* OYLER.

Olliff, Olliffe, Olliph *see* OLIFF.

Ollive, Olyet *see* OLIVE.

Olliver, Olver *see* OLIVER.

Olman *see* OLD.

O'Loyne *see* LANE.

Olyff, Olyffe *see* OLIFF.

O'Lynche, O'Lynchey, O'Lynchy, O'Lynseghane *see* LYNCH.

O'Melane *see* MACMILLAN.

O'Milligane *see* MILLIGAN.

O'Mollane *see* MACMILLAN.

O'Mollegane, O'Molleghan *see* MILLIGAN.

O'Moore, O'Mora *see* MOORE.

O'Moraine, O'Moran, O'Morane *see* MORAN.

O'Morcho, O'Morphy *see* MURPHY.

O'Moylane, O'Mullane *see* MACMILLAN.

O'Moylegane, O'Mullegan *see* MILLIGAN.

O'Mulrean, O'Mulrigan, O'Mulryan *see* RYAN.

O'Murphy *see* MURPHY.

O'Nea *see* NEVILLE.

O'Neal *see* NEIL.

O'Nee *see* NEVILLE.

O'Neil, O'Neilane, O'Neill, O'Nelane *see* NEIL.

O'Ney *see* NEVILLE.

O'Nillane *see* NEIL.

O'Noland, O'Nolane *see* NOLAN.

O'Nowan, O'Nown, O'Nowne *see* NOONAN.

O'Nowlan *see* NOLAN.

O'Phelane *see* WHELAN.

Opie, Oby (Cornish) Descendant of someone known by a pet form of *Osbert* or some similar name where the first element is an Old Norse word meaning 'god, divinity.'

O'Quin, O'Quine, O'Quyn see **Quinn.** **Orable, Arable, Errable, Orbel, Orbell** (Eng) Descendant of *Arabella,* formerly pronounced and spelt *Arbell.*

O'Rahilly *see* RILEY.

Oram *see* ORME.

Orbel, Orbell *see* ORABLE.

O'Realy, O'Reely, O'Reiley, O'Reilly, O'Riellie, O'Rielly *see* RILEY.

O'Reyley, O'Reyly *see* RILEY.

Orfaure, Orfeur *see* OFFER.

Orgill, Orgles *see* PROUD.

Orme, Oram, Ormes, Orrom, Orrum, Orum (Eng) Descendant of *Ormr*, an Old Norse personal name meaning snake, serpent.

Orneblow *see* HORNBLOWER.

Orrom, Orrum, Orum *see* ORME.

O'Ryan *see* RYAN.

O'Sheahan, O'Sheehan, O'Shehane, O'Shieghane *see* SHEEHAN.

Ostler, Horsler, Hoselur, Hosteler, Hosteller, Hostler, Hustler, Oastler, Osler, Ostiller (Eng) In the surname formation period an ostler would have been either the guest-master in a monastery, or an inn-keeper.

Ostrick, Ostridge *see* HORSEWREATH.

O'Sullivan *see* SULLIVAN.

Otemonger *see* OATMONGER.

Otis, Ott, Otten, Otton *see* OATEN.

Ould, Oulds *see* OLD.

Outlaw *see* LAWLESS.

Outram (Eng) Bardsley guesses reasonably that this is a form of 'outer ham, homestead,' but Outram is not found as an English place name.

Around 1800 Benjamin Outram made certain improvements to the narrow-gauge railway used in coal mines. According to Smiles's *Life of George Stephenson*, his system supposedly led to *Outram* roads, which phrase in turn was shortened to *tramroads* and gave us the word *tram*. This pleasant theory is hampered by the fact that *tram* had been in use for at least two centuries before Mr Outram appeared, though the word's sense development from 'handle of a barrow' to 'vehicle running on rails' was fairly complex.

Over, Noare, Nowers, Owers (Eng) Descendant of someone who lived near a steep slope or came from one of several English places named Over because of its slope.

Overal, Overall, Overell, Overill, Overhalt (Eng) Occupational name of a servant at the 'upper hall' or someone who lived there.

Overbeck (Eng) Descendant of someone who lived 'beyond the stream.'

Overell *see* OVERAL.

Overend (Eng) Descendant of someone who lived at the 'upper end' of a village.

Overfield (Eng) Dweller in or near the 'upper field'.

Overill, Overhalt *see* OVERAL.

Overman (Eng) Descriptive of a 'superior, leader'.

Overton (Eng) Someone who came from one of the many English places so-named because it was an 'upper settlement.'

Owen, Bowen, Bowing, Bowins, Owain, Owens, Owings (Welsh) Descendant of a man called *Owen,* which was itself (probably) a form of *Eugenios*, a Greek name meaning 'well born, noble.'

O'Whalen, O'Whealan *see* WHELAN.

Ox, Oxer, Oxman, Oxnard, Oxx (Eng) Occupational name of an oxherd.

Oxborough, Oxberry, Oxborrow, Oxbrow, Oxby, Oxburgh, Oxenberry, Oxenbury (Eng) Descendant of someone who originally came from Oxborough, Norfolk, 'settlement where oxen were kept.'

Oxenden, Oxendon (Eng) Descendant of someone who came from Oxendon, Northampton, 'ox-hill.'

Oxenford, Oxford (Eng) Dweller near an Oxford or someone from the city of Oxford, 'ford for oxen.'

Oxenham (Eng) From residence in Devonshire place, so-named because it was a 'water-meadow where oxen grazed.'

Oxer *see* Ox.

Oxford *see* OXENFORD.

Oxlade (Eng) Descendant of someone who lived in the 'oak valley'.

Oxman, Oxnard, Oxx *see* Ox.

Oyler, Oill, Olier, Ollier, Oyles (Eng) Occupational name of a dealer in (linseed) oil.

Pace *see* PEACE.

Pach, Pack, Packe *see* PASCHAL.

Packman, Pacheman, Packard, Packeman, Pakeman (Eng) An itinerant hawker, who carried the goods he was selling in a pack on his back.

Pacock *see* PEACOCK.

Paddey, Paddie, Paddison, Paddy *see* PATRICK.

Page, Padget, Padgett, Padgit, Paget, Pagett, Paige (Eng) A page, young boy acting as household servant.

Paice *see* PEACE.

Paige *see* PAGE.

Paik *see* PASCHAL.

Pain, Paine, Paines *see* PAYNE.

Painter, Paynter, Peyntour, Peyntur (Eng) A painter, mainly of windows and walls.

Paitrie *see* PETER.

Pakeman *see* PACKMAN.

Pakenham (Eng) From residence in the place so-named because it was '*Pacca's* homestead.'

Pakes *see* PASCHAL.

Palefray *see* PALFREY.

Palet *see* PALLET.

Palfrey, Palefray, Palfery, Palframan, Palfreeman, Palfreman, Palfreyer, Palfreyman, Palfry, Pallfrey, Palphramand, Palphreyman, Paphraman, Parfrement, Parffrey, Parfrey (Eng) Keeper of the palfreys, small saddle-horses mainly ridden by ladies.

Paliser, Palismaker, Palister *see* PALLISER.

Pallet, Palet, Pallat, Pallatt, Pallett (Eng) Maker of pallets (straw mattresses).

Pallfrey *see* PALFREY.

Palliser, Paliser, Palismaker, Palister, Pallies, Pallis, Pallister, Pallyster, Palser, Palyster (Eng) Maker and maintainer of palings and fences.

Palmer, Palmar, Palmere, Palmes, Paumier (Eng) Descendant of someone who had been on a pilgrimage to the Holy Land and had returned with a palm branch.

Harry Palmer was the British spy portrayed by Michael Caine in films based on novels by Len Deighton, including *The Ipcress File* and *Funeral in Berlin*.

Palphramand, Palphreyman *see* PALFREY.

Palser, Palyster *see* PALLISER.

Pane *see* PAYNE.

Pannifer *see* PENNYFATHER.

Panter, Panther, Pantler, Pantrey, Pantry (Eng) Steward in charge of the food store; official at a monastery who distributed bread to the poor.

Panyfader *see* PENNYFATHER.

Paphraman *see* PALFREY.

Paramour, Paramor, Paramore, Parramore (Eng) A paramour, lover, sweetheart.

Parden, Pardner *see* PARDON.

Pardoe, Pardew, Pardey, Pardieu, Pardy, Perdeu, Purday, Purdeu, Purdey, Purdie, Purdu, Purdue, Purdy, Purdye (Eng) Nickname for someone who made excessive use of *parde* or *pardy*, both forms of the French oath *par dieu* (by God). Those who used the same expression in its English version could likewise be known as **Bigod, Bigot, Bygod, Bygot,** etc.

Pardon, Parden, Pardner, Pardoner, Partener, Partner (Eng) A man licensed to sell the Pope's indulgences, which theoretically allowed one to escape divine punishment for one's sins.

Parell, Parenn *see* PETER.

Parfitt, Parfait, Parfect, Parfit, Perfect, Perfitt (Eng) Someone who had completed a period of training and was fully accomplished in his trade or profession.

Parfrement, Parffrey, Parfrey *see* PALFREY.

Paridelle *see* BEWES.

Park, Duparc, Parke, Parker, Parkers, Parkes, Parkhouse, Parkis, Parkman (Eng) Occupational name for a gamekeeper, official in charge of a deer park. See also PORTER, WILLIAMS.

The phrase *Nosey Parker*, describing someone who is constantly 'poking his nose' into other people's affairs, first appeared in the early 20th century. Many attempts have been made to identify the Parker concerned, on the assumption that the phrase alluded to a specific person. Harold Wheeler, in *How Much Do You Know?*, stated confidently that the reference was to Matthew Parker (1504-75), chaplain to Anne Boleyn and Henry VIII and later Archbishop of Canterbury. Stanley Rogers, in *From Ships and Sailors*, was equally certain that Richard Parker was meant, a man who was hanged in 1797 for leading a mutiny. However, common sense would appear to dictate that ordinary English people were hardly likely to start alluding in informal 20th century conversations to obscure sailors of the past, nor to archbishops who had been dead for centuries. If a real Parker was responsible for the expression, he must have been alive and well-known around 1910. No one named Parker who remotely fits the bill has been discovered. There may be a connection here with 'poke one's nose in.' The person who does so could be called a 'poker', and indeed the word is recorded in the sense of 'inquisitive person' from the 17th century. 'Nosey' is also recorded as an adjective describing such a person. The phrase 'nosey poker' would very clearly indicate an officiously inquisitive person and a humorous change to 'Nosey Parker' is easily imagined. This must remain pure speculation, since no printed example of 'nosey poker' has been found, but in the absence of a Parker who was famous for his nosiness, the conversion from word to name status of some such phrase deserves consideration.

A last will and testament of 1785, quoted in Chambers' *Book of Days*, read: 'I, Charles Parker, of New Bond Street, Middlesex, bookseller, give to Elizabeth Parker the sum of £50, whom, through my foolish fondness, I made my wife, without regard to family, fame, or fortune; and who, in return, has not spared, most unjustly, to accuse me of every crime regarding human nature, save highway-robbery.'

Parkhill (Eng) Dweller on a hill within a park.

197

Parkhouse *see* PARK.

Parkhurst (Eng) Dweller near a wood in a park, or someone who originally came from one of the places so-called, eg in Sussex.

Parkin, Parkins, Parkinson *see* PETER.

Parkinson's Law, which states that 'work expands so as to fill the time available for its completion,' was formulated by Cyril Northcote Parkinson, an English historian and political economist.

Parkis, Parkman *see* PARK.

Parkyn *see* PARKIN.

Parlabean, Parlby, Parlebien, Parlebeen, Parleby (Fre) A man who could *parle bien* 'speak well.'

Parramore *see* PARAMOUR.

Parratt, Parret, Parrett *see* PETER.

Parries *see* HENRY.

Parrot, Parrott *see* PETER.

Parry *see* HENRY.

Parson, Parsonage, Parsons, Parsonson (Eng) Servant or son of a parson.

Partener, Partner *see* PARDON.

Paschal, Pach, Pack, Packe, Paik, Paish, Pakes, Pascall, Pasco, Pascoe, Pash, Pashe, Pashson, Pask, Paske, Paskell, Pasket, Paskin, Paskins, Pasqual, Pasque, Pasquill, Pass, Passe, Patch, Patchell, Patchett, Patchen (Eng) These names all refer to Easter, probably to someone born at that time. Pascoe is especially associated with Cornwall.

Passage (Eng) Dweller in a narrow lane.

Passe, Patch, Patchell, Patchett, Patchen *see* PASCHAL.

Patching (Eng) Someone who originally came from *Patching*, Sussex, or *Patching Hall*, Essex.

Pate, Pateman *see* PATRICK.

Patel (Hindi) Descendant of a 'village-leader.'

Patrick, Paddey, Paddie, Paddison, Paddy, Pate, Pateman, Paterson, Pates, Patey, Patison, Patman, Paton, Patrickson, Patterson, Patteson, Pattinson, Pattison, Pattisson, Pattman, Patton, Pattrick, Pattyson, Paty (Eng) Descendant of *Patrick,* a name normally explained as 'patrician,' ie belonging to the Roman nobility. Patrick was a missionary ('the apostle of Ireland'), who became patron saint of that country. His name was much used there in his honour. Paddy is derived from the Gaelic form of Patrick, *Padraig*. *See* PETER.

Patrie, Patry *see* PETER.

Patten, Pattin *see* CLOG.

Patterson, Patteson, Pattinson, Pattison, Pattisson, Pattman, Patton, Pattrick, Pattyson, Paty see **Patrick**. For Patteson see also note one to GUNN.

Paul, Paule, Pauley, Paulin, Pauling, Paull, Paulling, Paully, Paulson, Pawle, Pawlyn, Pollins, Polson, Poulsom, Poulson, Powling, Powly (Eng) Descendant of a man named *Paul,* a given name from Latin *Paulus* 'small.' In the Bible it is the surname adopted by Saul of Tarsus after his conversion to Christianity. The name was also borne by other early saints. Paul has sometimes led to the surnames POOL, POWELL and PAWLEY, but Pool can also indicate an ancestor who lived near a pool or pond, while Powell is more frequently from Welsh *ap Howell* 'son of Hywel 'eminent.' **Pawley** is sometimes a form of the French place name *Pavilly*.

Paumier *see* PALMER.

Pauncefoot, Pauncefort, Pauncefote *see* PUDDY.

Pauper *see* POWER.

Paw, Pawe, Pawson *see* PEACOCK.

Pawle, Pawlyn *see* PAUL.

Pawley *see* PAUL.

Paxton (Eng) Someone who came from a place so-named because it was the 'settlement of *Paecc's* people.'

Pay *see* PEACOCK.

Paybody *see* PEABODY.

Payce *see* PEACE.

Paye, Payman *see* PEACOCK.

Payne, Pain, Paine, Paines, Pane, Payn (Eng) Descendant of a man called *Pain* or *Payn*, ultimately from Latin *paganus* 'country dweller as opposed to townsman.' In his *Etymological Dictionary of Modern English*, Ernest Weekley explains: 'The Roman soldier used *paganus* 'yokel' as a contemptuous name for a civilian or for an incompetent soldier and, when the early Church adopted *miles (Christi)* in the figurative sense 'soldier (of Christ)', *paganus* was also taken over from colloquial Latin as its natural opposite, to connote one who was not a good soldier of Christ. Thus the sense ('pagan') has developed from that of the Kiplingesque "lousy civilian".'

Pays, Payze *see* PEACE.

Payton (Eng) Someone who came from one of the several places so-named because it was the 'settlement of *Paega's* people.'

Pea *see* PEACOCK.

Peabody, Paybody, Peberdy, Pepperday, Pipperday (Eng) Presumably a nickname similar to PEACOCK. In early English pea was used for the bird, while -*body* in names usually means 'person.'

L.J. Davis, in *Walking Small*, writes: 'Her real name wasn't Lois Angeles, it was Linda Peabody, which struck him as a damn good reason for changing it to almost anything else you could think of.'

Peace, Pace, Paice, Payce, Pays, Payze, Peaceable (Eng) Nickname for a peaceful man, one of even temper. It could also refer to someone who played this role in a medieval miracle play. *See* VERITY.

Peacham (Eng) From residence in a place so-named because it was a 'homestead by a hill.'

Peacock, Pacock, Paw, Pawe, Pawson, Pay, Paye, Payman, Pea, Peacocke, Peaman, Pee, Peecock, Peyman, Pocock, Pococke, Poe, Powe, Pycock (Eng) Descendant or servant of someone whose nickname indicated that he dressed in an extravagant way or was considered to be as proud as a peacock.

Peaddie *see* PETER.

Peak, Peake, Peaker, Peakman (Eng) From residence near a peak, especially one who came from the Peak District. See also **Peck.**

Peale, Peele *see* PEEL.

Peaman *see* PEACOCK.

Pearce, Pears, Pearse, Pearson, Peat, Peatrie, Peattie *see* PETER.

Peberdy *see* PEABODY.

Peck (Eng) Probably an occupational name derived from the 'peck' which was a measure of dry goods, such as corn. The name could also be a form of PEAK.

An article in *Reveille* in 1970 reported that a policeman named Peck changed his name to Denham just before he married. His future wife's first name began with N, so that she would have become Mrs N. Peck.

Peddie, Pedrick *see* PETER.

Pee, Peecock *see* PEACOCK.

Peel, Peale, Peele, Peile, Piele (Eng) The name refers to a stake or pole, but the exact meaning is far from clear. An early bearer may have lived or worked in a stockade or small castle. He may have built fences of stakes: he may have earned a nickname for being a 'bean-pole.'

Whatever its precise meaning, this name had considerable social status in some parts of the country. Arnold Bennett writes, in *The Old Wives' Tale*: 'He bore the almost sacred name of Peel. His family had been distinguished in the district for generations. Peel! You could without impropriety utter it in the same breath with 'Wedgwood.' And 'Swynnerton' stood not much lower.'

Peers, Peet, Peirce, Peirs *see* PETER.

Pelham (Eng) From residence in the Hertfordshire place, so-named because it was '*Peotla's* homestead.'

Pell *see* PETER.

Pelter, Pelletier, Peltier (Eng, Fre) Occupational name for a furrier.

Pender (Eng) A pinner, man in charge of a pound or pinfold, in which stray cattle were kept.

Pendleton (Eng) Someone who came from one of the several places so-named because it was a 'settlement on a hill.'

Penfare *see* PENNYFATHER.

Pengelly, Pengilley (Cornish) From residence in a Cornish place of this name. *Pen-* in all such names means 'end, head, top.' The *-gelly* here refers to a copse. Similar names are PENDRY, PENFOUND, PENGLAZE, PENHALE, PENHALIGON, PENHALLOW, PENNECK, PENPRASE, PENRICE, PENROSE, PENTREATH, PENWARDEN. These are place names, where in all cases the second element refers to a natural feature, such as a hill, moor, wood, ford, meadow or beach.

Penifader, Pennefather *see* PENNYFATHER.

Penny, Penney, Pennie, Penniman, Penning, Pennings, Pennyman (Eng) There are a number of 'money' surnames, including DUCAT (Duckett), FARTHING and SHILLING as well as many based on penny, such as HALFPENNY, HALPENNY, TWOPENNY, TIPPENY, THICKPENNY,

MONEYPENNY. Medieval rolls reveal similar names that do not seem to have survived, such as *Brodepeny, Fivepeni, Godspeny, Nynpenyz, Twelpenes*. The name POUND normally refers to an animal pound or enclosure, Farthing may also refer to a 'fourth of an acre' rather than the coin, but names which indicate a specific sum of money cannot be explained in any other way. Unfortunately we have no way of knowing, except in very rare instances, why particular individuals received a name of this type as a nickname, but see BALL for a possible connection with field names.

An article in the *Church Times* once drew attention to the registers of St Mary Woolnoth where there is this entry: 'A male child was found in our parish with a penny in his hand and was named accordingly Henry Penny.' This was clearly an untypical naming, and speculation about other reasons for such names can lead to no firm conclusions.

Pennyfather, Pannifer, Panyfader, Penfare, Penifader, Pennefather, Pennyfeather (Eng) Nickname for a miserly man.

Evelyn Waugh's *Decline and Fall* has a conversation which runs: '"I suppose you're the new master?" he said. "Yes," said Paul, "I'm called Pennyfeather." The little boy gave a shrill laugh. "I think that's terribly funny," he said, and went away.'

Pennyman *see* PENNY.

Penprase, Penrice, Penrose *see* PENGELLY.

Penry *see* HENRY.

Pensil This name looks Cornish because of the *Pen-*, but there is no obvious Cornish source. It may be an American form of German **Penseler**, from *Pinsel* 'paint-brush,' used figuratively in modern German of a 'fat-head, duffer.'

The name occurs in Henry James's *The Portrait of a Lady*, where there is the exchange: 'Pensil. It's an odd name, but it isn't a bad one.' 'I think one name's as good as another.'

Pentreath, Penwarden *see* PENGELLY.

Peper *see* PIPER.

Pepperday *see* PEABODY.

Perce *see* PETER.

Perdeu *see* PARDOE.

Perell, Peret, Perett *see* PETER.

Perfect, Perfitt *see* PARFITT.

Periman *see* PERRY.

Perken, Perkin, Perkins, Perot, Perott, Perowne, Perrat, Perren, Perrens *see* PETER.

Perrett (Eng) Nickname for a man with a 'pear-shaped head.'

Perriman *see* PERRY.

Perrin, Perring, Perris, Perron, Perrowne *see* PETER.

Perry, Periman, Perriman, Perryman, Peryman, Pirie (Eng) Descendant of someone who lived near pear trees. The name is also said to derive from Welsh *ap Henry* or *ap Harry*, but these forms normally became PENRY, PARRY, not Perry. Pirie is Scottish, and may link with PETER rather than 'pear.'

Perryn, Perse, Persse *see* PETER.

Peryman *see* PERRY.

Perys *see* PETER.

Petain, Petard *see* BELCHER.

Peter, Paitrie, Parell, Parenn, Parkin, Parkins, Parkinson, Parkyn, Parratt, Parret, Parrett, Parrot, Parrott, Patrie, Patry, Peaddie, Pearce, Pears, Pearse, Pearson, Peat, Peate, Peatrie, Peattie, Peddie, Pedrick, Peers, Peet, Peirce, Peirs, Pell, Perce, Perell, Peret, Perett, Perken, Perkin, Perkins, Perot, Perott, Perowne, Perrat, Perren, Perrens, Perrin, Perring, Perris, Perron, Perrowne, Perryn, Perse, Persse, Perys, Peterken, Peterkin, Peterman, Peters, Peterson, Petherick, Pether, Pethers, Pethick, Petre, Petrie, Pierce, Piers, Pierse, Pierson, Pirret, Pither, Pithers, Pitkin, Purkins (Eng) These surnames are all related to *Peter* or one of its pet forms, with or without a diminutive ending such at *-ot, -el* or *-kin*. Normal pronunciation of Peter in medieval times was PIERS, influenced by French *Pierre*. In Scotland PATRICK became confused with Peter and Scottish surnames such as Petrie may refer to either name. PEDRICK, PETHERICK, PETHICK refer to *Petroc*, the 'father of Cornish saints.' Once again there is some doubt as to whether Petroc is a form of Peter or Patrick.

Petit *see* PETTY.

Petter, Pethard, Peton, Petot *see* BELCHER.

Petty, Petit, Pettet, Pettie, Pettit, Pettitt, Petyt, Pittet (Eng)

Nickname for a small person, or perhaps for a younger brother.

Peyman *see* PEACOCK.

Peyntour, Peyntur *see* PAINTER

Phalp *see* PHILIP.

Pharaoh, Pharo, Pharro *see* FARRAR.

Phear *see* FEAR.

Phelan *see* WHELAN.

Philip, Fill, Fills, Filson, Phalp, Phelips, Phelops, Phelp, Phelps, Phibbs, Philben, Philbin, Philcock, Philcott, Philcox, Philiphs, Philipp, Philippot, Philipps, Philippson, Philips, Philipse, Phillcox, Phillins, Phillip, Phillipp, Phillipps, Phillippse, Phillippson, Phillips, Phillipson, Phillis, Phillot, Phillott, Phillp, Phillpot, Phillps, Philott, Philp, Philpin, Philpot, Philpott, Philps, Philson, Phipard, Phippen, Phippin, Phipps, Phips, Phipson, Pilpot, Pot, Potkin, Potkins, Pott, Pottel, Pottle, Potts (Eng) Son or servant of *Philip,* a Greek name meaning 'horse-lover.' In medieval times the name was also written and pronounced *Phelip,* which could be contracted to Phelp. Pet forms were *Phil* and *Phip,* which themselves could be given diminutive endings. The name was obviously familiar as that of one of the apostles.

Pidgeon, Pidgen, Piggin, Pigeon (Eng) Nickname for someone who was, like the bird, 'easily plucked.' Since there were men who were professionally concerned with the hunting of wood pigeons, this could also be an occupational name. On occasion, however, the name has no connection with pigeons. Professor Reaney discovered references in 14th century documents to *Pijohan, Petiion* and *Petijohan* which clearly indicate that *Petit John* 'little John' could be a source of the name.

Pidgeon is more interesting and complex than it at first seems, but that does not affect modern reaction to it. When a character in Elizabeth Bowen's *The Death of the Heart* says 'His name was Pidgeon,' we are told that: 'Eddie tittered at this.'

Piele *see* PEEL.

Pierce, Piers, Pierse, Pierson *see* PETER.

Benjamin Franklin Pierce was better known as 'Hawkeye' in the television series *M*A*S*H*, based on the novels of Richard Hooker.

Piggin, Pigeon *see* PIDGEON.

Pike, Pyke (Eng) Several origins are possible, and it is impossible to know which one applies to a particular family. The name may indicate a pike fisherman, or a soldier who used a pike. It could be a nickname for someone as predatory as the fish, or as tall and thin as a pikestaff. A sharply pointed hill is also called a pike, and the surname may indicate residence on or near such a hill.

Pilbeam, Pilbean (Eng) Early forms of this name are of the form *de Peltebhem,* which indicate a place name, but no such place can be found. Professor Weekley therefore suggested that this was an occupational name for a 'peeler of trees,' who obtained the bark that was used for tanning leather.

Pilch, Pilcher (Eng) Occupational name for a dealer in 'pilches.' coarse leather garments with hair still visible on the skin. The word was later used for 'saddle rugs.'

Pilkington (Eng) Someone who came from a place so-named because it was the 'settlement of *Pileca's* people.'

Pillinger *see* BAKER.

Pilpot *see* PHILIP.

Pinch, Punch (Eng) Weekley ingeniously suggested that these names indicate someone who usually played the part of *Pontius Pilate* in a medieval religious play. Others connect Pinch with names like **Pinchen, Pinching, Pinck,** PINK, PINKETT, PINKS, PINSENT, PINSHON, PINSON and explain it as a nickname based on the cheerful qualities of the chaffinch (Welsh *pinc*, Old French *pinson* or *pineon*, Norman French *pinchon* 'finch'). The bird is variously known in dialect as a *pink, pinkety, pink-twink, spink, twink*, etc., in imitation of its call-note.

Tom Pinch is a Dickensian character in *Martin Chuzzlewit*. At one point Jonas Chuzzlewit says: 'Just attend to me for a bit, Mr Pitch, or Witch, or Stitch, or whatever your name is.' 'My name is Pinch,' Tom replies. 'Have the goodness to call me by it.' 'What!' says Jonas, 'you mustn't even be called out of your name, mustn't you? Pauper prentices are looking up, I think.'

Pine, Pyne (Eng) Descendant of someone who lived near a pine forest, though there is also the (unlikely) possibility of a nickname based on the appearance of the tree.

Chester Hines writes (none too seriously) in his novel

Pinktoes: 'Pine would carry on. Not for nothing was Pine named after the sturdy tree that had supplied the world with so many mighty poles. Pine would pick up the great fight.'

Pink *see* PINCH.

Pinkerton (Scot) *see* HAMILTON.

Pinkett, Pinks, Pinsent, Pinshon, Pinson *see* PINCH.

Piper, Peper, Pipar, Pipe, Pipes, Pipester, Pypar, Pyper (Eng) A player of bagpipes.

Pipperday *see* PEABODY.

Pirie *see* PERRY.

Pirkis, Pirkiss *see* PURCHASE.

Pirret, Pither *see* PETER.

Pitcher, Pitcherman, Pitchers (Eng) Occupational name of a man who used pitch to caulk the seams of a ship.

Pithers, Pitkin *see* PETER.

Pittet *see* PETTY.

Platesmith *see* SMITH.

Playfair, Playfer, Playfere (Eng) Probably a nickname for a keen sportsman, though Black suggests a connection with Playford in Sussex.

Ploughwright, Plowright, Plowsmith (Eng) Occupational name for a maker of ploughs.

Plumpton (Eng) Someone who came from one of the several places so-named because it was a 'settlement where plum trees grew.'

Pocock, Pococke, Poe *see* PEACOCK.

Polglaze (Cornish) An old saying is that 'by tre-, *pol-* and *pen-*, ye shall know most Cornishmen. Names which begin with *Pol-* indicate an ancestor who lived in a place named for its 'pool.' Polglaze is 'green or blue pool; POLMEAR, to take another example, is 'big pool.' Similar names are POLGREAN, POLGREEN, POLKINGHORNE, POLSUE, POLWHELE, POLWIN. The meaning of the second element is not always clear.

Pollins *see* PAUL.

Polly, Polley (Eng) Nickname from Old French *poli* for a 'polite' person.

The name can present difficulties for its bearer, as illustrated by

H.G. Wells in *The History of Mr Polly*. The hero, Alfred Polly, has a conversation with a little girl which runs: 'What are you called?' 'Polly.' 'Liar!' 'Why?' 'I'm Polly.' 'Then I'm Alfred.'

Polmear, Polsue, Polwhele, Polwin *see* POLGLAZE.

Polson, Pool *see* PAUL.

Pooler, Puller (Eng) Occupational name for a hen-keeper, from Old French *poulier* 'poulter,' the official in a large household who attended to the purchase of poultry.

Poor, Poore, Poorman *see* POWER.

Pope (Eng) Descendant of someone who played the part of the *Pope* in a medieval pageant.

This name is associated with poetry, thanks to Alexander Pope (1688-1744). Sir Thomas Pope seems also to have been a poet in his way. When James I came to visit him, he introduced his daughter to the king with these verses:

> See! this little mistress here
> Did never sit in Peter's chair,
> Neither a triple crown did wear,
> And yet she is a Pope!
> No benefice she ever sold,
> Nor did dispense with sin for gold;
> She hardly is a fortnight old,
> And yet she is a Pope!
> No king her feet did ever kiss,
> Or had from her worse looks than this,
> Nor did she ever hope,
> To saint one with a rope,
> And yet she is a Pope!
> A female Pope, you'll say, a second Joan?
> No, sure, she is Pope Innocent, or none.

Porcas, Porkess *see* PURCHASE.

Porter (Eng) Occupational name for a door-keeper, or carrier of goods.

Jimmy Porter was the hero of John Osborne's ground-breaking play *Look Back in Anger*.

A less obvious bearer of the name is Tarzan's beloved Jane, in the novels of Edgar Rice Burroughs. She is the daughter of

Professor Archimedes Q. Porter of Baltimore. When played by Maureen O'Sullivan in several film versions, she was wrongly named Jane Parker.

Pot, Potkin, Potkins, Pott, Pottel *see* PHILIP.

Potter, Potmaker (Eng) maker of pots – earthenware, clay or metal.

Pottle, Potts (Eng) Descendant of *Philpot*, a diminutive form of *Philip*.

> Evelyn Waugh's *Decline and Fall* has the exchange: '"I had a great friend called Potts." "Potts!" said Lady Circumference, and left it at that.'

Poulsom, Poulson *see* PAUL.

Pound, Pounder, Pounds, Pund (Eng) Descendant of someone who lived near an animal pound, or occupational name of someone whose job was to round up stray animals and impound them. *See* PENNY.

Powe *see* PEACOCK.

Powell *see* PAUL.

Power, Poor, Poore, Poorman, Powers (Eng) Nickname for a 'poor' person, or descendant of someone who came from Picardy, in France. PAUPER is also found.

Powling, Powly *see* PAUL.

Pratt, Pratman, Pratten, Pratlett, Prett, Pritt (Eng) Nickname for someone who was 'clever, astute,' perhaps at the expense of others, though the name of an early Prat was explained as 'because, when captured by the enemy, he often escaped by cunning.'

> The British actor William Pratt adopted the stage-name Boris Karloff.

Prebble, Preble (Eng) Possibly a form of a French place name, such as *Préval*, 'old meadow.'

> P.G. Wodehouse has fun with this name in *The Rise of Minna Nordstrom*: 'Vera Prebble was engaged in writing on a sheet of paper a short list of names, one of which she proposed as a *nom de théatre* as soon as her screen career should begin. She wrote Ursuline Delmaine, Theodora Trix, Uvula Gladwyn. None of them seemed to her quite what she wanted. She pondered. Possibly something a little more foreign and exotic. Greta Garbo. No, that had

been used. And then suddenly inspiration descended upon her and, trembling a little with emotion, she inscribed on the paper the one name that was absolutely and indubitably right. Minna Nordstrom.'

Preece *see* PRICE.

Preston (Eng) Someone who came from one of the several places so-named because it was the 'settlement of the priests.'

Pretlove *see* CATCHLOVE.

Prett *see* PRATT.

Price, Brice, Bryce, Preece, Pryse, Rease, Reece, Rees, Reese, Reice, Rhys, Rice (Welsh) Descendant of a man named *Rhys*, Old Welsh *Ris* 'fiery The forms in *B-* and *P-* are from *ab Rhys* or *ap Rhys* 'son of Rhys.' Price and Preece are occasionally English names of independent origin, perhaps from Old French *pré(s)* 'price, prize,' in which case the reference could be to a prized member of the community, or an arbitrator who fixed prices. Another possible origin, according to Weekley, is French *pré(s)* 'meadow.' *See* JONES.

Prichard, Pritchard (Welsh) From *ap Richard* 'son of Richard.
An epitaph in an Essex churchyard reads:

> Here lies the man Richard
> And Mary his wife
> Whose surname was Prichard
> They lived without strife
> And the reason was plain
> They abounded in riches
> They had no care or pain
> And his wife wore the breeches.

Priddle *see* BEWES.

Pride *see* PROUD.

Prior, Prier, Pryer, Pryor (Eng) A reference to the monastic official, probably to his servant rather than the man himself.

Pritchard *see* PRICHARD.

Pritlove *see* CATCHLOVE.

Pritt *see* PRATT.

Probart, Probat, Probate, Probert, Probett, Probin, Probyn *see* ROBERT.

Proger, Progers *see* ROGER.

Pronty *see* BRONTË.

Proper, Propert *see* ROBERT.

Prosser *see* ROGER.

Proud, Proude, Proudfellow, Proudfit, Proudfoot, Proudfut, Proudman, Proudy, Prout, Prowdfut, Prudfut (Eng) Nickname for a proud or haughty man. Prout is the Cornish form of the name. PRIDE is found in the Welsh border counties. Its form suggests that it was given to someone who had played the part of *Pride* in a medieval pageant. The French equivalent of such names, from *orgeuil*, takes such forms as ORGILL, ORGLES.

Prunty *see* BRONTË.

Pryer *see* PRIOR.

Prykkelove *see* CATCHLOVE.

Pryor *see* PRIOR.

Pryse *see* PRICE.

Puddy (Eng) Nickname for a 'podgy or pudgy person, round-bellied.' The same Middle English word occurs in compound names like PUDDEPHAT, PUDDEFOOT, PUDDIFOOT, PUDEPHAT, PUDIFOOT, PUTTIFOOT, where the second element is perhaps 'vat,' and the whole name is meant to conjure up an image of a barrel. However, Weekley thought that the original form was *Puddifoot* and that the nickname described someone who had a swollen foot, making him an English equivalent of *Oedipus*. In support of this he cited other compound surnames such as BARFOOT, BURFOOT 'bare foot,' BROADFOOT, LIGHTFOOT 'fast runner,' LONGFOOT, PROUDFOOT 'someone who walked in an arrogant way,' WHITEFOOT. Weekley also mentioned *Pauncefoot (Pauncefote, Pauncefort)* without glossing it, but here the first element means 'stomach, paunch' and the *-foot* must be another word, probably *vout* or *vaut* 'arched, rounded.'

Pugh, Pughe *see* HUGH.

Puller *see* POOLER.

Pullinger *see* BAKER.

Punch *see* PINCH.

Pund *see* POUND.

Purchase, Pirkis, Pirkiss, Porcas, Porkess, Purchas, Purches, Purchese, Purkess, Purkis, Purkiss (Fre) The earliest meaning of Old French purchas was 'pursuit,' and the name was used for couriers and messengers. In the more general sense of 'acquisition' the name was perhaps borne by the official responsible for buying supplies for a manor house or monastery.

Purday, Purdeu, Purdey, Purdie, Purdu, Purdue, Purdy, Purdye *see* PARDOE.

Purkess *see* PURCHASE.

Purkins *see* PETER.

Purkis, Purkiss *see* PURCHASE.

Puttifoot *see* PUDDY.

Pycock *see* PEACOCK.

Pyke *see* PIKE.

Pyne *see* PINE.

Pypar, Pyper *see* PIPER.

Quaggin (Manx) A form of Gaelic *MacDhubhagain* 'son of *Dubhagán, d*iminutive of *dubhan* 'black.' The same Gaelic name gave rise to **Duggan.** See also **Keogh.**

Quaife, Coyfe, Queyfer (Eng) Occupational name for a maker/seller of *coifs*, close fitting caps. This could also have been a nickname for someone, such as an ecclesiastic, who habitually wore a coif.

Quail, Quaile, Quails, Quale, Quayle (Eng) Nickname associated with the bird, which is reputedly amorous but timid. However, families of this name from Gaelic-speaking regions would derive it from Irish *MacPhoil,* Scottish *MacPhail*, Manx *MacPhayl* 'son of *Paul.*'

Quaint, Quant, Quantrell, Quantrill, Quintrell (Eng) These names are based on early senses of 'quaint,' referring either to a finely dressed person, a dandy, or someone thought to be clever, knowing.

Quaintance (Eng) The usual explanation of this name is that it indicates an 'acquaintance, friend.' It might also be '*Quentin's,*' ie 'a devotee of St Quentin.' Quaintance seems to have established itself in America. Bardsley noted it in Philadephia, Bowditch in Boston. It also occurs in early records as *Cointance*.

Quainton From residence in the Buckinghamshire place, so-named because it was the 'Queen's settlement.'

Qualter, Qualters (Eng) Descendant of a man who was the 'son of *Walter.*'

Qualtrough (Manx) Clan of *Walter*'s son. The ending of this name is a form of *-ach,* added to Gaelic names to mean 'family or clan.'

Quane (Manx) From Gaelic *MacDhubain* 'son of *Dhubán, a* personal name meaning 'black.'

Quant, Quantrell, Quantrill *see* QUAINT.

Quark (Manx) From Manx *MacWark*, a form of Gaelic *MacMhairc* 'son of *Mark*.'

Quarles (Eng) Someone who originally came from the place of this name in Norfolk. The place name appears to refer to a prehistoric stone circle, though all signs of it have disappeared.

There is a character of this name in *Elmer Gantry*, by Sinclair Lewis, which gives rise to the comment: 'The president, old Quarles – quarrels is right, by golly, ha, ha, ha!'

Quarell, Quarrell (Eng) This name could refer either to a maker or user of crossbow bolts, where '*quarrel*' refers to the bolt's 'square' head, or to someone who was a quareller, or troublemaker.

Quarry, Quarrie (Eng) Worker in a quarry, or resident near a quarry. The name could also be a form of French *Carré,* referring to a squarely-built, thick-set man. In a Gaelic-speaking context it is a form of *MacGuaire,* 'son of *Guaire*,' a personal name meaning 'noble.'

Quartermain, Quartermaine, Quarterman, Quatermain (Fre) The name means 'four hands.' The reference is probably to the habitual wearing of heavy mailed gloves, though C.M.Matthews, in *English Surnames,* says that 'it seems more like a name for a very dexterous person.' Ernest Weekley said that it was 'perhaps bestowed on a very acquisitive person.'

H. Rider Haggard bestowed the name Quatermain, for his part, on the hunter-hero of *King Solomon's Mines*.

Quatermass (Fre) C. L'Estrange Ewen, in his *History of Surnames* of the British Isles, suggests that this is a form of a Norman place name, *Quatremare*. In this case *Quatre* would not mean 'four', as one might expect. Early forms of the place name show that it was *Guitricmara* 'pond belonging to *Witerich*.' Others have linked Quatermass to QUATERMAIN.

Quaye (Manx) From Gaelic *MacAodha*, son of *Aodh* 'fire.' KAY, KAYE and KEE are other forms of this name.

Quayle *see* QUAIL.

Queen, Quene, Queneson (Eng) Probably a descendant of some-one who had played the part of 'Queen of the May' in a rural celebration. Bardsley pointed out that in the USA Queen and QUINN have become almost interchangeable in modern times, though the latter name has nothing to do with the origin of Queen.

'Ellery Queen' is a literary curiosity in being both an authorial pen-name and name of the hero in many stories about a New York detective. The pen-name concealed the identities of Manfred B.Lee and Frederick Dannay.

Quenby (Eng) From residence in the Leicestershire place, so-named because it was the 'Queen's (or woman's) estate.'

Quentin *see* QUINTON.

Quick, Quicke, Quickman (Eng) Nickname for a lively person; or someone who worked at a cow-wick, a dairy farm; or dweller near aspens or poplars. The name is frequent in Cornwall and Devon, where it relates to Cornish *gwyk*, referring to a wood, found in place names such as Polquick and Gweek.

Quilleash (Manx) A Manx form of *MacPhaluis,* 'son of *Paulus (Paul)*'.

Quilliam (Manx) A form of *MacWilliam,* 'son of *William*'

Quill (Gaelic) From **MacCuill**, 'son of *Coll*,' a personal name based on a Gaelic word meaning 'hazel.'

Quiller (Eng) Probably a form of the French surname *Cuiller,* found also as **Cullier, Cuilhé, Cuilerier, Cuilleron, Culleron,** all referring to a 'maker and seller of spoons.' The senses 'one who makes quills (pens)' or 'one who quills material into ruffs' cannot apply to the surname, since these meanings of 'quill' only came about long after the surname-formation period.

Quillin (Manx) A form of *O'Cuilinn*, descendant of *Cuileann*, from a Gaelic word meaning 'holly.'

Quilt, Quilter, Quilty (Eng) Occupational name of a maker of quilts, mattresses and quilted garments.

Quin *see* QUINN.

Quinard, Quinaud, Quinault (Fre) Probably 'descendant of *Jacquinard, Jacquinaud,*' diminutive forms of *Jacques.*

Quine (Manx) From *MacSveinn* 'son of *Sveinn*,' an Old Norse personal name meaning 'boy, page, servant.' In Ireland Quine is 'descendant of a man named *Conn,*' a Gaelic personal name meaning 'leader.'

Quinn, O'Quin, O'Quine, O'Quyn, Queen, Quin, Quine,

Quinney (Irish) Descendant of a man named *Conn*, a personal name from a Gaelic word meaning 'leader.'

Quinton, Quentin, Quintin (Eng) Someone who originally came from one of the places with this name, which refers to the 'Queen's settlement;' or from a place named in honour of Saint Quentin.

Quintrell *see* QUANT.

Quirk, Quirke (Manx) A form of Gaelic *MacCuirc*, 'son of *Corc*,' from a Gaelic word meaning 'heart.'

Rabb, Rabbatts, Rabbets, Rabbetts, Rabbits, Rabbitt, Rabbitts, Rabe, Rabett, Rabjohn, Rabjohns, Rablan, Rablen, Rablin *see* ROBERT.

Rafe, Raff *see* RALPH.

Raiment *see* RAYMOND.

Rain, Raine, Raines, Rayne (Eng) Descendant of someone who bore a male Germanic personal name which began with the element *ragin* 'counsel.' There was also a female name *Reine* 'queen' in the Middle Ages which could have led to this name.

Chambers, in his *Book of Days*, quotes a poem addressed to a lady named *Rain*:

> Whilst shivering beaux at weather rail,
> Of frost, and snow, and wind, and hail,
> And heat, and cold, complain,
> My steadier mind is always bent
> On one sole object of content –
> I ever wish for Rain!
> Hymen, thy votary's prayer attend,
> His anxious hope and suit befriend,
> Let him not ask in vain;
> His thirsty soul, his parched estate,
> His glowing breast commiserate –
> In pity give him Rain!

Rainey, Rainie, Rainnie, Rainy, Raney, Rannie, Reaney, Reanney, Reanny, Reany, Reinny, Reney, Renison, Rennie, Renny, Reyney, Ryney (Irish, Scottish) Descendant of *Reynold* 'counsel – rule.' Edward Maclysaght, in *The Surnames of Ireland*, explains *O Raighne*, which is Anglicized in the forms quoted above, as 'a form of *Reginald*,' the latter name merely a Latinized form of *Reynold*. Reaney can have a different origin – *see* REAGAN.

Raisin (Eng) Descendant of a man who was the 'reeve's son.' The reeve was either a magistrate or chief steward of an estate.

Ralph, Rafe, Raff, Ralf, Ralfe, Ralfs, Ralphs, Ralphson (Eng) Descendant of *Ralph*, a form of Old Norse *Rathulfr* or Norman *Radulf, Raulf* 'counsel-wolf.'

Ramsay, Ramsey (Scot) Descendant of someone who originally came from an English or Scottish place so-named. In England the place name means 'low-lying land with wild garlic.' The Scottish Ramsey is '*Ram's* island.'

Ramsbottom, Ramsbotham (Eng) Descendant of someone who came from the place of this name in Lancashire. The second element refers to the bottom of a valley. The first element is not what it seems, but a form of Old English *hramsa* 'wild garlic.'

    In 1971 a research team at Sussex University stated that children sometimes developed psychiatric disorders because their surnames were ridiculed. Names with -bottom, such as Ramsbottom, *Shufflebottom* and *Winterbottom*, were cited as names that made children more likely to end up at the bottom of the class. *Smellie, Snooks* and *Sex* were also described as 'troublesome.' Molly Bloom, in James Joyce's *Ulysses*, had already said in her famous monologue that Bloom was at least better than 'those awful names with bottom in them Mrs Ramsbottom or some other kind of a bottom.'

Ramsey *see* RAMSAY.

Randolph, Fitzrandolph, Randall, Randell, Randerson, Randlesome, Randle, Randles, Randoll, Randy (Eng) Descendant of *Randolph,* an Old Norse name composed of elements meaning 'shield' and 'wolf,' or the equally common Old German name *Rannulf* 'raven wolf.'

Raney, Rannie *see* RAINEY.

Raper, Rapier *see* ROPER.

Rasch *see* ASH

Ray, Raye (Eng) In some instances this name is the equivalent of KING, from Norman French *rey, roy* 'king', given for the same reasons. It can also be a nickname comparing someone to a *ray* 'female roe deer,' presumably because of that person's shyness. Ray can also be a variant of RYE.

Rayman *see* RYE.

Raymond, Raiment, Rayment, Raymont, Redmonds (Eng) Descendant of someone who bore the Norman personal name *Raimund*, composed of elements meaning 'counsel' and 'protection.' Redmonds is an Irish form of this name, also found as MACREMON, MACREDMOND.

Rayne *see* RAIN.

Rea *see* RYE.

Read, Red, Reed (Eng) A nickname commenting on redness of complexion or hair. In Scotland the name is usually spelt REID.

Reagan, Regan (Irish) Anglicized forms of Gaelic *O Riagain,* a personal name of uncertain meaning though 'impulsive' is often mentioned as a possibility.

Ronald Reagan pronounced his name *Reegan* while an actor, but changed to *Raigan* when he became President. Perhaps he was influenced by Professor Reaney, a great authority on surnames, who said of his own name: 'The correct pronunciation is *Rainey*, now being replaced by the spelling pronunciation *Reeney*.' Profesor Reaney also went on to say that his name was ultimately from Old Norse *hrafn-haugr* 'raven-hill,' and was not to be included with the Rainey group of names.

Really, Realy *see* RILEY.

Reaman *see* RYE.

Reaney *see* RAINEY, REAGAN.

Reanney, Reanny, Reany *see* RAINEY.

Reaper *see* RIPPER.

Rease *see* PRICE.

Reatchlous *see* RECKLESS.

Reay *see* RYE.

Rebert *see* ROBERT.

Reckless, Reatchlous, Rickless (Eng) Nickname for a person who behaved recklessly.

Red *see* READ.

Redhead (Eng) A descriptive nickname.

Redmonds *see* RAYMOND.

Reece *see* PRICE.

Reed *see* READ.

Reely *see* RILEY.

Rees, Reese *see* PRICE.

Regan *see* REAGAN.

Jack Regan was the flying squad detective, played by John Thaw, in *The Sweeney* television series. The name of the series was derived from Cockney rhyming slang, Sweeney Todd for 'flying squad.'

Reice *see* PRICE.

Reid *see* READ.

Reinny *see* RAINEY.

Remington, Rimmington (Eng) Someone who came from one of the places so-named because it was a 'settlement on a boundary stream.'

Reney, Renison *see* RAINEY.

Rennell, Rennells *see* REYNOLD.

Rennie *see* RAINEY.

Rennold, Rennolds *see* REYNOLD.

Renny *see* RAINEY.

Reynalds, Reynell *see* REYNOLD.

Reyney *see* RAINEY.

Reynold, Rennell, Rennells, Rennold, Rennolds, Reynalds, Reynell, Reynolds, Reynoldson (Eng) Descendant of *Reynold*, a Germanic personal name composed of elements meaning 'counsel' and 'rule.'

Rhoser, Rhosier *see* ROGER.

Rhys *see* PRICE.

Rian *see* RYAN.

Ricard, Ricarde, Ricards, Riccard *see* RICHARD.

Rice *see* JONES, PRICE.

Richard, Deakes, Deek, Deekes, Deeks, Deex, Dekin, Dekiss, Dick, Dickason, Dicke, Dickels, Dicken, Dickens, Dickenson, Dickerson, Dickeson, Dicketts, Dickin, Dickings, Dickins, Dickinson, Dickison, Dickons, Dicks, Dickson, Digg, Diggan, Diggen, Diggens, Digges, Diggin, Diggins, Diggle, Diggles, Diggon, Dix, Dixon, Dixson, Dykins, Hedgcock, Hedgecock, Hedgecoe, Hick, Hickes, Hickeson, Hickin, Hickish, Hicklin, Hickling, Hickman, Hickmer, Hickmet, Hickmore, Hickmott, Hicks, Hickson, Higgens, Higgett, Higgins, Higginson, Higgit, Higgons, Higgot,

Higgs, Higman, Higson, Hiscock, Hiscocks, Hiscoke, Hiscott, Hiscox, Hiscutt, Hiskett, Hitch, Hitchcock, Hitchcoe, Hitchcott, Hitchcox, Hitchen, Hitchens, Hitcheon, Hitches, Hitchin, Hitching, Hitchings, Hitchins, Hitchisson, Hitchman, Hitchmough, Hitchon, Hix, Hixon, Hixson, Hytch, Prichard, Pritchard, Ricard, Ricarde, Ricards, Riccard, Rich, Richardes, Richards, Richardson, Richarson, Riche, Riches, Rick, Rickard, Rickardes, Rickards, Rickeard, Rickerd, Rickert, Ricket, Rickets, Rickett, Ricketts, Ricks, Rickson, Ritch, Ritchard, Rix, Rixom, Rixon, Rixson (Eng) Descendant of *Richard*, a Germanic name composed of elements meaning 'power' and 'brave.' Introduced to Britain by the Norman barons, amongst whom it was very popular, it was soon taken up by the lower social classes, though the latter quickly shortened it to *Rich* or *Rick*. Because they had difficulties coping with the initial *R-* sound, as pronounced by the Normans, they also changed the name to *Dick, Hick* and *Hich* before adding diminutive suffixes. In Wales *ap Richard* 'son of Richard' was reduced to PRICHARD, PRITCHARD.

Rickless *see* RECKLESS.

Ricks *see* RICHARD.

Ridley (Eng) Someone who originally came from one of the many places so-named because of a 'channel clearing' or a 'clearing with reeds.'

This is apparently one of those surnames which can cause problems for its bearers. A *Daily Mail* correspondent some years ago complained that she had often been addressed by such diverse forms as *Riddle, Wrigley, Radlet* and *Wiggly*.

Rigby (Eng) Someone who came from one of the several places so-named because it was a 'farm on a ridge.'

Riley, O'Rahilly, O'Reyley, O'Reyly, O'Realy, O'Reely, O'Reiley, O'Reilly, O'Riellie, O'Rielly, Really, Realy, Reely (Irish) Descendant of someone who bore the Gaelic personal name *Raghailleach*. A suggested meaning of this name is 'rakish, sporting, unsettled.'

Rimmington *see* REMINGTON.

Ringsmith *see* SMITH.

Ripper, Rippier, Reaper (Eng) Occupational name connected with baskets in some way, from Old English *hrip* 'basket.' The *Ripper* could have made and sold baskets, or carried goods such as fish in them.

Ritch, Ritchard, Rix, Rixom, Rixon, Rixson *see* RICHARD.

Roak, Roake *see* OAK.

Robatham, Robathan *see* ROWBOTTOM.

Robert, Dabbs, Dabinett, Dabs, Dabson, Dobb, Dobbe, Dobbie, Dobbin, Dobbing, Dobbings, Dobbins, Dobbinson, Dobbison, Dobbs, Dobby, Dobbyn, Dobey, Dobie, Dobieson, Dobing, Dobinson, Dobson, Doby, Dobyn, Dopson, Dubbin, Dubin, Hob, Hobb, Hobbes, Hobbin, Hobbins, Hobbis, Hobbiss, Hobbs, Hobkin, Hobkins, Hoblin, Hobling, Hoblyn, Hobson, Hopkin, Hopkins, Hopkinson, Hopp, Hopson, Nobb, Nobbs, Nobes, Nokkins, Nopps, Nops, Probart, Probat, Probate, Probert, Probett, Probin, Probyn, Proper, Propert, Rabb, Rabbatts, Rabbets, Rabbetts, Rabbits, Rabbitt, Rabbitts, Rabe, Rabett, Rabjohn, Rabjohns, Rablan, Rablen, Rablin, Rebert, Robart, Robarts, Robb, Robbens, Robberds, Robbie, Robbings, Robbins, Robbs, Robe, Robearts, Robelyn, Robens, Roberds, Robers, Roberson, Roberts, Robertson, Robeson, Robey, Robin, Robinent, Robinett, Robins, Robinson, Robison, Robjant, Robjohns, Roblett, Roblin, Robson, Roby, Robyns (Eng) Descendant of *Robert*, a Germanic name composed of elements which mean 'fame – bright.' It was introduced to Britain by the Normans and quickly taken up in great numbers. Robert had the pet forms *Dob, Hob, Nob, Rab* and *Rob,* which in turn could acquire diminutive endings. The forms of the surname beginning with *P*- are Welsh, from *ap Robert*, 'son of Robert.' *See* JONES.

Robinson occurs in the well-known phrase 'before you could say Jack Robinson.' No one has been able to trace an actual person who might have been responsible for the saying.

Robotham, Robottom *see* ROWBOTTOM.

Rochester, Rogister, Rossiter (Eng) Usually someone who originally came from the Kentish Rochester. The *-chester* indicates a Roman military camp; the first element is a contracted form of the original British name, which meant 'fortress bridge.' Bardsley suggested that Wroxeter, in Shropshire, might also be the source.

Edward Rochester is the brooding hero of Charlotte Brontë's *Jane Eyre*, of whom Jane famously says: 'Reader, I married him.'

Rock, Rocke, Rocks (Eng) Dweller near an outcrop of rocks.

Rockefeller (Ger) This name was taken to the USA by German emigrants. The original bearers of the surname would have come from Rockenfeld in the Rhineland, named because rye was grown in its fields.

P.G. Wodehouse jokes about a similar name (though it is one which he presumably invented) in *Carry On, Jeeves*: 'He had this aunt in Illinois; and, as he had been named Rockmeteller after her (which in itself, you might say, entitled him to substantial compensation) and was her only nephew, his position looked pretty sound.'

Rocker, Rokker, Rooker, Rucker (Eng) A wool-spinner, or maker/seller of the distaffs on which the wool was wound.

Rocks *see* ROCK.

Rodger, Rodgers, Rodgerson, Rodget, Rodgier, Rodgman *see* ROGER.

Roebotham *see* ROWBOTTOM.

Roger, Dodge, Dodgen, Dodgeon, Dodgin, Dodshon, Dodshun, Dodgson, Dodson, Doidge, Doige, Dudgeon, Dudson, Hadgkiss, Hochkins, Hodge, Hodgen, Hodgens, Hodgeon, Hodges, Hodgeskinson, Hodgess, Hodgett, Hodgetts, Hodgin, Hodgins, Hodgkiess, Hodgkin, Hodgkins, Hodgkinson, Hodgekinson, Hodgkiss, Hodgkisson, Hodgeon, Hodgshon, Hodgskins, Hodgson, Hodkin, Hodshon, Hodskin, Hodkinson, Hodskins, Hodgson, Hodson, Hotchkin, Hotchkins, Hotchkiss, Proger, Progers, Prosser, Rhoser, Rhosier, Rodger, Rodgers, Rodgerson, Rodget, Rodgier, Rodgman, Rogers, Rogerson, Roget, Rogett, Roggeman, Rogger, Roginson, Roser, Rosser, Rudge (Eng) Descendants of a man named *Roger,* who was likely to be known as *Dodge* or *Hodge,* or diminutive forms of these names. These forms of the name reflected the difficulty English-speakers had reproducing the initial French *r-* sound. In Welsh Roger was pronounced *Rosser* because there was no *j* sound in that language. When the initial *R-* was aspirated it led to Rhoser, Rhosier. Welsh *ap Rosher* 'son of Roger' also led to Prosser. It has been suggested that 'educated' Welshmen, familiar with English, were able to pronounce Roger in the usual way, so that *ap* or *ab Roger* led to Proger. Roger itself is a Germanic personal name composed of elements meaning 'fame' and 'spear.' It was introduced to Britain by the Normans, replacing an Old English name *Hrothgar* of similar meaning. HOGGINS may belong here, a form of Roger analogous to HUGGINS from HUGH, HIGGINS from RICHARD.

Rogister *see* ROCHESTER.

Roke *see* OAK.

Rokeby (Eng) Someone who came from a place so-named because it was a 'village where rooks were plentiful.'

Rokker *see* ROCKER.

Roncin *see* RUNCIE.

Roobottam *see* ROWBOTTOM.

Roof, Rover, Ruffer (Eng) A roof-worker.

Rook *see* OAK.

Rooker *see* ROCKER.

Roper, Raper, Rapier, Rope, Ropes, Roop, Roope, Rooper (Eng) Occupational name for a man who made and sold rope.

Rose (Eng) Scholarly opinions differ widely about the origin of this name. In Jewish surnames, on its own or as part of a longer name, *Rose* means the flower. This may be the case with the English name, indicating someone who lived in a place where wild roses grew. The name could indicate more specifically someone who lived at the sign of the Rose. Basil Cottle preferred to look for a Gaelic original meaning something like 'wood' or 'moor.' There is also the (female) name of a tenant recorded in *Domesday Book* as *Rothais* 'renown - kind, sort' which led to ROYCE, ROYSE and perhaps Rose.

Bearers of this name smile weakly when someone quotes 'a rose by any other name would smell as sweet.' The quotation is often used in other contexts to suggest that Shakespeare thought that names were of no importance, one was as good as another. But he puts the words into Juliet's mouth at a time when she is desperately trying to convince herself that it is only Romeo's name that is causing a problem, not the fact that he belongs to a family which is the deadly enemy of her own. Even as she utters the words she knows full well that there is more to it than that. There is no reason whatsoever to think that Shakespeare really thought that a rose by any other name would smell as sweet.

Roser *see* ROGER.

Ross (Scot, Eng) Descendant of someone who came from any of the places where the name is based on Gaelic *ros* 'moorland' or 'promontory.' Such places are found in Scotland, England and Wales.

Rosser *see* ROGER.

Rossiter *see* ROCHESTER.

Roubottom *see* ROWBOTTOM.

Rough, Ruff (Eng) Nickname for an uncouth man, or dweller on rough ground.

Roughhead, Rowed, Ruffhead (Eng) Nickname for a man with shaggy hair.

Rouse, Rous, Rousel, Rousell, Roussel, Roussell, Rowse, Rowsell, Russ, Russel, Russell, Russill (Eng) A nickname commenting on someone's red hair, from Old French *rous* 'red.' Rousel was a diminutive form.

Rover *see* ROOF.

Rowbottom, Robatham, Robathan, Robotham, Robottom, Roebotham, Roobottam, Roubottom, Rowbotham, Rowbottam (Eng) From residence at 'the bottom of a rough (overgrown) valley.' See also **Longbottom.**

Rowed *see* ROUGHHEAD.

Rowedder *see* FOULWEATHER.

Rower, Royer (Eng) Occupational name of a wheelwright.

Rowse, Rowsel *see* ROUSE.

Royce *see* ROSE.

Royer *see* ROWER.

Royse *see* ROSE.

Rucker *see* ROCKER.

Rudd, Ruddy, Rudman (Eng) A nickname commenting on a man's red complexion or hair.

Rudge (Eng) From residence near a ridge, or a nickname commenting on someone's red complexion or hair, or descendant of ROGER.

Rudman *see* RUDD.

Ruff *see* ROUGH.

Ruffer *see* ROOF.

Ruffhead *see* ROUGHHEAD.

Runcie, Roncin, Runcieman, Runchman, Runciman, Runcy, Runsyman (Fre) Occupational name based on Old French *roncin* 'horse.' This word became 'rouncy' in English, but early quotations do not make it clear what kind of horse was meant. Modern French *roussin* is defined historically as a 'charger,' the type of horse which would have been ridden by an officer going into battle, but the contemporary meaning is more like 'pack-horse.' The surname Runcy also appears to have been a nickname for a porter, a human beast of burden. These names, in any case, refer to someone who was in charge of horses of one kind or another.

Russ, Russel, Russell, Russill *see* ROUSE.

Rutherford (Scot) Descendant of someone who came from the Scottish place of this name near Roxburgh.

Black cites a typical folk etymology, which explains a word or name by a vivid use of the imagination rather than serious research. Rutherford has thus been explained in terms of a battle between Scots and English in which the latter were routed, being driven back across a ford of the Tweed. The spot was then supposedly named 'rue the ford.'

Ryan, Rian, O'Ryan (Irish) A simplified form of MULRYAN (also found as MULRAIN, MULRINE, MULROYAN, MULRYNE, O'MULREAN, O'MULRIGAN, O'MULRYAN. Anglicized form of Gaelic *O Maoil-Riaghain*, descendant of the 'devotee of St *Riaghan*.' The meaning of the latter name is not clear, though a diminutive of a word meaning 'king' has been suggested.

Rye, Rayman, Rea, Reaman, Reay, Ryman (Eng) From Middle English phrases such as *atter ye* 'at the island' or *atter eye* 'at the river,' indicating where the name-bearer lived. There could also be a connection with Old English *ryge* 'rye.' The meaning would then be someone who lived near a field where rye was grown, or someone who grew rye.

Ryney *see* RAINEY.

Saddler, Sadler, Sadleir, Sadlier (Eng) A maker and seller of saddles.

Sage (Eng) Nickname for someone thought to be exceptionally wise.

Sailor, Sailer, Sayler, Seiler, Seiller, Seyler (Fre) A professional dancer or acrobat. The mariner sense of sailor only occurs after the surname-formation period.

Saint, Sant, Sants, Saunt (Eng) Nickname (though perhaps ironic) for a saintly person.

Salisbury, Salisberry, Salesbury, Salsbury, Salusbury (Eng) From Salisbury, in Wiltshire. Lancashire families of this name were originally from Salesbury, near Blackburn.

Salmon (Eng) Descendant of a man who bore this name, a contracted form of *Salomon* or *Solomon*, Greek forms of the Hebrew *Shelomoh* 'the peaceful.'

Salmonella, the genus of bacteria associated with food poisoning, is named after its discoverer, the vetinarian Dr Daniel E. Salmon (1850-1914).

Samper, Simper (Fre) Descendant of someone who lived in a placed named in honour of *Saint Pierre (Peter)*.

Samways (Eng) Nickname for someoneone considered to be half-witted, from Old English *sam* 'half' plus *wis* 'wise'.

In Dorset dialect a 'fool' is a *sammy*. *Sam-sodden* means 'half-boiled,' or 'half-baked' as a Londoner might say.

Sand, Sande, Sands, Sandys (Eng) Sometimes a descendant of *Alexander*, but probably more often an indication that an ancestor lived on sandy soil. Similar names where *sand* has the latter meaning are SANDFORD, SANDHAM, SANDILANDS, SANDY, SEND.

Sandars, Sandeman, Sander, Sanderman, Sanders, Sandeson,

Sandieson, Sandison *see* ALEXANDER.

Sandford, Sandham, Sandilands, Sandy, Sandys *see* SAND.

Sant, Sants *see* SAINT.

Saunder, Saunders, Saunderson *see* ALEXANDER.

Saunt *see* SAINT.

Sawer *see* SAWYER.

Sawright (Eng) Occupational name for a maker of saws.

Sawyer, Sawer, Sawyers (Eng) Occupational name of a man who sawed wood.

Mark Twain's *Tom Sawyer* is one of the world's best-known literary characters, along with his friend Huckleberry Finn.

Saxby (Eng) Someone who came from one of the several places so-named because it was '*Saxi*'s village.'

Sayler *see* SAILOR.

Scambler (Eng) A maker of 'scambles,' or benches.

Scattergood (Eng) It is not clear why this nickname was bestowed. The man concerned could have been someone who carelessly squandered his possessions. He could just as well have been a philanthropist who gave them freely to the poor.

Schmidt *see* FABER.

Schwarz, Schwart, Schwartz, Schwartzer, Schwarzer, Swartz (German) A nickname equivalent to **Black,** from German *schwarz* 'black.' **Schwarzkopf** 'black head' also occurs.

Scott, Scotson, Scotts (Eng, Scot) Descendant of a man who was Scottish, especially one who spoke Gaelic.

Screech (Eng) Possibly a nickname for someone who tended to screech. Bowditch, in his *Suffolk Surnames,* oddly includes Screech in his collection of 'musical' names. *See* STAMP.

Scruton, Scrutton (Eng) Someone who came from one of the several places so-named because it was the 'settlement of *Scurfa*'s people.'

Sealey, Seeley *see* SILLY.

Seath *see* SHAW.

Seaton (Eng) Someone who came from one of the several places so-named because it was a 'settlement near a lake.'

Arthur Seaton is the working-class hero of Allan Sillitoe's 1958 novel *Saturday Night and Sunday Morning*, brought to life in the screen version by Albert Finney.

Sefton (Eng) Someone who came from one of the several places so-named because it was a 'settlement where rushes grew.'

Seiler, Seiller *see* SAILOR.

Seivwright *see* SIEVWRIGHT.

Selby (Eng) Someone who came from a place so-named because it was a 'farm near willow trees.'

Sellerman (Eng) Man responsible for the cellar, originally a store for provisions above or below ground.

Selly *see* SILLY.

Send *see* SAND.

Seppanen *see* FABER.

Seth *see* SHAW.

Settle (Eng) Descendant of someone who originally lived in the Yorkshire place of this name. Old English *setl* meant 'seat, abode.'

There was an 18th century playwright of this name, which for some reason John Wilkes disliked. He is quoted in Boswell's *Life of Johnson* as saying: 'There is something in names which one cannot help feeling. Now Elkanah Settle sounds so queer, who can expect much from that name? We should have no hesitation to give it for John Dryden in preference to Elkanah Settle, from the names only.'

Severwright *see* SIEVWRIGHT.

Sewer, Sewter, Souter, Sowter, Suetor, Suiter, Suter (Eng) Occupational name of a shoe-maker. Most of these forms influenced by Latin *sutor* 'sewer.'

Sex, Sexsmith (Eng) A maker of knives or daggers. Sex is one of the surnames that tends to be changed because of the comments it evokes, but some families retain it. See further on surnames that cause problems at RAMSBOTTOM.

Sexauer, Sexaur (Ger) This name is listed in a *New Dictionary of American Family Names,* by Elsdon C. Smith, where it is explained as someone who came from *Sexau*, Germany.

Mr Smith does not record the anecdote about someone telephoning a company and asking the receptionist: 'Do you have a Sexauer there?' The receptionist replied: 'Sexauer! We don't even have a coffee break.'

Sexsmith *see* SEX.

Seyler *see* SAILOR.

Shacklady, Shakelady *see* LOVELADY.

Shackleton (Eng) Someone who came from a place so-named because it was a 'settlement on a tongue of land.'

Shackshaft *see* SHAKESPEARE.

Shafe *see* SHAW.

Shakespeare, Shackshaft, Shakelance, Shakeshaft, Shakesheff, Shakeshift (Eng) Probably a nickname for a soldier, or someone who was a quarrel-monger, constantly challenging others by metaphorically brandishing his spear. A more bawdy explanation is possible, since the 'spear,' 'shaft' may have been a euphemistic reference to the male member. This would perhaps make the name a reference to vigorous sexual activity. Although we cannot be certain of the exact reason why someone should have been called a 'spear-shaker,' there is no reason to think that Shakespeare is a corruption of words other than those. Absurd suggestions have nevertheless been made – that the name is really *Sigisbert,* or that it is a form of *Jacques-Pierre*, that it is from a place name of the type Shachsburgh, Saxby or French *Saquespée*, that it is Celtic *Shacspeir* 'dry shanks,' or Saxon *Seaxberht,* or a form of *Schalksboer* 'the knave's farm.' The wide variety of medieval names similar in form to Shakespeare make it quite clear that verb + noun was a common formula.

Shakespeare itself had existed as a surname for several centuries before William Shakespeare inherited it. A William *Sakespere* was convicted of robbery and hanged in 1248. In the 15th century a Hugo *Shakspere* changed his surname to Sawndare, explaining that Shakspere 'has an evil reputation.'

Shakespeare still exists as a surname, and some men who bear it are called William. An article in *The Reader's Digest* of August, 1936, went into some of the problems that the writer had experienced because he was a modern William Shakespeare. They included being thrown into prison for a minor traffic violation because the police were convinced he had given them a false name.

Shank, Shanks (Eng) Nickname for someone with long or unusual legs.

Sharer, Sharman *see* SHEARER.

Sharp, Sharpe, Sharps (Eng) Nickname for a smart, quick person.

Smart is a similar name.

Thackeray fitted name to character when he created Becky Sharp in *Vanity Fair*. Becky is smarter than most people she meets, though she eventually gets her come-uppance.

Sharples, Sharpless (Eng) Descendant of someone who came from Sharples Hall, near Bolton, so-named because of its 'steep pasture.'

This name is frequently found in Lancashire, but is known throughout Britain thanks to Ena Sharples, the busybody in *Coronation Street*.

Shatswell, Shatwell, Shawell (Eng) From residence in Shawell, Leicestershire, earlier *Schathewell, Shathewell*, so-named because of its 'boundary stream.'

In *The Watch that ends the Night*, Hugh Maclennan has: '"A chap with the name of Shatwell," he explained, "learns rather early on that things are likely to go against him, you understand. I thought of changing the old name once, but I'd become rather attached to it, you understand, so I decided to make do".'

Shaw, Shafe, Shave, Shaves, Shawe, Shay, Shays, Shea, Sheye (Eng, Scot) A shaw is a 'small wood, copse.' This surname in its various forms indicates someone who lived near a shaw, or in a place named because of its copse. Reaney gives *shay* as a Yorkshire dialect form of the word, and *Shafe* and *Shave* as Devonshire variants. Black tells us that the Shaws who live in the Highlands derive their name instead from a Gaelic name meaning 'wolf' which happens to sound something like shaw. The Gaelic name has also been Anglicized in various parts of Scotland as SEATH, SETH, SHEACH, SHIACH, SITHACH, SITHEAG, SITHECH and SYTHAG.

Shea *see* SHAW.

Shawell *see* SHATSWELL.

Shea *see* SHAW.

Sheahan, Shean *see* SHEEHAN.

Shearer, Sharer, Sharman, Sheara, Shearman, Shears, Sheerman, Sherer, Sherman, Shirer, Shurman (Eng) A sheep-shearer, or one who trimmed the nap of woollen cloth with shears.

Sheehan, O'Sheahan, O'Sheehan, O'Shehane, O'Shieghane, Sheahan, Shean, Sheean, Sheen, Shine (Irish) Descendant of *Síodhachán,* a Gaelic personal name meaning 'peaceful.'

Sheepy *see* BIRDSEYE.

Sheerman *see* SHEARER.

Shepobotham *see* SHIPPERBOTTOM.

Sherer *see* SHEARER.

Sherlock, Shurlock (Eng) Nickname for a man with a lock of fair, shining hair.

Sherman *see* SHEARER.

Sheye *see* SHAW.

Shilling *see* PENNY.

Shine *see* SHEEHAN.

Shinn, Shinner *see* SKINNER.

Shipperbottom, Shepobotham, Shipplebotham, Shipowbotham, Shoebottom, Shoebotham, Shovelbottom, Shubotham, Shufflebotham, Shufflebottom, Shupplebotham (Eng) Shipperbottom in Lancashire was named because it was the bottom of a valley where there was a 'sheep well,' used for washing sheep. *See* LONGBOTTOM.

Shipton (Eng) Someone who came from one of the several places so-named because it was a 'settlement with sheep.'

Shipwright (Eng) Occupational name for a ship-builder.

Shirer *see* SHEARER.

Shoebottom, Shoebotham *see* SHIPPERBOTTOM.

Shoesmith *see* SMITH.

Shooter, Shotter, Shut, Shuter, Shutt, Shutte, Shutter, Shutts (Eng) An archer. In some instances the reference may be to someone who lived in a shut, a narrow street. A connection with suitor (litigant) has also been suggested.

Shore (Eng) Descendant of someone who lived near a sea-shore. *See* NIGHTINGALE.

Shoreham (Eng) From residence in the Kentish place, so-named because it was a 'homestead near a steep shore.'

Short, Shortman (Eng) Nickname for a short man.

Shorthouse, Shorters, Shorthose, Shortis (Eng) Nickname for someone with a short neck, *-house* being a form of *hals* 'neck,' or for someone who wore 'short hose.'

Shortman *see* SHORT.

Shotter *see* HOOTER.

Shovelbottom *see* SHIPPERBOTTOM.

Shrapnel (Eng) Weekley equated this name with French *Charbonnel* 'little coal,' having found an 'intermediate' *Sharpanel*. Dauzat explains the French name as 'charcoal seller.' The Oxford *Dictionary of Surnames* prefers to think of it as a nickname for a man with a 'swarthy complexion.'

A *Dictionary of Eponyms*, by Cyril Leslie Beeching, says that: 'Henry Shrapnel (1761-1842) was a British army officer who invented and gave his name to the shrapnel shell . . . filled with explosive and ball shot.' The meaning of shrapnel was later extended to 'fragments of an exploding shell, bomb or mine.'

Shubotham, Shufflebotham, Shufflebottom, Shupplebotham *see* SHIPPERBOTTOM.

Shurlock *see* SHERLOCK.

Shurman *see* SHEARER.

Shut, Shuter, Shutt, Shutte, Shutter, Shutts *see* SHOOTER.

Shynn *see* SKINNER.

Sidebottom, Sidebotham (Eng) Someone who came from a place so-named because it was a 'wide valley bottom.' See also **Longbottom.**

Siegel (Ger) Descendant of a man who bore a Germanic personal name beginning with the popular element *sigi* 'victory,' such as Sieghard, Siegert, Siegfried, Siegmund, Siegward.

The New York poet Eli Siegel wrote his celebrated poem 'One Question' in 1925. It runs:

> I.
> Why?

Oddities and Curiosities of Words and Literature, edited by C.C. Bombaugh, quotes an even shorter anonymous poem, though its title ('Reactions to a Statement by Kruschev that the Soviet Union has no desire to meddle in the internal affairs of other Nations') rather cancels out its brevity. The poem itself is:

> O,
> So?

Sievwright, Seivwright, Severwright, Sivewright (Eng) Occupational name for a maker of sieves.

Silly, Ceeley, Cely, Sealey, Seeley, Selly, Silley, Sillifant, Zealey,

Zelley (Eng) Descriptive of someone who was silly in the word's original sense – 'happy, fortunate, blessed.'

Silverbird *see* WHITBREAD.

Silverlock (Eng) Nickname for a man with silver hair.

Silversmith *see* SMITH.

Silvery *see* BIRDSEYE.

Simon, Fitzsimmons, MacImmie, MacKimmey, MacKimmie, Sim, Simcock, Simcocks, Simcox, Sime, Simes, Simkin, Simeon, Simeons, Simion, Simkin, Simkins, Simm, Simmens, Simmins, Simmonds, Simmons, Simnel, Simnett, Simond, Simonds, Simons, Simonson, Simpkin, Simpkins, Simpkinson, Simpson, Simson, Sym, Symcox, Symes, Symmons, Symms, Symon, Symonds, Symondson, Symons, Syms, Syson (Eng) Descendant of *Simon* or *Simeon*, or someone who was known by a diminutive or derivative of these names, such as Sim or Simcock. The name is from Hebrew *Shim'on* and means '(Yah) has heard.' In the Bible *Simeon, Symeon* (Old Testament) and *Simon* (New Testament) are Greek forms of the name, the latter becoming confused with another Greek name from *simos* 'snub-nosed.' In Scottish Gaelic 'son of Simon' became *MacShimidh*, then MACKIMMEY, etc. The great poularity of the name in the Middle Ages was due to its frequent occurrence in the Bible (eighteen different men, including two Apostles and a "brother" of Christ).

Simper *see* SAMPER.

Simpkin, Simpkins, Simpkinson, Simpson, Simson *see* SIMON.

Singleday *see* DOUBLEDAY.

Singleton (Eng) Someone who came from one of the several places so-named because it was a 'settlement on shingly soil.'

Sithach, Sitheag, Sithech *see* SHAW.

Sitwell (Eng) Probably an occupational name for someone who sold the drug obtained from the root of 'setwall,' otherwise known as 'zedoary.' It has properties similar to ginger. In *The Miller's Tale* Chaucer says: 'And he himself as sweete as is the roote lycorys, or any cetewale.'

Sivewright *see* SIEVWRIGHT.

Sixsmith (Eng) Occupational name for a maker of sickles or 'socks', *see* SOCKSMITH.

Skegg, Skeggs (Eng) Nickname for a bearded man, *skegg* being the Old Norse word for 'beard.'

Skelton (Eng) Someone who came from one of the several places so-named because it was a 'settlement on a bank or hill.'

Skinner, Shinn, Shinner, Shynn, Skin, Skyner, Skynner (Eng) Occupational name of a man who skinned animals, producing hides that could be tanned. The -*k*- spellings are from the Old Norse word *skinn*. The Old English word of the same meaning was *shinn*.

This name is discussed by Scottish characters in Jane Duncan's *My Friend Flora*: '"Take Jock Skinner's name, now. Skinner is not a bonnie word at a-all. Do you think that is because Jock himself is not bonnie or is it chust an ugly word whateffer?" "It is not a bonnie noise of a word," Tom concluded, "besides making you think on beasts being skinned at the slaughter-house, poor craiturs. Of course, there might be some very nice people off the name off Skinner for all that".'

Skmiton *see* FABER.

Slater, Slate, Slates, Slator, Slatt, Slatter (Eng) Occupational name for a man who slated roofs.

Slaughter, Slaughterer (Eng) Occupational name for a slaughterer of animals. However, there are English places called Slaughter and the surname may indicate someone who originally came from such a place. The place-name meaning is derived from Old English *slohtre* 'muddy place.'

Slay, Slaymaker, Slee (Eng) Occupational name for a maker of 'slays,' an instrument used in weaving.

Sleath *see* SLY.

Slee *see* SLAY.

Sleeman, Sleith, Slemming, Slemmings, Slemmonds, Sligh *see* SLY.

Slight (Eng) Nickname for a slender person or one who was clever. In the latter sense the name is similar to SLY.

Sliman, Slimming, Slimmon *see* SLY.

Slingsby (Eng) Someone who came from a place so-named because it was '*Sleng's* village.'

Sloper, Slopier (Eng) Occupational name for a maker of 'slops,' loose breeches of knee length or shorter. In Shakespeare's *Romeo* *and Juliet* Mercutio comments on Romeo's fashionable French slops.

Trollope has a character named Slope in *Barchester Towers*. The author says: 'Of the Rev. Mr Slope's parentage I am not able to say much. I have heard it asserted that he is lineally dscended from that eminent physician who assisted at the birth of Mr T. Shandy (ie Dr Slop, in Laurence Sterne's *Tristram Shandy*), and that in early years he added an "e" to his name for the sake of euphony, as other great men have done before him.'

Sly, Sleath, Sleeman, Sleith, Slemming, Slemmings, Slemmonds, Sligh, Sliman, Slimming, Slimmon, Slybody, Slye, Slyman (Eng) A nickname for someone who was considered to be 'skilful, clever' in a good sense, or 'cunning, crafty' in a bad sense.

The man who was born Leonard Slye changed his name to Dick Weston, then changed it again to Roy Rogers when he became 'the singing cowboy.'

Small (Eng) Nickname for someone who was smaller than average. *Smale* is a Cornish form of the name.

Smalley *see* BIRDSEYE.

Smart *see* SHARP.

Smeatham (Eng) From residence in a place so-named because it was a 'homestead with a smithy.'

Smeaton (Eng) Someone who came from one of the several places so-named because it was a 'settlement with a smithy.'

Smed *see* FABER.

Smellie (Eng) Perhaps a descendant of someone who originally lived in Smalley, Derbyshire, so-named because of a 'narrow clearing in a wood,' though the name could also mean what it says and refer to an especially smelly person. *See* RAMSBOTTOM.

Pennethorne Hughes remarks in *Is Thy Name Wart*: 'Fortunately the bearers of this name at my school were able to assert themselves.'

Erica Jong also refers to the name in *Fanny*: 'Dr Smellie, whose very name, i'faith, seem'd so comical to me that I should surely commence laughing the moment he came to attend me.'

Smiler, Smiles, Smiley, Smylie (Eng) The word smile had its modern meaning in the Middle English period, so these names

236

could be descriptive of someone who smiled a great deal. They could also be euphemistic alterations of SMELLIE. Professor Weekley offered the ingenious suggestion that Smiles could be a contracted form of *St Miles*. He added that **Smirk** could then conceivably be from *St Mark*.

Schoolboy humour says that Smiles is by far the longest English surname because there's a 'mile' between the first and last letters.

George Smiley is the British Intelligence chief in the novels of John le Carré, someone made very real by Alec Guinness in filmed versions of the novels.

Smith, Smither, Smithers, Smithson, Smyth, Smythe, Smythson (Eng) A metal worker or his son. Every village needed its smith, who made both agricultural and domestic tools in periods of peace as well as swords, armour, etc at times of conflict. In some instances the name may refer to residence near a smithy. Many surnames refer more precisely to a worker in iron **Blacksmith, Shoesmith**, copper, **Brownsmith, Coppersmith**, lead **Greensmith**, silver **Silversmith**, gold **Goldsmith**, or tin **Tinsmith, Whitesmith. Sixsmith, Sexsmith** probably refers to a maker of scythes or sickles. A **Sucksmith** made ploughshares.

A large collection of compound surnames based on Smith can be found in *The Book of Smith*, by Elsdon C. Smith, Nellen Publishing Inc, New York, 1978. In some cases the original meaning of the name is obscure. Examples, with variants in brackets, include Ainsmith (Aimsmith), Aldersmith, Anchorsmith (Ankelsmith, Ankersmith), Armsmith, Arrowsmith (Arasmith, Arousmyth, Arowsmith, Arrasmith, Arsmith, Arusmyth), Axsmith, Bellsmith (Balismith, Balysmyth, a smith who worked with bellows), Billsmith (axe or sword smith), Bladesmith (Bladsmith), Boltsmith, Bowsmith (Bowersmith, Boyersmith), Bucklesmith (Bucksmith), Clocksmith, Coopersmith, Fieldsmith, Goodsmith, Gunsmith, Hammersmith, Harrowsmith, Highsmith, Hoopersmith, Hudsmith (maker of hoods, helmets), Knifesmith, Locksmith, Messersmith (a form of German Messerschmidt, a maker of knives), Moneysmith, Nailsmith (Naismith, Nasmyth, Naysmith, Neasmith), Platesmith, Plowsmith, Ringsmith, Spearsmith, Youngsmith.

One problem with Smith is its apparent lack of social status. Jane Austen comments ironically in *Persuasion*: 'A mere Mrs Smith, an every day Mrs Smith, of all people and of all names in the world, to be the chosen friend of Miss Anne Elliot. Mrs Smith, such a name!'

John Fowles, in *The French Lieutenant's Woman*, writes in similar vein: '"Do but think," he had once said to her, "how disgracefully plebeian a name Smithson is." "Ah, indeed – if you were only called Lord Brabazon Vavasour Vere de Vere – how much more I should love you"!'

In *Mike*, P.G. Wodehouse dealt with the Smith problem in his own inimitable way: 'If you ever have occasion to write to me, would you mind sticking a P at the beginning of my name? *P-s-m-i-t-h*. See? There are too many Smiths, and I don't care for Smythe. I've decided to strike out a fresh line. In conversation you may address me as Rupert (though I hope you won't), or simply Smith, the P not being sounded.'

Smith is notoriously used as an alias. Even the French king Louis-Philippe, when he abdicated and fled for his life, assumed the name William Smith. It was also sporadically used by Greta Garbo (see GARBO). In P.M Hubbard's novel The Tower a man whose name is John Smith registers at a hotel, but thinks that the receptionist is suspicious. He comments: 'That was the trouble with John Smith. They always expected you to bring in a giggling blonde with the wrong initials on her suitcase.'

All this was countered by G.K.Chesterton in *Heretics*. Writing at a time when a blacksmith still plied his trade in every village, he said: 'Even the village children feel that in some dim way the smith is poetic, as the grocer and the cobbler are not poetic, when they feast on the dancing sparks and deafening blows in the cavern of that creative violence. The brute repose of Nature, the passionate cunning of man, the strongest of earthly metals, the weirdest of earthly elements, the unconquerable iron subdued by its only conqueror, the wheel and the ploughshare, the sword and the steam-hammer, the arraying of armies and the whole legend of arms, all these things are written, briefly indeed, but quite legibly, on the visiting-card of Mr Smith. Yet our novelists call their hero "Aylmer

Valence," which means nothing, or "Vernon Raymond," which means nothing, when it is in their power to give him this sacred name of Smith – this name made of iron and flame.'

Smollett (Eng) Nickname for a man with a 'small head.'

Smylie *see* SMILER.

Smyth, Smythe, Smythson *see* SMITH.

Snawley (Eng) This looks like a transferred English place name, but no trace of such a place can be found.

Dickens makes quiet fun of the name in *Nicholas Nickleby*: '"My name is Snawley, sir," said the stranger. 'Squeers inclined his head, as much to say, "And a remarkably pretty name, too".'

Snell, Snelling, Snelman, Snellman, Snelson (Eng) The Middle English *snell* meant 'lively, active' and this would originally have been a nickname for such a person.

An epitaph from an English churchyard suggests that the name Snell is not always an apt one:

Poor Martha Snell, she's gone away

She would if she could but she could not stay

She'd two bad legs and a baddish cough

But her legs it was that carried her off.

Snoddie, Snoddy (Scot) A nickname based on a northern dialectal word *snod* 'neat, smart.'

This name does not sound especially attractive in itself, but the person who bears it may make up for that. Lorene Snoddy, (together with Alberta *Futch*, Flora *Sleeper* and Roberta *Tarbox*) were bathing beauties who took part in the Miss America contest.

Snooks (Eng) Several surname authorities accept that this surname derives ultimately from the place name Sevenoaks, through an intermediary form such as *Sinnocks*. Professor Weekley cites a 16th century reference to the Kentish town as *Senock*. Bardsley mentions early examples of Senenoke and *Snouk*. Cottle, followed by Hanks and Hodges, prefers to look to a Middle English word *snoke* 'projecting piece of land.'

H.G. Wells, in the meantime, had based his amusing story, *Miss Winchelsea's Heart*, on the problems created by Snooks. Miss Winchelsea, a very refined young lady, is attracted to a young man – until she learns his name: 'Snooks! The name struck Miss

Winchelsea like a blow in the face . . . Of all offensive surnames –
Snooks! From the moment that it first rang upon her ears, the dream
of her happiness was prostrate in the dust. All the refinement she
had figured was ruined and defaced by that cognomen's unavoid-
able vulgarity . . . She conceived herself being addressed as Snooks
by all the people she liked least, conceived the patronymic touched
with a vague quality of insult. She figured a card of grey and silver
bearing "Winchelsea" triumphantly effaced by an arrow, Cupid's
arrow, in favour of "Snooks." She imagined the terrible rejoicings
of certain girl friends, of certain grocer cousins from whom her
growing refinement had long since estranged her. How they would
make it sprawl across the envelope that would bring their sarcastic
congratulations. Would even his pleasant company compensate for
that? "It is impossible," she muttered; "impossible! Snooks"!' The
young man marries Miss Winchelsea's friend. Eventually, at the
request of his wife, he deals with the Snooks problem by restoring
it to the respectable Sevenoaks.

Snooks became for a time the name applied to a hypothetical
person, rather like *Joe Bloggs*. Hotten's *Dictionary of Slang* (1860)
had an entry: 'Snooks, an imaginary personage often brought forward as the answer to an idle question, or as the perpetrator of a
senseless joke.' As late as 1959 *The Times*, in an article on answer-
phones, was reporting: 'The recommended formula goes something
like this: "This is Flaxway 5768. Mr. Snooks is out. If you wish to
leave a message, go ahead." Snooks, returning eventually to base,
presses a button, and the machine reels off all the messages.'

Socksmith, Sixsmith, Sucksmith (Eng) Occupational name for a
maker of 'socks,' a word used in dialect to mean a 'ploughshare.'

Solace, Sollas *see* COMFORT.

Souter *see* SEWER.

South, Southern, Sotherton (Eng) Descendant of someone who
lived south of a village, or who had come there from further south.
See WEST.

Southam (Eng) From residence in one of the places so-named
because it was the 'southern homestead.'

Southern, Sotherton *see* SOUTH.

Sowerby (Eng) Someone who came from one of the several places so-named because it was a 'farm with muddy ground.'

Sowter *see* SEWER.

Sparrow (Eng) A nickname from the bird, commenting on some aspect of behaviour, such as chirpiness, that the sparrow suggests. Marie de L. Welch associated the sparrow with arrogance:

> The viewpoint of the sparrow
> Is arrogant and narrow,
> He knows that he excels.
> He is selfishly obsessed;
> He would not give an ostrich best.
> His children leave the shells
> Puffed to their very marrows
> With pride at being sparrows.

Spence, Despenser, Spencer, Spens, Spenser (Eng) Occupational name for a dispenser of provisions, a household servant very similar to a butler or steward.

The short jacket called a *spencer* was first worn by Earl Spencer, an 18th century contemporary of John Montagu, 4th Earl of Sandwich, after whom the sandwich is named. An anonymous humorist of the time was responsible for:

> Two noble earls, whom, if I quote,
> Some folks might call me sinner,
> The one invented half a coat,
> The other half a dinner.
> The plan was good, as some will say
> And fitted to console one,
> Because in this poor starving day
> Few can afford a whole one.

Michael Crawford's portrayal of an accident-prone Frank Spencer in the television series *Some Mothers Do 'Ave 'Em* was very popular in the 1970s.

Spendlove, Spendlow, Spenlow *see* CATCHLOVE.

Spens, Spenser *see* SPENCE.

Spicknell, Spickernell (Eng) An occupational name, describing the legal official who was 'a sealer of writs.'

Spiller, Spillman (Eng) Occupational name of a 'juggler, tumbler, actor.'

Spindler (Eng) A maker and seller of spindles.

Spindlowe *see* CATCHLOVE.

Spittle, Spital, Spitall, Spittel, Spitteler, Spittler, Spittles (Eng) Occupational name of someone who worked in a 'hospital,' originally a house of rest for pilgrims, travellers and strangers.

Spooner (Eng) Occupational name for a maker of spoons. As Canon Bardsley pointed out, this was an important trade in the Middle Ages, when no forks were used and meals often consisted of stews and soups.

The Rev. W.A. Spooner, Warden of New College, Oxford, occasionally transposed initial letters, or syllables, or even words, but most spoonerisms that are quoted today (and all those that are ribald) are modern inventions. Attributed to him is the comment: 'I remember your name perfectly well, but I just can't think of your face.'

Stainer, Stainman, Steiner, Steinor (Eng) Occupational name of a man who dyed fabrics or glass.

Stamp, Stamps (Norman) A name which links with *Etampes* (earlier *Estampes*) in Normandy. This ancient place was settled before Roman times and has a Celtic name of obscure meaning.

The modern English surname is interpreted quite differently, of course. The *Financial Times* mentioned in 1970 that 'there is a Post Office near Shaftesbury run by a Mr and Mrs Stamp and their daughter Penny.' The same article claimed to have discovered dentists named *Tooth, Screech* and *Fillingham*, as well as a Belgian journalist called Schoop. The dental roll-call was matched by the three doctors named *Aiken, Sorrow* and *Paine* who once worked in the same hospital.

Stanley, Stanleigh, Standly, Stanly (Eng) Descendant of someone who came from any of the English places named because it was a 'stony clearing.' *See* BROWN.

Stansfield, Stansfeld (Eng) From residence in the Yorkshire place so-named because it was '*Stan's* pasture' or because it was 'stone field,' ie one with a monolith.

Stansfield was the family name of Gracie Fields, the immensely popular English singer and entertainer. Her mother shortened the surname when a theatrical agent said it would be too long to fit on posters. For exactly the opposite view, *see* VALENTINE.

The rather similar name FAIRFIELD, also found as FEARFIELD, refers to a 'dweller by a fair field' and is the real name of the British novelist Rebecca West.

It would seem that surnames with -field as a second element are not popular, though the American actress Jayne Mansfield saw nothing wrong with them. She had been born Vera Jayne Palmer, but was glad to be known by her married name MANSFIELD – indicating someone who originally came from the English place of that name which means 'open land by the Mam (name of a hill.') There are many other place-names turned surnames which end in *-field*, often of obvious meaning: BEACONSFIELD, DITCHFIELD, GREENFIELD, WESTFIELD, but DANGERFIELD (see that entry) is not what it seems. *Copperfield* appears to be a Dickensian invention.

Stapleton (Eng) Someone who came from one of the several places so-named because it was a 'settlement with a boundary post.'

Starbeck, Starbuck (Eng) From residence in Starbeck, Yorkshire, a place so-named because of its 'sedge brook.'

L.J. Davis, in *Walking Small*, writes: ' "My mother's grandmother was a Starbuck." Coffin had always thought that the name Starbuck had been made up by the guy who wrote *Moby Dick* – or at least by the guy who wrote the movie script for *Moby Dick* – and not even made up very well.' As it happens, Melville could certainly have come across a real life Starbuck after whom he could name the chief mate on the *Pequod* in *Moby Dick*. The name occurs in American directories.

Starkweather *see* FOULWEATHER.

Starns *see* STERN.

Statham (Eng) From residence in the Cheshire place, so-named because it was a 'homestead with landing-stage.'

Steady (Eng) Probably a nickname for a man of steady character.

Stearn, Stearne, Stearns *see* STERN.

Steeve, Steeves, Steve, Steves, Stief, Stiff (Ger) The Steeves of North America claim that they are all descendants of Heinrich and Rachel *Stief*, who arrived in America from Germany in 1766. They had seven sons to help them perpetuate the anglicized form of their name, which meant 'stiff, unbending.'

Some years ago there was a Steeves reunion, hosted by the British Columbia branch of the family. Representatives of the estimated 200,000 people who now bear a form of this name gathered appropriately in Steveston, named in the 19th century after William Herbert Steves. Clan gatherings, of people sharing the same surname, occur fairly regularly, but it is rare for them to claim descent with certainty from the same ancestors.

Steiner, Steinor *see* STAINER.

Stern, Starns, Stearn, Stearne, Stearns, Sterne (Eng) Nickname for a man of stern disposition.

Steve, Steves *see* STEEVE.

Steward, Steuart, Stewardson, Stewart, Stewartson, Stuart (Eng, Scot) An official who controlled the domestic affairs of a manor, an estate manager. At its highest level, a stewardship referred to control of the royal household – the Lord High Steward of Scotland was the king's first officer – but most modern bearers of this name have a less exalted ancestor.

Stickler (Eng) Weekley thinks that this name referred to an umpire, but *stickle* in the sense of 'act as a referee' is only recorded from the 16th century. The surname perhaps derives from a Middle English word of similar meaning.

Stiddard *see* STODDARD.

Stidolf, Stidolph (Eng) Descendant of *Stithwulf,* an Old English personal name composed of elements meaning 'hard' and 'wolf.'

Stief, Stiff *see* STEEVE.

St Maur *see* BROWN.

Stoat *see* STOTT.

Stoddard, Stiddard, Stodart, Stoddart, Stodhart, Stothard, Stothart, Stothert, Studart, Studdard, Studdeard, Studdert, Stuttard, Stuttert (Eng) Occupational name for a 'keeper of stots.' A *stot* was used both of a horse and a young steer. The first element in some of these names may be 'stud,' as in a stud of horses, though this meaning of 'stud' is not otherwise recorded until well after the surname-formation period.

Stone, Stoneman, Stones (Eng) Descendant of someone who lived in one of the many places named because of its stony ground, rocky outcrop, or hundred-stone, marking a boundary. **Stoneham** 'stone homestead' is a similar place name which led to a surname. **Stonehouse** is self-explanatory. Stone could also indicate the occupation of a stone-mason.

Stothard, Stothart, Stothert *see* STODDARD.

Stott, Stoat, Stote (Eng) Nickname comparing a man to a *stot*, a young bullock, perhaps because of wild behaviour.

Strange, Lestrange, Strainge, Stranger (Eng) Nickname for someone who was a newcomer to the district, a stranger. STRANGEMAN, however, is a form of STRONGMAN. Lestrange is a Norman form of Strange.

This is obviously a name which attracts 'witty' comments. It also figures in the well-known verses:

> At a tavern one night
> Messrs Moore, Strange and Wright
> Met to drink, and their good thoughts exchange;
> Says Moore, 'Of us three
> Everyone will agree
> There's only one fool, and that's Strange.'
> Says Strange, rather sore,
> 'I'm sure there's one Moore,
> A most terrible knave, and a fright,
> Who cheated his mother,
> His sister and brother . . . '
> 'Oh, yes,' replied Moore, 'that is Wright.'

Strangeways, Strangeway, Strangewick, Strangways (Eng) Strangeways 'strong wash, current' is the name of a place near Manchester. Most bearers of the surname have an ancestor who once lived there.

The writer Nicholas Blake made the donnish detective who appears in many of his crime novels Nigel Strangeways.

Film buffs will remember Peter Sellers in the role of *Dr Strangelove*. This surname appears to be the invention of the scriptwriters Stanley Kubrick and Terry Southern.

Stratton (Eng) Someone who came from one of the several places so-named because it was a 'settlement on a Roman road.'

Streaker (Eng) This may be a nickname connected with the Middle English word streke 'severe, unyielding,' though this normally led to **Streek** and **Streake** as surnames. There was also a kind of dog bred for hunting, already known as a *streaker* by the 13th century. A nickname based on the dog would presumably have referred to the ability to run quickly, though not, as with the modern 'streaker,' unclothed and in a public place in front of thousands of spectators.

Dickens describes a Streaker in *The Haunted House*. She is a housemaid, 'a mere distillery for the production of the largest and most transparent tears I have ever met with.'

Strickland (Eng) Descendant of someone who originally came from the Cumberland place so-named because it was a 'bullock pasture.'

Strongitharm *see* ARMSTRONG.

Stuart *see* STEWARD.

Studart, Studdard, Studdeard, Studdert, Stuttard, Stuttert *see* STODDARD.

Sucksmith *see* SOCKMITH.

Suetor, Suiter, Suter *see* SEWER.

Sullivan, O'Sullivan, Sullevan (Irish) Descendant of *S£ilehabh†n,* a Gaelic personal name meaning 'black eyed' or 'keen-eyed.'

Summer, Summerhayes, Summerland, Summerleys, Summers (Eng) Descendant of someone who lived on land used for summer grazing.

Sutton (Eng) Someone who came from one of the several places so-named because it was a 'southern settlement.'

Swan, Swann (Eng) In some cases a form of **Swain,** which was a Scandinavian personal name *Sveinn* as well as a noun describing a 'servant' or sometimes a 'peasant.' A swan was used as a house-sign in medieval times; the surname may, therefore, indicate someone who lived 'at the sign of the swan.' If Swan is a nickname based on the bird, it is a comment on refinement. The swan was a royal bird and was tightly protected.

A Dictionary of English and Folk Names of British Birds, edited appropriately by H. Kirke Swann, says that the medieval punishment for stealing a swan's egg was imprisonment for a year and a day, plus a fine. The birds themselves were fattened for the tables of the privileged in 'swan-pits.' Many legends and superstitions surrounded the birds; they were thought to live for 300 years, sing when about to die (hence 'swan-song'), and so on. 'I will play the swan, and die in music' says Emilia, in Shakespeare's *Othello*.

Swanton (Eng) Someone who came from one of the several places so-named because it was a 'swain's settlement.'

Swart (Eng) Nickname for a swarthy person.

Swindell, Swindells, Swindle (Eng) Probably from residence in Swindale, Yorkshire, where the place name means 'wild boar valley.'

Swindler *see* SWINGLER.

Swinderby (Eng) Someone who came from a place so-named because it was a 'southern village.' The first part of the name is Old Scandinavian *sundri* 'southern.'

Swinerd, Swinnard (Eng) Occupational name of a swineherd.

Swingler, Swindler (Eng) Occupational name for a beater of flax or hemp. He would have used a *swingle*, a wooden instrument resembling a sword, to cleanse the material. A swingle was so-called because it was swung like a flail.

Swinton (Eng) Someone who came from one of the several places so-named because it was a 'settlement with pigs, a pig farm.'

Sym, Symcox, Symes, Symmons, Symms, Symon, Symonds, Symondson, Symons, Syms, Syson *see* SIMON.

Sythag *see* SHAW.

Taffee, Taffie *see* DAVID.

Taillefer *see* TELFER.

Tailour *see* TAYLOR.

Talbot, Talbott, Talbut (Eng) This name is of disputed origin. A *talbot* was formerly a breed of hunting dog, but it is thought to have been named for a Talbot family, of Norman descent, which included a dog in its armorial bearings. This therefore negates the explanation that the surname derives from someone living 'at the sign of a talbot.' A derivation from French *taille-botte* 'cut faggot' has also been suggested but does not meet with scholarly approval. It is perhaps from a Germanic personal name composed of the elements *tal* 'destroy' and *bod* 'message,' which Hanks and Hodges interpret as 'messenger of destruction.' *See* BROWN.

Talboys, Tallboy, Tallboys (Fre) Occupational name from Old French *tailler bosc (bois)*, referring to a woodcutter.

Talbut *see* TALBOT.

Taleford, Taylforth (Eng) Someone who originally came from Taleford, in Devon, a place named as a 'ford over the river Tale.'

Talfourd *see* TELFER.

Tallboy, Tallboys *see* TALBOYS.

Tallifer *see* TELFER.

Tamblin, Tambling, Tamblyn, Tamlin, Tamlyn, Tamplin *see* THOMAS.

Tancock, Tandy *see* ANDREW.

Tanner (Eng) Occupational name of a tanner of skins.

The name is associated by many with Elsie Tanner, leading lady of the long-running and highly successful British television series *Coronation Street*.

George Bernard Shaw had earlier created John Tanner as the

freethinking hero of *Man and Superman.*

Tapper, Tapster, Tipler (Eng) Occupational name for someone who tapped casks of ale, a beer-seller or tavern keeper. Tapster refers to a woman who pursued this trade. The earliest sense of *tippler* was also 'seller of alcohol,' though it is perhaps easy to see how the later sense of 'hard drinker' came about.

Tarbock, Tarbox, Tarbuck, Terbocke (Eng) Descendant of someone who came originally from Tarbock, Lancashire, named for its 'thorn bushes' and 'brook.' *See* SNODDIE.

Tasch *see* ASH.

Tayler, Taylerson *see* TAYLOR.

Taylforth *see* TALEFORD.

Taylor, Tailour, Tayler, Taylerson, Taylorsmith, Taylorson, Taylour (Eng) Occupational name of a tailor. Taylorsmith is a corrupt form of **Taylorsmaugh**, where the second element refers to a relative by marriage.

Teacher (Eng) Occupational name of a teacher.

Teacher's Whisky owes its name to the founder of the company, William Teacher, a Glaswegian who started his working life in a factory at the age of seven.

Tebb, Tebbell, Tebbett, Tebbitt, Tebble, Tebbs, Teed *see* THEOBALD.

Telfer, Taillefer, Talfourd, Tallifer, Telfair, Telford, Tolver, Tulliver (Fre) A man who could *taille fer* 'cut iron,' presumably the armour worn by his enemy.

Tellwright (Eng) Occupational name for a maker of tiles, bricks.

Temirzi *see* FABER.

Temple, Templar (Eng) There is usually a connection with the Knights Templar, eg a reference to someone who worked at one of the houses maintained by the Knights.

Between 1728 and 1755 Temple was the name was given to 104 foundlings who were baptized at the Temple Church, in London. Many families bearing this name must therefore have an ancestor named in such a manner.

A well-known fictional character was Paul Temple, hero of a BBC radio series which ran for thirty years and a subsequent television series, starring Francis Matthews in the title role. Even better known is the fictional hero Simon Templar, otherwise known as the Saint, created by Leslie Charteris.

Templeton (Eng) Someone who came from one of the several places so-named because it was a 'settlement belonging to the Knights Templar.'

Tenison, Tennyson *see* DENNIS.

Terbocke *see* TARBOCK.

Tesche, Tesh *see* ASH.

Thatcher, Thacker, Thaxter, Theaker (Eng) Occupational name for a roof-thatcher, Thacker and Theaker being northern English forms of the southern Thatcher. Thaxter would originally have referred to a woman who plied this trade.

Theobald, Deeble, Dibble, Diboll, Dybald, Dyball, Dybell, Tebb, Tebbell, Tebbett, Tebbitt, Tebble, Tebbs, Teed, Theed, Theobalds, Theobold, Tibb, Tibballs, Tibbett, Tibbetts, Tibbins, Tibbitts, Tibble, Tibbles, Tibbots, Tibbs, Tidbald, Tidball, Tidboald, Tidbold, Tippetts, Tippins, Tipple, Tipples, Tipson, Tudball (Eng) Descendant of a man named *Theobald,* a Germanic personal name composed of elements meaning 'people' and 'bold.' *Tibbald* was the earlier pronunciation, reflecting Norman French usage. Old French forms of the name included Teobaud, Tibaut as well as *Thibaut, Theobald* and the initial *Th-* would always have been pronounced *T-* by French speakers. *See* TUBB.

Thickpenny *see* PENNY.

Thirlby (Eng) Someone who came from a place so-named because it was the 'village of the thralls, or bondmen, in bondage to a lord or master.'

Thomas, Tamblin, Tambling, Tamblyn, Tamlin, Tamlyn, Tamplin, Thom, Thomaset, Thomasson, Thomazin, Thomerson, Thomline, Thomlinson, Thompsett, Thompson, Thoms, Thomsett, Thomson, Tolson, Tom, Tomalin, Tomas, Tombleson, Tomblin, Tombling, Tomblings, Tombs, Tome, Tomes, Tomkies, Tomkin, Tomkins, Tomkinson, Tomkys, Tomlin, Tomline, Tomlins, Tomlinson, Tomsen, Tompkin, Tompkins, Tompkinson, Tompset, Tompson, Tomsett, Tomson, Toombes, Toombs, Toulson, Towlson, Townson (Eng) Descendant of *Thomas,* an Aramaic name meaning 'twin.' As the name of one of the Apostles it was much used in mediaeval times, with dialectal variations in pronunciation and spelling. There seems to be little doubt about the origin of these names, but R.A.McKinley says in his *Norfolk Surnames in the Sixteenth Century*: 'The surname Thompson is no doubt often a patronymic, but it must also at times be derived from the Norfolk village of Thompson, earlier *Tumeston* or *Thompston*, as the occurrence in the sixteenth century of the forms *Thompston* or *Tompston* indicates.'

In 1832 Joseph Thompson, a farmer who had been married for three years, made a public announcement in Carlisle that his wife was for sale. He duly sold her at an auction that day to a man named Henry Mears for twenty shillings and a Newfoundland dog. These wife-auctions occurred regularly at the beginning of the 19th century, usually with the wife's agreement, because the marriage had broken down. It was commonly believed in rural areas that such sales were the equivalent of a legal divorce. By coincidence, it is recorded that another Thompson offered his wife for sale in 1858, at Little Horton near Bradford, though some years earlier, in Yorkshire, a man had been committed to prison and hard labour for a month for attempting to dispose of his wife in this way. Thomas Hardy commented on this practice in *The Mayor of Casterbridge*. In the novel Henchard sells his wife Susan and their daughter Elizabeth Jane for five shillings to a sailor.

Thornton (Eng) Someone who came from one of the several places so-named because it was a 'settlement where thorn bushes grew.'

Thoroughgood, Thorogood, Thorowgood (Eng) A complimentary nickname for someone who was 'thoroughly good, good throughout.'

Thorp, Thorpe, Thripp, Thrupp (Eng) Descendant of someone who lived in a *thorp*, an Old Norse word for 'village,' or came from one of the many places called Thorp, Thorpe.

Threadgold, Threadgill, Thridgould, Tredgold (Eng) It was the task of an embroiderer to 'thread gold.'

Thrift *see* FIRTH.

Thrower (Eng) An occupational name, of several possible origins. The earliest sense of throw was twist or turn. A thrower could have turned wood on a lathe, used a potter's wheel, or twisted raw silk into thread.

Thurston (Eng) Someone who came from a place so-named because it was the 'settlement of *Thori's* people.'

Tibb, Tibballs, Tibbett, Tibbetts, Tibbins, Tibbitts, Tibble, Tibbles, Tibbots, Tibbs *see* THEOBALD.

Tickle, Tickel, Tickell (Eng) From residence in Tickhill, Yorkshire, so-named because it was '*Tica's* hill.'

In *The Glory of the Hummingbird*, Peter de Vries explains Tickler in an American context: ' "Tickler is a rather unusual name," he said. I made what has necessarily become a set speech. "It's an Americanization of Tichelar," I said, spelling it out. "Tichel is the Dutch word for brick, tichelaar for tile worker or brick-layer. Anyway, I might as well have been sea-changed into Jimmy Bricklayer – or James Mason – as Jimmy Tickler, which is simply a phonetic spelling of the way the name has always been pronounced here in this country.'

Tidbald, Tidball, Tidboald, Tidbold *see* THEOBALD.

Tidmas, Tidmus *see* TITMARSH.

Till, Tille, Tillet, Tillot, Tillotson, Tills, Tilson (Eng) Descendant of *Matilda* 'might - battle.' *See* MAUDE.

Tingle, Tingler (Eng) A maker of 'tingles,' small nails.

Tiplady *see* LOVELADY.

Tipler *see* TAPPER.

Tippeny *see* PENNY.

Tippetts, Tippins, Tipple, Tipples, Tipson *see* THEOBALD.

Tipton (Eng) Someone who came from a place so-named because it was the 'settlement of *Tibba's* people.'

Titmarsh, Tidmas, Tidmus, Titmass, Titmouse, Titmuss (Eng) Probably from residence in Tidmarsh, Berkshire, a place so-named because it was '*Tydda's* marsh.' **Titchmarsh** also exists as an English place name, indicating '*Ticcea's* marsh.' This too could have given rise to the surname. By this explanation, the Titmouse variants would merely be altered spellings. They might instead represent a nickname based on the bird, commenting on a person's small size.

Thackeray has a *History of Samuel Titmarsh*, in which occurs: '"Mr Titmarsh," says the Commissioner, with a peculiar sarcastic accent on the Tit-'.

Todd, Tod (Eng, Scot) *Tod* is a dialectal word for a fox. The surname probably began as a nickname for someone who was 'foxy,' ie cunning, or having the colouring of a fox. **Todhunter** also exists as a surname, and is of obvious meaning. **Todkill** looks equally obvious, but in fact means 'descendant of a man named *Theogild*, a Germanic personal name composed of the elements 'god' and 'pledge.'

When the 1936 film version of the *Sweeney Todd* story was made, the role of the 'demon barber' of Fleet Street, who turned the bodies of his victims into meat pies, was appropriately played by an actor named Tod Slaughter.

Togod *see* TOOGOOD.

Tolson *see* THOMAS.

Tolver *see* TELFER.

Tom, Tomalin, Tomas, Tombleson, Tomblin, Tombling, Tomblings, Tombs, Tome, Tomes, Tomkies, Tomkin, Tomkins, Tomkinson, Tomkys, Tomlin, Tomline, Tomlins, Tomlinson, Tomsen, Tompkin, Tompkins, Tompkinson, Tompset, Tompson, Tomsett, Tomson *see* THOMAS.

Toogood, Togod, Tougod, Towgood, Tugwood, Twogood (Eng) Literally, a reference to someone who was 'too good,' but more likely to be a sarcastic comment than a sincere one.

Toombes, Toombs *see* THOMAS.

Tooth (Eng) Nickname for someone whose teeth (or tooth) attracted particular attention. For the inevitable dentist of this name, *see* STAMP.

Topham (Eng) From residence in a place perhaps so-named because it was '*Toppa's* homestead.'

Toplady, Toplass, Topley, Topliss *see* LOVELADY.

Tougod, Towgood *see* TOOGOOD.

Toulson, Towlson *see* THOMAS.

Townley, Towneley, Townsley (Eng) Someone originally from Towneley, Lancashire, a place named because it was a 'settlement in a clearing.'

'I wish, my dear,' says a character in Samuel Butler's *The Way of all Flesh*, 'you could cultivate your acquaintance with Towneley, and ask him to pay me a visit. The name has an aristocratic sound.'

Townsend, Townend, Townshend (Eng) Names indicating an

ancestor who lived on the outskirts of a village.

Townsley *see* TOWNLEY.

Townson *see* THOMAS.

Toy, Toye (Eng) A northern English name for a maker of 'toys' (close-fitting caps).

Tracey, Tracy (Eng) Descendant of someone who originally came from places called *Tracy* in Normandy, named in their turn after a Roman called *Thracius*.

Dick Tracy was the widely syndicated comic-strip detective created by Chester Gould. The British press reported in the early 1990s that the male colleagues of a woman police constable called Tracy had nicknamed her Dickless Tracy.

Women like the constable whose first name is Tracy or Tracey probably owe the name indirectly to Philip Barry, who wrote a play called *The Philadelphia Story* in which there was a character called Tracy Samantha Lord. In the filmed musical version of this play, *High Society*, Grace Kelly played this part and launched both Tracy and Samantha (as well as Kelly) as first names in Britain.

Treacher (Eng) Uncomplimentary nickname for a 'trickster' or 'traitor,' from Old French *trecheor,* modern French *tricheur.*

Shakespeare uses *treacher* to mean 'traitor' in *King Lear*: 'Knaves, thieves, and treachers by spherical predominance.'

Trebell (Cornish) From residence in the Cornish place, so named because it was a 'distant homestead.' The element *tre* 'homestead' occurs as a first element in many other Cornish place names that have become surnames. The meaning of the second element cannot always be deciphered. Typical names are **Trebarthen, Trebilcock, Tredinnick, Tredrea, Tredray, Tredwen, Treen, Treffry, Frefusis, Tregale, Treganowan, Tregarthen, Tregaskes, Tregaskis, Tregea, Tregay, Tregeagle, Tregagle, Tregear, Tregenna, Tregunna, Tregenza, Tregilgas, Treglown, Tregoning, Trehane, Trehearne, Trelawney, Trelawny, Trelease, Treleaven, Treleven, Tremaine, Tremayne, Trembeth, Tremelling, Tremethick, Tremewan, Trenance, Trenear, Trenhaile, Trenwith, Trestain, Trestrail, Trethowan, Trevain, Trevan, Treverton, Trevean, Trevelyan, Trevenna, Trewen, Trewin.** Bearers of such names should see further such works as *A Handbook of Cornish Surnames*, by G. Pawley White.

Tredgold *see* THREADGOLD.

Trimble *see* TURNBULL.

Trohy, Troy (Irish) Forms of the Gaelic *O Troighthigh* 'foot sol-dier.' Edward MacLysaght points out in his *Surnames of Ireland* that *Troyswood* in Co. Kilkenny was named after the **De Troys**, an Anglo-Norman family. The name in this case would refer to a French place name such as Troy, Troyes or Troyon.

Evelyn Waugh has the following exchange in *Unconditional Surrender*: 'What's her name?' 'Troy, I think. It was when I last saw her.' 'Mrs Troy?' 'Yes.' 'Funny name.'

Trumble, Trumbull *see* TURNBULL.

Truslove, Truslow, Trussler *see* CATCHLOVE.

Tubb, Tubbs, Tubby (Eng) Descendant of a man called *Tubbi*, an Old Norse personal name, or of Theobald, as suggested by Bardsley in his *Dictionary of English and Welsh Surnames*.

Tucker, Tuckwell (Eng) A fuller, who cleaned and thickened fresh-ly woven cloth. Compare FULLER and WALKER.

Tudball *see* THEOBALD.

Tugwell (Eng) Possibly a form of TUCKWELL, or a reference to a wrestler.

Tugwood *see* TOOGOOD.

Tulliver *see* TELFER.

Tully (Irish) Anglicized form of a Gaelic name. If the original name was *Teathleach* the meaning would be 'peace-loving,' but the traditional derivation is from the Gaelic word *tuile*, 'flood.'

Tupper (Eng) A herdsman in charge of 'tups,' uncastrated male sheep.

Turnbull, Turnbill (Eng) A nickname for a strong man, able to throw down a bull, or another form of TRUMBULL, TRUMBLE, TRIMBLE, where the meaning is strong and brave.

Turner, Turnor, Turnour (Eng) Normally an occupational name of a wood-turner. In rare instances the name was originally *Turnhare*, referring to a man who could run faster than a hare and turn it back. 'Operator of a turnspit' or 'official in charge of a tournament' are also possible. The derivation that has been proposed from French *la tour noire* 'the black tower,' hinting at occupation of a Norman castle, is pure fantasy. *See* DUCK.

Tweddle, Twaddle, Tweddell, Tweedale, Tweedle (Eng) Indicating an ancestor who lived in the dale (valley) of the River Tweed.

Twiceaday *see* DOUBLEDAY.

Twining, Twineham, Twinham, Twyning (Eng) From residence in one of the places so-named because it was 'between the streams.' In *Naming Day in Eden*, Noah Jonathan Jacobs quotes:

> It seems as if Nature had curiously planned
> That our name with our trades should agree.
> There's Twining, the Tea-man, who lives in the Strand,
> Would be whining if robbed of his T.

The opposite view was long ago expressed by James Smith. The first two verses (of seven) of his poem run:

> Men once were surnamed from their shape or estate
> (You may all from History worm it);
> There was Lewis the Bulky, and Henry the Great,
> John Lackland, and Peter the Hermit.
> But now, when the door-plates of Misters and Dames
> Are read, each so constantly varies
> From the owner's trade, figure, and calling,
> Surnames seem given by the rule of contraries.
> Mr Box, though provoked, never doubles his fist,
> Mr Burns, in his grate, has no fuel;
> Mr Playfair won't catch me at hazard or whist,
> Mr Coward was wing'd in a duel.
> Mr Wise is a dunce, Mr King is a whig,
> Mr Coffin's uncommonly sprightly,
> And huge Mr Little broke down in a gig,
> While driving fat Mrs Golightly.

Twogood *see* TOOGOOD.

Twopenny *see* PENNY.

Ugo *see* HUGH.

Uncle, Uncles, Ungles (Eng) In some instances this is *uncle*, the term of relationship. The earlier word in English of the same meaning was *eme,* which gave rise to the surnames EAMES, HEAMS, HEMES. The Sussex Uncles derive their surname from someone who bore the Old Norse personal name *Ulfketell* 'wolf cauldron.'

Underhill, Undrell (Eng) From residence in a place so-named because it was 'at the bottom of a hill.' **Underdown** is a similar name.

Underwater (Eng) From residence 'south of a stream or river.'

Underwood (Eng) From residence in one of the places so-named because it was below a wood on a hillside. It could also refer to someone who lived within a wood, under its trees.

Undrell *see* UNDERHILL.

Unthank (Eng) From residence in one of the places so-named because it was occupied 'without permission.' Ekwall, in *The Oxford Dictionary of English Place Names,* glosses the name as 'squatter's farm.'

Unwin, Hunwin (Eng) In some instances this name refers to somebody considered to be an enemy, literally an 'un-friend.' But there was an Old English personal name *Hunwin* composed of elements meaning 'bear-cub' and 'friend.' Some bearers of this name, including those who spell it without the initial *h*, are 'descendants of a man called Hunwin.'

Upham (Eng) From residence in a place so-named because it was the 'upper homestead.'

Upjohn (Eng) A form of Welsh *ap John* 'son of John.'

Upton (Eng) Someone who came from one of the several places so-named because it was an 'upper settlement.'

Urquhart (Scot) From the barony of this name on Loch Ness, Inverness-shire. Black says in his *Surnames of Scotland* that the name is normally pronounced *Orchar, Urchard* being an earlier spelling.

William Faulkner claims (see **Ingram**) that Urquhart became *Workitt* in Mississippi.

Usherwood *see* ISHERWOOD.

Ustinov *see* JUSTIN.

Vahy *see* MACBETH.

Vairow *see* FARRER.

Vale, Vail, Vaile (Eng) From residence in a valley.

Valentine, Valentin, Vallentin, Vallentine (Eng) Descendant of a man named *Valentine,* Latin 'to be strong, healthy.'

There are two saints of this name, but Donald Attwater, in *A Dictionary of Saints*, remarks that 'there is nothing in either Valentine legend to account for the custom of choosing a partner of the opposite sex and sending "valentines" on 14 February.'

One of the great names in the history of the cinema is Rudolph Valentino. A character in Garson Kanin's novel *Moviola* comments: 'Alan Bolt? Nothing. Let's get a name for him, somebody. A long one. That one is too short. It's over before you know it. I like long names. They look bigger on the billing. People think they are getting more for their money. Like Rudolph Valentino, now there's a good name.' The speaker would obviously have been pleased with Valentino's real name, which was Rodolpho Alfonzo Raffaelo Pierre Filibert Guglielmi di Valentina d'Antonguolla.

Valiant (Eng) Nickname for a valiant man.

Vallentin *see* VALENTINE.

Vallet, Vallett, Vallette (Eng) Occupational name of a 'manservant, a valet.' **Valley** may also belong here, if it does not indicate residence in a valley.

Valois, Vallis (Fre) Descendant of someone who came from Valois in northern France.

Van, Vance, Vane, Vann, Vanne *see* FENN.

Vanner, Vannah, Vannar *see* FANNER.

Vanns *see* Fenn.

Varah *see* FARRER.

Vardy *see* VERITY.

Varey, Varro, Varrow *see* FARRER.

Varty *see* VERITY.

Vary, Varyer *see* FARRER.

Vaughan, Vaughn (Eng) Anglicized form of Welsh *Fychan*, itself a mutated form of *Bychan* 'little,' used to distinguish a father and son of the same name.

Vavasour, Vassar, Vawser (Eng) Old French *vavassour* originally referred to a feudal tenant ranking immediately below a baron, but his status declined after the 12th century.

Veigh *see* MACBETH.

Velden *see* FIELD.

Venables (Eng) Descendant of someone who came from the French place of this name, which was once a 'hunting ground.'

Venn, Venning *see* FENN.

Venner (Eng) In some instances a doublet of FENNER, indicating someone who lived in a fen. In other cases a French version of Hunter, Old French *veneour* having that sense.

Vergin, Vergo *see* VIRGIN.

Verity, Vardy, Varty (Eng) Descendant of someone who played the role of *Veritas* 'truth' in a medieval miracle play. The amateur actors in these religious plays probably repeated their role each year, so that the name stuck to them. Personifications of abstract ideas were a feature of the plays, other characters including *Death, Mercy, Justice, Peace,* all of which led to surnames.

Vernon (Eng) Descendant of someone who came from a French place of this name, which is based on a word meaning 'alder tree.'

Villiers (Eng) Descendant of someone who came from any of the French places named for its 'outlying farm.'

Vincent, Vincett, Vinsen, Vinson (Eng) Descendant of *Vincent* 'conquering.' It was the name of several saints and used in all Christian countries. In Italy, for example, it led to surnames such as *De Vincenzo* and *Da Vinci*.

Virgin, Vergin, Vergo, Virgo, Virgoe (Eng) Perhaps a descendant of someone (it would have been a young man) who played the part of the *Virgin Mary* in a medieval pageant. Residence near a statue of the Virgin has also been suggested. Basil Cottle remarks in his

Penguin Dictionary of Surnames that it may be an 'impudent joke,' presumably referring to a chaste man or ironically to one who was a lecher.

Voller *see* FULLER.

Vowell, Vowells, Vowels, Vowles see FOWLE. Lower relates in his *Patronymica Britannica* that 'when the eccentric Dr Barton, Warden of Merton College, Oxford, was informed that Dr Vowell had died he remarked: "Let us be glad 'tis neither *u* or *i*".'

Vowler *see* FOWLER.

Vowles *see* FOWLE.

Vreede *see* FIRTH.

Waddington (Eng) Someone who came from one of the several places so-named because it was the 'settlement of *Wada's* people.' The Surrey place of this name was originally a 'wheat hill.'

Wade, Wadeson, Waide, Waidson (Eng) Descendant of someone who lived by a ford, or of a man who bore the Old English name *Wada*, from *wadan* 'to go.' Wade was known as the name of a sea-giant, 'dreaded and honoured by the coast tribes of the North Sea' according to Chambers.

Wader, Wadman, Wademan, Waider, Wodeman (Eng) Occupational name for a gatherer and seller of 'woad,' a plant which gives a blue dye. The ancient Britons made use of it to dye themselves.

Wadman *see* WADER.

It is Widow Wadman who hilariously tries to seduce Tristram's uncle in Laurence Sterne's *Tristram Shandy*.

Wadsworth, Wardsworth, Wordsworth (Eng) From residence in Wadsworth, Yorkshire, a place so-named because it was '*Waeddi's* enclosure.'

Bardesley pointed out the curious coincidence of Wadsworth being Henry Wadsworth Longfellow's middle name, giving the name an even stronger link with poetry than that provided by William Wordsworth.

Wafer (Eng) Occupational name of a wafer-maker, especially the thin bread used in communion services. But 'wafers' were also thin cakes, spiced or sweetened.

Wagstaff, Wagstaffe (Eng) Occupational name of a functionary, such as a beadle, who wielded a staff of office. The editors of *A Dictionary of Surnames* (Oxford University Press) make the suggestion that these names, along with **Waghorn, Waghorne** and even SHAKESPEARE, might also have been obscene nicknames for a medieval flasher, 'one who brandished his "staff" publicly.' There is no direct evidence, however, that words like *staff* and *horn* meant 'penis' in the slang of the surname-formation period. If such evidence exists, it seems to have eluded Eric Partridge, who spent a lifetime studying the bawdy slang of previous generations. Nor do any quotations in the *Oxford English Dictionary* support such a statement.

Perhaps Groucho Marx was reading an obscene meaning into the name when he said, in *Horse Feathers*: 'You're a disgrace to our family name of *Wagstaff*, if such a thing is possible.'

Waide *see* WADE.

Waider *see* WADER.

Waidson *see* WADE.

Wailer *see* WHEEL.

Wainwright, Wainewright, Wainwrigt, Wenwright, Winwright (Eng) Occupational name for a wagon-maker.

Waistcoat *see* WESTBROOK.

Walker (Eng) Occupational name for someone who fulled cloth by walking on it to make it cleaner and thicker. Some bearers of the name owe it to an ancestor who came from Walker in Northumberland, so-named for its '(Roman) wall and marsh.'

Wallace, Walch, Wallice, Wallis, Walsh, Walshe, Waugh, Welch, Welsh (Scot, Irish, Eng) From an Anglo-Norman French *waleis,* connected with Old English *wealh* 'foreign,' ie 'a Celt.'

Walsingham (Eng) From residence in the Norfolk place, so-named because it was '*Waels's* homestead.'

Walter, Fitzwalter, Fitzwater, MacWalter, MacWatters, Walters, Water, Waters, Watkin, Watking, Watkins, Watkinson, Watlin, Watling, Watt, Wattis, Watts, Watters, Watterson, Whatling (Eng) Descendant of *Walter,* a Germanic personal name composed of elements meaning 'rule' and 'army.' The Normans who introduced the name to England often used the form *Wauter*. In ordinary speech the *-l-* in the name was not pronounced.

This was still the case in the 17th century, hence the comment by Suffolk in Shakespeare's *2 Henry VI*, when as a prisoner he meets Walter Whitmore:

Thy name affrights me, in whose sound is death.
A cunning man did calculate my birth
And told me that by water I should die.

Waltham (Eng) From residence in one of the places so-named because it was a 'homestead in a wood.'

Walton (Eng) Someone who came from one of the several places so-named because it was the 'settlement of the Britons' or 'settlement with a wooden wall' or 'settlement near a welling stream.'

Isaak Walton, regarded as the Father of Angling because of his work *The Compleat Angler*, also wrote several biographies. One of them, appropriately, was of Richard HOOKER.

Wane *see* GAVIN.

Warburton (Eng) Someone who came from a place so-named because it was the 'settlement of *Waerburg's* people.'

Ward, Warde, Wardman, Wards (Eng) Occupational name of a watchman or guard, or descendant of someone who lived near a guard-house or prison.

Warner, Warren, Warrender, Warrener, Warrent, Warriner (Eng) Occupational name of a game-keeper. A warren was originally an enclosed area of land where animals were bred.

Warrington (Eng) Someone who came from one of the several places so-named because it was a 'settlement near a weir.'

Wart, Wartman, Warts, Warty (Eng) Bowditch found many examples of these names in American directories. They are presumably English versions of the German names *Warth, Warthe, Warther* and *Wartmann*, which Hans Bahlow, in his *Deutsches Namenlexikon,* explains as referring to a 'watchman, guardian.' The Old Norse element present in some English place names (*see* WARTH) has a similar basic meaning.

Shakespeare seems to have been familiar with Wart as a surname, since he makes Thomas Wart one of Falstaff's recruits in *2 Henry IV,* Falstaff puns on the names of all the men during the recruitment scene, and asks 'Is thy name Wart?' 'Yea, sir.' 'Thou art a very ragged wart,' says Falstaff, with an allusion to the ragwort plant.

In 1965 James Pennethorne Hughes made *Is Thy Name Wart?* the title of his little book on 'the origins of some curious and other surnames.' One curious name for which he forgot to offer an explanation was Wart.

Warth (Eng) From residence in one of the places with the Old Norse element *vartha* 'beacon' as an element in its name.

Washington (Eng) Someone who came from one of the two English places of this name, which means the 'settlement of *Wassa's* people.'

Water, Waters *see* WALTER.

Waterston, Waterton (Eng) Someone who came from a place so-named because it was '*Walter's* settlement.'

Watkin, Watking, Watkins, Watkinson, Watlin, Watling, Watson, Watt, Wattis, Watts, Watters, Watterson see **Walter.**

Dr John Watson is theoretically the admiring chronicler of Sherlock Holmes's investigative triumphs, though Arthur Conan Doyle also had a hand in the matter.

Waugh *see* WALLACE.

Wayler *see* WHEEL.

Weafor *see* WEAVER.

Weather, Weathers (Eng) Occupational name of a shepherd, who tended the *wethers* 'castrated rams.' It has also been suggested that this could be a nickname for someone who was like a wether, though in this case it is difficult to see how the name could have been passed on.

Weaver, Weafer, Weavers (Eng) Occupational name for a weaver, or someone who lived near the River Weaver in Cheshire.

Webb, Webber, Webster, (Eng) Occupational name for a weaver. *See* DUCK.

Welby (Eng) Someone who came from a place so-named because it was '*Ali's* village.' The same Old Norse personal name is found in the place name or surname AILBY.

Well, Wellen, Weller, Wellerman, Wellin, Welling, Wellings, Wellman, Wellon, Wells, Welman (Eng) From residence near a welling stream or pool. In some instances, however, the meaning of Wellerman and Wellman may be 'descendant of *Guillemin* or *Willemin*,' diminutives of *Guillaume* 'William.' Yet another explanation becomes possible in a Welsh context, *see* LEWIS.

Dickens made the name of Samuel Weller famous in *The Pickwick Papers*. He no doubt took the name from Mary Weller, a servant who looked after him when he was a child.

Welch, Welsh *see* WALLACE.

Wells, Welman *see* WELL.

Wenham (Eng) From residence in a place so-named because it was a 'homestead in a meadow.'

Wennell (Eng) Descendant of *Wynhild,* an Old English personal name with elements meaning 'joy' and 'war.'

Wentworth (Eng) From residence in one of the places so-named because it was a 'settlement inhabited only in winter,' though it might also be the 'settlement of *Wintra's* people.'

Sir Walter Elliot in Jane Austen's *Persuasion* remarks: 'Wentworth? Oh, ay – Mr Wentworth, the curate of Monkford. You misled me by the term "gentleman." I thought you were speaking of some man of property: Mr Wentworth was nobody, I remember; quite unconnected; nothing to do with the Strafford family. One wonders how the names of many of our nobility become so common.'

Wenwright *see* WAINWRIGHT.

Werberserch-Piffel *see* LANE.

Wescot, Wescott, Weskett *see* WESTBROOK.

Wesley, Westley, Westly (Eng) Descendant of someone who came from any of the many places named in connection with a 'western wood or clearing.'

West, Wester, Westerman, Western, Westman (Eng) Descendant of someone who lived to the west of a settlement or came from somewhere further west. It is claimed that West occurs far more frequently as a surname than NORTH, SOUTH or EAST.

Westbrook, Westbrooke, Westbrock (Eng) Descendant of someone who came from any of the places named for its 'western brook'. Similar names are **Westbury** 'west fortress' **Westby** 'west settlement' **Wescot, Wescott, Weskett, Westacott, Westcoate, Westcot, Westcote, Westcott,** WESTICOTT 'west cottage' WESTGATE, WESTHEAD 'west headland' **Westrop** 'west village' **Westwood**. The curious name **Waistcoat** also belongs here, as a variant of Wescot.

Wester, Westerman, Western *see* WEST.

Westfield *see* STANSFIELD.

Westicott, Westgate, Westhead *see* WESTBROOK.

Westlake *see* EASTLAKE.

Westley, Westly *see* WESLEY.

Westman *see* WEST.

Weston (Eng) Someone who came from one of the several places so-named because it was the 'western settlement.'

Westrop, Westwood *see* WESTBROOK.

Whaler *see* WHEEL.

Wharton (Eng) Someone who came from one of the several places so-named, either because it was a 'settlement on the river *Waefer*' or 'settlement by an embankment.'

Whatling *see* WALTER.

Wheel, Wailer, Wayler, Whaler, Wheal, Wheale, Whealer, Wheals, Wheele, Wheeler, Wheeller, Wheels, Wheelwright, Wheler, While, Whiler, Wiler, Wilesmith, Wyler (Eng) Occupational name for a maker of wheels. In rare instances the reference may be to someone who lived near a water-wheel, as in Wheelhouse.

Wheelan *see* WHELAN.

Wheele, Wheeler, Wheeller, Wheels, Wheelwright *see* WHEEL.

Whelan, Fylan, O'Feolane, O'Folane, O'Fylan, O'Phelane, O'Whalen, O'Whealan, Phelan, Philan, Wheelan (Irish) Descendant of *Faolán,* a Gaelic personal name based on *faol* 'wolf.'

Wheler *see* WHEEL.

Whild, Whilde *see* WILD.

While, Whiler *see* WHEEL.

Whitbread (Eng) Occupational name of a baker, or nickname of a man with a white beard. Weekley quotes an example of the same man who is recorded in the 13th century as *Whitbred* and *Whytberd*. FAIRBEARD and BLACKBEARD also exist as surnames, the latter perhaps also as BLACKBIRD, since SILVERBIRD is almost certainly 'silver beard.' MASSINGBIRD and its variant MASSINGBERD belong to this group, indicating a 'brass-coloured beard.' The surname BEARD (*Beart*) itself probably refers to an especially noticeable beard.

Whitby (Eng) Someone who came from a place so-named because it was a 'white village,' ie one with houses built of white stone. Similar place names turned surnames are WHITECROSS, WHITEFORD, WHITFORD, WHITEHORN 'white house' WHITEHOUSE, WHITELAW 'white hill' WHITELEY 'white clearing' WHITFIELD, WHITMARSH, WHITWELL.

White, Whiteing, Whites, Whiteson, Whiting, Whitson, Whitsun, Whitt, Whitte, Whitting, Whyte, Witt, Witting, Witts (Eng) Nickname for someone white of hair or complexion. *See* DUCK.

Whitecross *see* WHITBY.

Whitefoot *see* PUDDY.

Whiteford *see* WHITBY.

Whitehead (Eng) A descriptive nickname of someone with white hair.

Whitehouse *see* WHITBY.

Whiteing, Whites, Whiteson *see* WHITE.

Whitelaw *see* WHITBY.

Whitey *see* BIRDSEYE.

Whitfield *see* WHITBY.

Whitford *see* WHITBY.

Whiting *see* WHITE.

Whitmarsh *see* WHITBY.

Whitson, Whitsun, Whitt, Whitte, Whitting *see* WHITE.

Whittingham (Eng) From residence in one of the places so-named because it was '*Hwita's* homestead.'

Whittington (Eng) Someone who came from one of the several places so-named because it was the 'settlement of *Hwita's* people.'

Whitwell *see* WHITBY.

Whyte *see* WHITE.

Wick, Wicks (Eng) Descendant of someone who lived in an out-lying dairy farm, or in one of the places named for such a farm.

Wickerson *see* WILLIAMS.

Widdow, Widdas, Widders, Widdesson, Widderson, Widdess, Widdison, Widdowes, Widdows, Widdowson, Widowson (Eng) The reference is normally to a *widow* in the modern sense, but in dialectal use widow was also formerly used for *widower*. The name could refer to the person concerned or to her/his son or servant.

Wilberforce, Wilberfoss (Eng) From residence in the Yorkshire Wilberfoss, a place so-named because it was '*Wilburg's* foss (ditch).' The same feminine personal name occurs in Wilbraham 'Wilburg's homestead' and Wilburton 'Wilburg's settlement.'

Wilberforce is familiar to P.G. Wodehouse fans because it is Bertie Wooster's middle name. In *Much Obliged, Jeeves*, the hero tells his aunt Dahlia: "Concentrate on the sticky affairs of Bertram Wilberforce Wooster.' 'Wilberforce,' she murmured, as far as a woman of her outstanding lung power could murmur. 'Did I ever tell you how you got that label? It was your father's doing. The day before you were lugged to the font looking like a minor actor playing a bit part in a gangster film he won a packet on an outsider in the Grand National called that, and he insisted on you carrying on the name. Tough on you, but we all have our cross to bear.'

Wilcock, Wilcocke, Wilcocks, Wilcockson, Wilcox, Wilcoxen, Wilcoxon, Wilcoxson see WILLIAMS.

In *A Temporary Life* David Storey writes: 'I back towards the window. "Wil-cox be in fashion this year?" someone has written on the paintwork.'

Wild, Whild, Whilde, Wilde, Wilder, Wildman, Wyld, Wylds, Wylde, Wyldes (Eng) Nickname for a man who behaved in a wild fashion, or indicating someone who lived on a wild, uncultivated piece of land.

Wildey see BIRDSEYE.

Wildgoose, Wildgust, Willgoss (Eng) A nickname based on the wild (grey lag) goose. The nickname could refer simply to someone who was both a 'goose,' ie silly, and 'wild' in behaviour.

This is the goose which flies in a V formation and never attempts to overtake the leader, hence the later expression 'wild goose chase' for something which one cannot obtain.

Wildlove see LOVE.

Wiler, Wilesmith see WHEEL.

Wilford (Eng) From residence in the Nottinghamshire place, so-named because of its 'ford near willow trees.'

Dickens makes use of a name rather similar to this in *Our Mutual Friend*, where the hen-pecked Reginald Wilfer is over-run by his wife and daughters. There is the comment: 'Reginald Wilfer is a name with a rather grand sound, suggesting on first acquaintance brasses in country churches, scrolls in stained glass windows, and generally the de Wilfers who came over with the Conqueror. For it is a remarkable fact in genealogy that no DeAny ones ever came over with Anybody else.' Dickens is rather off the mark here, since very few French place names (or surnames) begin with a *W*. A name beginning *Ville-* would have been more accurate.

Wilfred, Wilfrith (Eng) Descendant of *Wilfrith,* an Old English personal name composed of elements meaning 'will-power' and 'peace.'

Willgoss *see* WILDGOOSE.

Williams, Wickerson, Wilcock, Wilcocke, Wilcocks, Wilcockson, Wilcox, Wilcoxen, Wilcoxon, Wilcoxson, Wilkerson, Wilkes, Wilkey, Wilkie, Wilkin, Wilkins, Wilkinson, Wilks, Willan, Willans, Willet, Willets, Willett, Willetts, Williamson, Willies, Willimott, Willin, Willing, Willings, Willins, Willinson, Willis, Willison, Williss, Wills, Willson, Willyams, Wilmot, Wilmott, Wilson, Wyling, Wyllis (Eng) Descendant of *William,* a name introduced to England by the Normans and composed of elements meaning 'will-power' and 'protection.' Many of the surnames are based on the pet form *Will* and a diminutive ending. William quickly became very popular as a first name, no doubt in deference to William the Conqueror. *See* DUCK *and* JONES.

A character in Anthony Powell's novel *Casanova's Chinese Restaurant* remarks: 'Carolo's real name is Wilson or Wilkinson or Parker, something rather practical and healthy like that. A surname felt to ring too much of plain common sense.'

Willoughby (Eng) Someone who came from one of the several places so-named because it was a 'village among willow trees.'

In *Sense and Sensibilty* Jane Austen writes: 'His name, he replied, was Willoughby, and his present home was at Allenham . . . Every circumstance belonging to him was interesting. His name was good, his residence was their favourite village.'

Wilman (Eng) *William's* servant.

Wilmot, Wilmott, Wilson *see* WILLIAMS.

Wilton (Eng) Someone who came from one of the several places so-named because it was a 'settlement among willow trees.'

Wimmer, Wimmers, Wynmer (Eng) Descendant of *Winmaer,* an Old English personal name meaning 'friend-famous.'

Windham *see* WYNDHAM.

Winney, Winny (Eng) Descendant of *Wyngeofu,* an Old English personal name meaning 'joy-battle.'

Winwright *see* WAINWRIGHT.

Winter, Winterman, Winters, Winterson, Wintour, Wynter, Wynters (Eng) Nickname for a gloomy person. Dr Reaney explains: 'Medieval houses often had their walls painted with scenes from biblical history, romances, etc., or allegorical subjects such as the Wheel of Fortune or the representation of Winter "with a sad and miserable face", which Henry III had painted over the fireplace in one of his rooms.'

Theodore Hook is in his usual punning mood when he writes of a tax-inspector named Winter:

Here comes Mr Winter, inspector of taxes,
I advise you to give him whatever he axes;
I advise you to give him without any flummery,
For though his name's Winter his actions are *summary*.

Names like Winter are found in other Germanic languages. In *The Glory of the Hummingbird*, Peter de Vries makes a comment on the Dutch name *Wintermoots*, transposed to the USA: '"What's your name?" "Amy." "What kind of Amy?" She drew a deep breath, as though stealing herself for an ordeal. "Wintermoots," she said, with visible strain. Then the smile broke out again, and she heaved her shoulders with a charming sigh. "Well! It's always a relief to get that over with."'

Winterbottom, Winterbotham (Eng) Resident in a settlement named because it was at the bottom of a valley used for habitation only in winter. *See* Longbottom.

Winterbourne (Eng) From residence in one of the many places so-named for its 'winter stream,' ie one which dried up in summer.

Winterton (Eng) From residence in one of the places so-named because it was a 'winter settlement' or the 'settlement of *Winter* (someone bearing that personal name).

Wintour *see* Winter.

Witt, Witting, Witts *see* White.

Wodeman *see* Wader.

Wodehouse *see* Woodhouse.

Wodhams *see* Woodall.

Wolton *see* Hamilton.

Wood, Attwood, Bywood, Wode, Woode, Wooder, Woodin, Wooding, Woodings, Woodman, Woods (Eng) In nearly all cases, descendant of someone who lived near (or in) a wood, or occupational name for someone who worked as a forester. However, there are early records of the type Adam the Wood, William the Wood, where the reference is to the Old English word *wod* 'frenzied, wild.' Wood can therefore be a nickname. *See* DUCK.

It is the secondary meaning of wood which allows the punning remark by Demetrius, in Shakespeare's *A Midsummer Night's Dream*: 'Here am I, and wood within this wood.'

Woodall, Woodhall (Eng) Descendant of someone who lived in one of the many places so-called, referring to a hall in a wood. There are many other compound names with *Wood* as the first element. **Woodard** is probably occupational for someone who tended a herd of animals in a wood. WOODCRAFT is a variant of WOODCROFT 'someone who lived in a croft by a wood.' Similar names which indicate where someone lived include WOODEND, WOODHAM, WOODHAMS, WODHAMS 'village near a wood', WOODGATE, WOODHEAD, WOODLAND, WOODSIDE. Occupational names connected with work in a wood include WOODER, WOODGER, WOODIER, WOODYEAR, WOODYER 'wood-cutter', WOODMAN, WOODWARD 'forester.'

Woodcock, Woodcocks (Eng) In some instances a nickname based on the bird's reputation for gullibility and stupidity. The name is too frequent for that to be the only origin, however, and Reaney suggested that it could also be a form of **Woodcote** 'cottage in a wood,' indicating someone who originally lived in such a cottage or in a place of that name.

Woodcraft, Woodcroft, Woodend, Wooder, Woodgate, Woodger, Woodhall, Woodham, Woodhams, Woodhead *see* WOODALL.

Woode, Wooder *see* WOOD.

Woodhouse, Wodehouse, Woodus (Eng, Scot) Descendant of someone who came from one of the many places named because of a wooden house.'

This is a highly literary name, borne by the comic novelist P.G. Wodehouse and by eg Jane Austen's character Emma Woodhouse in *Emma*.

This could also be described as a diabolic surname. In *Rosemary's Baby*, by Ira Levin, the young mother who gives birth to the Devil's child is Rosemary Woodhouse.

Woodier *see* WOODALL.

Woodin, Wooding, Woodings, Woodman, Woods *see* WOOD.

Woodland, Woodman, Woodside *see* WOODALL.

Woodus *see* WOODHOUSE.

Woodward, Woodyear, Woodyer *see* WOODALL.

Woolfield (Eng) Descendant of *Wulfhild*, an Old English personal name with elements meaning 'wolf' and 'war.'

Wordsworth *see* WADSWORTH.

Workman (Eng) Occupational name of a man who worked the soil. Reaney also discovered a gloss which explained 'workman' as someone who was ambidextrous. This special sense is not mentioned in the *Oxford English Dictionary* and it is difficult to know how widely the word would have been understood or used in such a sense.

Worship, Worthship (Eng) Complimentary nickname for someone who descerved respect or esteem.

Worthington (Eng) From residence in one of the places so-named because it was the 'settlement of *Wurth's* people.' Worthing in Sussex has a similar meaning.

As a surname Worthing would indicate someone who originally came from that place, though in *The Importance of Being Earnest*, by Oscar Wilde, it meant someone who was going there: 'The late Mr Thomas Cardew found me, and gave me the name of Worthing, because he happened to have a first class ticket for Worthing in his pocket at the time.'

Worthship *see* WORSHIP.

Wraight, Wraighte, Wraith, Wrate, Wreath, Wreight *see* WRIGHT.

Wren, Wrenn (Eng) Nickname from the bird, probably alluding to someone's smallness.

Sir Christopher Wren (1632-1723) is one of the world's best-known architects. A well-known 'clerihew' by E.C. Bentley runs:

Sir Christopher Wren.
Said: 'I am going to dine with some men:
If any one calls,
Say I am designing St Paul's.

Wright, Wraight, Wraighte, Wraith, Wrate, Wreath, Wreight,

Wrighte, Wrightson, Wrixon (Eng) Occupational name of a wood-worker, or worker in other materials. Compound names ending in -*wright* are not always 'worker' names, *see* ARKWRIGHT.

Jokes about a woman who marries her Mr Right, or two Wrights making a wrong, are hardly original, but have to be endured by those who bear the name. For punning verses about Wright *see* STRANGE, DUCK.

The following anonymous poem, quoted in Chambers' *Book of Days*, is entitled 'On Meeting an old Gentleman Named Wright:

What, Wright alive! I thought ere this
That he was in the realms of bliss!
Let us not say that Wright is wrong,
Merely for holding out so long;
But ah! 'tis clear, though we're bereft
Of many a friend that Wright has left,
Amazing, too, in such a case,
That Wright and left should thus change place!
Not that I'd go such lengths as quite
To think him left because he's
Wright: But left he is, we plainly see,
Or Wright, we know, he could not be:
For when he treads Death's fatal shore,
We feel that Wright will be no more.
He's therefore Wright, while left; but, gone,
Wright is not left; and so I've done.

Wyatt, Whyatt, Guyat, Guyatt, Gyatt (Eng) Descendant of someone who bore a form of the Old English personal name *Wigheard* 'war brave.' This had developed into *Wyot* and *Gyot* by the Middle Ages.

Wyld, Wylds, Wylde, Wyldes *see* WILD.

Wyler *see* WHEEL.

Wyling, Wyllis *see* WILLIAMS.

Wyndham, Windham (Eng) From residence in the Sussex place so-named because it was '*Winda's* low-lying meadow.'

Wynmer *see* WHIMMER.

Wynter, Wynters *see* WINTER.

Yale (Welsh) Indicating an ancestor who came from *Ial*, in Denbighshire.

Yap, Yapp (Eng) Nickname for a cunning, sly or astute person, from an Old English word which earlier meant 'curved, bent.'

Yardley (Eng) From a place name which occurs in various counties, originally indicating a forest used for timber.

Yarmouth (Eng) Descendant of someone who came from the Norfolk town, at the mouth of the River Yare.

Yarrow (Eng) Descendant of someone who lived near the River Yarrow (Lancs).

Yate, Yates, Yatman, Yeates, Yeatman, Yeats, Yetman, Yetts (Eng) Dweller near a town gate, or gate-keeper.

Yeldham (Eng) From residence in a place so-named because it was a 'tax-paying homestead.'

Yelland (Eng) Someone from any of the places of this name, which originally indicated 'old (long-cultivated) land'.

Yelverton (Eng) Someone who came from a place so-named because it was the 'settlement of *Geldfrith's* people.'

Yeowell *see* YULE.

Yetman, Yetts *see* YATE.

Yeuell *see* YULE.

Yewen, Yewens *see* EWAN.

Yoell *see* YULE.

Yong, Yonge (Eng) *see* YOUNG.

Yorick (Danish) Possibly meant to be a form of *Jorgen,* Danish *George*, as suggested by Murray J. Levith in *What's In Shakespeare's Names*. But *Roricus* was the name of Hamlet's maternal grandmother, according to Saxo Grammaticus, and this would have given *Rorick*.

Although this is a famous name, it is not one that is likely to be found in the telephone directory. Shakespeare uses it in *Hamlet* for the jester with whom the young Hamlet used to play.

Yorick was later taken up by Laurence Sterne for use in his *Tristram Shandy*. Sterne says there that 'Yorick was this parson's name, and, what is very remarkable in it (as appears from a most ancient account of the family) it had been exactly so spelt without the least variation or transposition of a single letter, for I do not know how long; which is more than I would venture to say of one half of the best surnames in the kingdom; which in the course of years, have generally undergone as many chops and changes as their owners. Has this been owing to the pride, or to the shame of the respective proprietors? In honest truth, I think sometimes to the one, and sometimes to the other, just as the temptation has wrought. But a villainous affair it is, and will one day so blend and confound us altogether, that no one shall be able to stand up and swear 'That his own great gradfather was the man who did either this or that.' Sterne implies that changes in spelling and pronunciation have been deliberate, whereas for the most part, they were due to the illiteracy of those who bore the names and the semi-literacy of those who recorded them.

York, Yorke (Eng) Someone who originally came from the city of *York*.

Youel, Youels, Youhill *see* YULE.

Youings *see* EWAN.

Youle, Youles, Youll *see* YULE.

Young, Younge, Younger, Yong, Yonge (Eng) Probably this name originally described a son who bore the same first name as his father.

Verse and Worse, an anthology compiled by Arnold Silcock, quotes the following epitaph:

Beneath this stone
A lump of clay
Lies Arabella Young
Who on the 21st of May 1771
Began to hold her tongue.

Youngsmith *see* SMITH.

Yule, Yeowell, Yeuell, Yoell, Youel, Youels, Youhill, Youle, Youles, Youll, Yuell, Yuill, Yuille, Yulle (Eng) Descendant of someone who was born at *Yule-tide*.

Zappa (Italian) Occupational name of a farm worker, from *zappa* 'hoe, mattock.'

Zealey, Zelley *see* SILLY.

Zhivago (Russian) Nickname for somone 'full of life.' The name literally means 'living.'

This is one of the better-known Russian names in the English speaking world, thanks to the novel by Boris Pasternak (1957), winner of a Nobel Prize for Literature. The novel was made into a film in 1965. The central character is Yuri Zhivago, who suffers greatly during the civil war.

Anyone with a special interest in Russian names should consult B.O. Unbegaun's comprehensive *Russian Surnames*, published by Oxford University Press in 1972.

Zimmermann (Ger) Occupational name of a carpenter. See also note 2 at CHAMBERLAIN.

Zola (Italian) This is usually explained in terms of Italian *zolla* 'clod, bank of earth,' found as a place name which then became a surname. In *Our Italian Surnames*, Joseph G. Fucilla points out that it could also be from a diminutive ending in names ending in -*zo,* such as *Lorenzo*. This becomes *Renzo*, then *Renzola. Franzola* is also a pet form of *Francesco*.

Zola is also used as a first name, as in the case of the South African athlete Zola Budd. Her father once said in an interview that he liked the idea of a name beginning with Z-, and had Zero in mind for a boy.

Appendix 1: Curious and Obsolete surnames

A great many surnames borne by our medieval ancestors no longer exist. They are mostly names which would be classed as 'odd' had they survived; a few would be considered obscene. In his *History of British Surnames*, for instance, C. L'Estrange Ewen mentions the following:

J. Brasskettle, Maudlyn Brickbatt, Dorothy Bucktrout,
J. Bullymore, Rob. Buttermouth, Rich. Catskin,
Nick. Childman, W. Cockesbrayn, Rich. Cokeye,
Thom Cockfyssh, Odo Dimpel, Hugh Doggetail,
Geoff. Drinkedregges, Thom Drinkmilk, J. Drunken,
Ralph Dunghul (Dunghill), Alan Evilchild, J. Feveryear,
Hugh Findesilver, Sam. Fullpot, Anne Godhelpe,
Serle Gotokirke, Gilb. Greyschanke, J. Hackewude (Hackwood),
Rob. Hanging, W. Harepyn, Edw. Havejoy, Sarra Hopshort,
W. Horsepet (Horsefart), Rich. Hotgo, Rich. Hurlbatt,
J. Ingoal (probably 'in gaol'), Mary Isbroke, Rich. Lateboy,
Harvey Leapingwell, W. Lickberd (Lickbeard),
Geoff Lickefinger, Simon Likelove, Rob. Litelbodi,
J. Litelskill, Maud Lusshefish, Rob. Midniht,
Rog. Milksoppe, Rich. Nettlebed, W. Oldflesh, J. Onehand,
Alice Peckecheese, Rich. Pitchfork, Grace Pluckrose,
J. Pokepot, Hugh Pudding, J. Quartale, Jos. Quickfall,
J. Ratellbagge, Thom. Rhubarb, Rch. Ringgebelle,
J. Rotenhering, Geo. Sawhell, Hen. Scrapetrough,
J. Shepewassh, Geo Shotbolte, W. Smalwryter,
Ch. Smartknave, Ann Spearpoint, Aug'tine Spurnewater,
J. Standeven, W. Strokelady, Thom. Swetemouth,
Jacob Tiplady, Hen. Tukbacon, J. Underdonne, Eliz. Wagtail,
Walt. Wakewel, Walt. Wanderbug, J. Waytelove,

Thom. Whalebelly, Rob. Witheskirtes.

Ernest Weekley provides a similar list in his *Surnames*, though he says that 'to save space I have omitted the baptismal names.' Examples from his list are:

Baisedame (Kiss woman), Bayseboll (Kiss the bowl – which would be full of liquor), Baysers (Kiss arse), Besecu (*Baise cul* 'kiss arse'), Blouhorn, Brekedishe, Brechehert (Breakheart), Cachehors (Chase horse), Cachemay (Chase maiden), Chaceporc (Chase pig), Chanteben (Sing well), Chasehare, Chipawey, Chopfox, Countefoghel (Count birds), Coupne (Cut nose), Crakpot, Curedame, Cutfox, Cuthog, Drawespere, Etebred (Eat bread), Etebutter, Etelof, Etemete, Fernon (Fear none), Findesilver, Gnawpeny, Gobefore, Godsendus, Gointhewynd, Grindelove, Gripchese, Hackenose, Hoppeschort, Hotgo, Kepecat, Laughwell, Lenealday (Lean all day), Levetoday, Locout (Look out), Makebeverage, Makeblisse, Makeblythe, Makefair, Makehayt, Makejoy, Mangebacun (Eat bacon), Mendfaute, Paynlow (Torture wolf), Parlefrens (Speak French), Pikebone, Pikechin, Rerepaunch, Rivegut, Robechild, Romefare (Traveller to Rome), Schitebroch (Shit breeches), Serveladi, Shavetail, Sparegod, Spekelitel, Spilblod, Stelecat, Stepwrong, Sturpot, Swetinbedde, Tendhogge, Tosseman, Tredewater, Trussebut, Tukbacon, Wantemylk, Wastepeny, Wetebedde, Winnelove, Wipetail.

Yet more names which families have abandoned are listed by P.H. Reaney in *The Origin of English Surnames*. They include:

Roger Blakeballoc (Black testicle), Walter Brekebak (Break back), Adam Brekeleg, William Brekewomb, William Cacchemayde (Chase maid), William Cachepeni (Chase penny), Godwin

Clawcunte, Symon Cuttepurs (Cut purse, a pickpocket, thief), William Doggepintel (Dog penis), Henry Drinkalup, William Etecroue (Eat crow), Adam Fayrarmful (Fair armful, nickname for a short person), John Fillecunt, John Gedirstanes (Gatherstones), Roger Gildynballokes (Golden testicles), Serle Gotokirke, Ralph Hackbon (Hack bone), Geoffrey Hakkeches (Hack cheese, a cheese-seller), Adam Hanggedogge, John Hucketrout (Trout seller), Hugo Humpintel (Honey penis), Peter Hunitail, Adam Le Lechur (The lecher), Roland Le Pettour (The Farter), John Levetoday, Leofric Liccedich (Lickdish), Roger Louestycke (Lovestick, an obscene reference), Ralph Lycorys (Lecherous), John Makebeter, Richedon Makedance, Ralph Makelittel, Robert Mangebien (Eatwell), Adam Pickpese (Pick peas), Richard Pilecat (Steal cat), Richard Playndeamours (Full of love), Philip Pleywel, Ernald Pokestrong, John Prikehard, Adam Richeandgod, Richard Scittebagge (Shitbag), Adam Singsmal (Sings badly), Agnes Singalday, John Skipop (Skip up), Geoffrey Sitadun, William Spillebred (Waste bread), John Spylwater, John Strokelady, John Swetpintel (Sweet penis), Osbert Triphup, Roger Waspail (Wash pail), John Washewhite, Mucheman Wetebede (Wet the bed), Bele Wydecunthe.

George F. Black added a few Scottish examples to this collection in the Introduction to his *Surnames of Scotland*:

Adam Aydrunken (Always drunk), William Conquergood, Johannes Excommunicatio, Andro Goddiskirk, Ricardus Hangpudyng, Robert Luggespick (Ear pick), Patrick Morselmouthe, John Out with the sword, John Sowlug (Pig ear), Will Spurncurtoys (Spurn courtesy), George Swynhouse, John Unkutheman (Unknown man).

APPENDIX 2: SURNAME DISTRIBUTION

In his *Homes of Family Names in Great Britain*, published in 1890, Henry Brougham Guppy gave the results of surveys he had made into the distribution of surnames. Most names were spread over a wide area, but of particular interest are the names that at the end of the 19th century were 'peculiar to one county,' as Guppy described them. The latter give strong clues to those interested in their family history as to where to pursue their searches. The 'peculiar' names are listed below in Guppy's original groupings. Some names appear in more than one of the Scottish groups.

BEDFORDSHIRE
Battams, Breary, Brightman, Buckmaster, Claridge, Cranfield, Darrington, Dillamore, Duncombe, Fensom, Foll, Hallworth, Harradine, Hartop, Inskip, Kempson, Malden, Mossman, Negus, Quenby, Scrivener, Scroggs, Stanbridge, Stanton, Timberlake, Whinnet.

BERKSHIRE
Adnams, Benning, Buckeridge, Bunce, Corderoy, Corderey, Crockford, Dormer, Fairthorne, Freebody, Frogley, Froome, Halfacre, Headington, Izzard, Keep, Kimber, Lanfear, Lay, Lonsley, Lyford, Maslen, Napper, Pither, Poyey, Shackel, Tame, Tyrrell, Wilder.

BUCKINGHAMSHIRE
Belgrove, Boughton, Brazier, Dancer, Darvell, Darvill, Dover, Dwight, Edmans, Fountain, Fountaine, Ginger, Gomm, Holdom, Horwood, Ing, Kingham, Plaistowe, Purssell, Roads, Sare, Sear, Slocock, Startford, Syratt, Sirett, Tapping, Tattam, Tofield, Tomes,

Tompkins, Varney, Viccars, Warr, Willison, Wilmer, Wooster.

CAMBRIDGESHIRE

Bays, Chivers, Clear, Collen, Coxall, Dimmock, Dimock, Doggett, Elbourn, Frohock, Fullard, Fyson, Ground, Grounds, Haggar, Hagger, Hurry, Ivatt, Jonas, Maxwell, Murfitt, Mustill, Purkis, Ruston, Sallis, Shepperson, Skeels, Stockdale, Thoday, Vawser, Wayman, Yarrow.

CHESHIRE

Acton, Adshead, Allman, Ankers, Ardern, Astbury, Aston, Basford, Baskerville, Basnett, Bebbington, Birtles, Blackshaw, Boffey, Bolshaw, Bracegirdle, Bradock, Broadhurst, Broster, Callwood, Cash, Chesters, Done, Dooley, Duton, Eden, Erlam, Etchells, Furber, Gallimore, Gleave, Goddier, Goodier, Gresty, Hankey, Hassall, Hassell, Henshall, Hickson, Hockenhall, Hockenhull, Hocknell, Hollinshead, Hooley, Hopley, Houlbrook, Huxley, Jeffs, Jepson, Kennerley, Kinsey, Leah, Leather, Littler, Major, Marsland, Minshall, Minshull, Mottershead, Mounfield, Mountfield, Mullock, Newall, Noden, Norbury, Oakes, Okel, Oulton, Pimlott, Pownall, Priestner, Rathbone, Ravenscroft, Rowlingson, Ruscoe, Sandbach, Scragg, Sheen, Shone, Shore, Siddorn, Snelson, Sproston, Stelfox, Stockton, Summerfield, Swinton, Tapley, Thompstone, Thornhill, Tickle, Timperley, Trickett, Trueman, Urmston, Wheelton, Whitelegg, Whitlow, Witter, Woddall, Woollam, Woollams, Wych, Yarwood.

CORNWALL

Benny, Berriman, Barryman, Bice, Biddick, Blarney, Boaden, Boase, Bolitho, Borlase, Brendon, Brenton, Budge, Bullmore, Bunt, Burnard, Cardell, Carlyon, Carne, Carveth, Cawrse, Chenoweth, Clemow, Clyma, Clymo, Coad, Cobbledick,

Cobeldick, Congdon, Couch, Cowling, Crago, Cragoe, Craze, Crowle, Cundy, Curnow, Dingle, Dunstan, Dunstone, Eddy, Eva, Freethy, Galtey, Geach, Geake, Gerry, Gillbard, Glasson, Goldsworthy, Grigg, Grose, Gynn, Hambly, Hawke, Hawken, Hawkey, Hayne, Hearle, Henwood, Higman, Hodge, Hollow, Hotten, Ivey, Jane, Jasper, Jelbart, Jelbert, Jenkin, Jose, Julian, Julyan, Keast, Kerkin, Kestle, Kevern, Kitto, Kittow, Kneebone, Laity, Lander, Lanyon, Lawry, Lean, Liddicoat, Littlejohn, Lobb, Lory, Lug, Lyle, Mably, Maddaford, Maddiver, Magor, Mayne, Morcom, Morkam, Moyle, Mutton, Nance, Oates, Oats, Odger, Odgers, Old, Olver, Opie, Oppy, Pascoe, Paynter, Pearn, Pedlar, Pedler, Pender, Pengelly, Pengilly, Penna, Penrose, Peter, Pethick, Philp, Pinch, Polkinghorne, Prisk, Raddall, Raddle, Rapson, Retallack, Retallick, Rickard, Rodda, Roose, Roseveare, Rosewarne, Roskelly, Roskilly, Rouse, Rowse, Rundle, Runnalls, Sandercock, Sandry, Scantlebury, Seccombe, Skewes, Spargo, Tamblyn, Tinney, Tippett, Toll, Tom, Tonkin, Trebilcock, Tregear, Tregellas, Tregelles, Tregoning, Treleaven, Treloar, Tremain, Tremayne, Trembath, Trerise, Tresidder, Trethewey, Trevail, Treweeke, Trewhella, Trewin, Tripcony, Trounson, Trudgen, Trudgeon, Trudgian, Truscott, Tyack, Tyacke, Uren, Vellenoweth, Venning, Verran, Vivian, Vosper, Wearne, Wellington, Whetter, Wickett, Woodley, Woolcock, Yelland.

CUMBERLAND AND WESTMORLAND
Beattie, Beaty, Burns, Carruthers, Dalzell, Dalziel, Donald, Faulder, Fearon, Fleming, Johnston, Martindale, Mossop, Mounsey, Patinson, Routledge, Sim, Simm, Spotterswood, Thomlinson, Topping.

DERBYSHIRE
Alton, Bark, Barnsley, Beardsley, Biggin, Boam, Bowmer,

Briddon, Brocksopp, Broomhead, Burdikin, Byard, Chadfield, Clewes, Clews, Copestake, Crookes, Cupit, Cutts, Drabble, Dronfield, Eley, Else, Fearn, Fitchett, Foulke, Fowke, Fretwell, Gent, Graton, Gyte, Hadfield, Handford, Hartle, Hawley, Henstock, Housley, Hulland, Jerram, Joule, Knifton, Knott, Limb, Litchfield, Longden, Ludlam, Lynam, Mallinder, Marchington, Marples, MaskeryMaskrey, Mortin, Murfin, Nadin, Oakden, Outram, Peat, Plackett, Pursglove, Purslove, Rains, Renshaw, Revell, Revill, Rowarth, Saint, Seal, Shacklock, Sherwin, Shirt, Sidebottom, Skidmore, Smedley, Spalton, Staley, Staniforth, Stoppard, Storer, Tagg, Towndrow, Townrow, Townroe, Turton, Tym, Tymm, Udall, Wager, Wallwin, Waterfall, Waterhouse, Wetton, Wheatcroft, Whittingham, Wibberley, Wigley, Winson, Wragg.

DEVONSHIRE

Addems, Alford, Amery, Anning, Arscott, Babbage, Balkwill, Balman, Balsdon, Bastin, Bater, Beedell, Beer, Besley, Bickle, Blatchford, Blowey, Bloye, Bolt, Boundy, Bovey, Bradridge, Brag, Braund, Brayley, Breayley, Bridgman, Brimacombe, Broom, Bucknell, Burgoin, Burgoyne, Burrough, Burrow, Cawsey, Chaffe, Charnings, Chammings, Channin, Channing, Chave, Cheriton, Chowen, Chown, Chubb, Chugg, Cleverdon, Coaker, Cockram, Cockeram, Colwill, Coneybeare, Conybear, Connibear, Coombe, Copp, Courtice, Crang, Crimp, Crocombe, Cuming, Dallyn, Damerell, Darch, Dare, Dart, Dayment, Densem, Densham, Dicker, Dimond, Dymond, Doble, Doidge, Dommett, Dufty, Earl, Earle, Easterbrook, Estabrook, Eggins, Ellacott, Ellicott, Elston, Elworthy, Endacott, Eveleigh, Evely, Fairchild, Fewings, Foale, Foss, Friend, Furneaux, Furse, Furze, Gammon, German, Gidley, Gillard, Gloyn, Gorwyn, Grendon, Halse, Hamlyn, Hannaford, Hartnell, Hartnoll, Hayman, Headon,

Health, Heaman, Heard, Heddon, Heggadon, Helmer, Hext, Heyward, Heywood, Hillson, Hilson, Hockridge, Honniball, Hookway, Hurrell, Huxham, Huxtable, Irish, Isaacs, Jackman, Kerslake, Kingwell, Knapman, Lambshead, Lang, Langman, Langworthy, Lear, Lerwill, Lethbridge, Letheren, Ley, Lidstone, Littlejohns, Loosemoor, Loosmoor, Lovering, Luscombe, Luxton, Madge, Manley, Maunder, Melhuish, Melluish, Metherall, Metherell, Mildon, Mill, Millman, Milman, Mogford, Mugford, Mortimore, Mudge, Nancekivell, Nancekeville, Nankevil, Netherway, Newcombe, Norrish, Northam, Northmore, Nosworthy, Oldreave, Oldreive, Paddon, Palfrey, Palk, Parkhouse, Pavey, Pearcey, Penwarden, Perkin, Perrin, Petherbridge, Petherick, Pinhay, Pinhey, Powlesland, Prettejohn, Prettyjohn, Pring, Pugsley, Pym, Quance, Rabjohns, Raymont, Raymount, Reddaway, Reddicliffe, Retter, Rew, Ridd, Routley, Seldon, Sellek, Sercombe, Seward, Shapland, Sharland, Shorland, Sherill, Sherwill, Shopland, Slader, Slee, Slugget, Smale, Smallbridge, Smallridge, Smaridge, Smerdon, Smyth, Soby, Soper, Spurrell, Spurle, Squance, Stanbury, Stidston, Stoneman, Tancock, Taverner, Toms, Tope, Tozer, Tremlett, Trick, Trott, Trude, Tuckett, Tully, Underhay, Underhill, Vallance, Vanstone, Venner, Voaden, Vodden, Vooght, Wadland, Wakeham, Ware, Waycott, Were, Westacott, Westaway, Westcott, Western, Westren, Wheaton, Whiteaway, Whiteway, Widdicombe, Willing, Withecombe, Witheycombe, Witheridge, Wonnacott, Woolland, Wotton, Wrayford, Wreford, Wroth.

DORSETSHIRE

Antell, Ballam, Bastable, Besent, Bowditch, Brickell, Brine, Bugg, Bugler, Caines, Cake, Chilcott, Cluett, Dominy, Dorey, Dunford, Durden, Ensor, Fifett, Fooks, Foot, Gatehouse, Genge, Gillingham, Guppy, Hames, Hann, Hansford, Hayter, Homer, Honeyfield,

Hounsell, Jesty, Kellaway, Keynes, Kingman, Larcombe, Legg, Lodder, Loder, Mayo, Meaden, Meatyard, Meech, Milledge, Munckton, Peach, Pomeroy, Rabbets, Ridout, Ross, Rossiter, Samways, Scutt, Shute, Spicer, Sprake, Studley, Swaffield, Symes, Topp, Trowbridge, Tuffin, Wakely, Walden, Wareham, Wrixon.

DURHAM

Applegarth, Beadle, Bruce, Bullman, Bulman, Burdon, Callender, Coatsworth, Eggleston, Greenwell, Heppell, Hepple, Hewitson, Hopps, Jameson, Jamieson, Kirkup, Kirton, MacLaren, Makepeace, Mallam, Pallister, Pease, Proud, Quelch, Shotton, Surtees, Tarn, Tinkler, Walburn, Wearmouth.

ESSEX

Basham, Beddall, Belcham, Bentall, Byford, Cant, Caton, Challis, Christy, Dowsett, Eve, Fairhead, Felgate, Fenner, Folkard, Gowlett, Halls, Hasler, Hockley, Housden, Hutley, Kemsley, Ketley, Kettley, Lagden, Littlechild, Lucking, Marriage, Maskell, Mathams, Meeson, Metson, Milbank, Millbank, Mott, Muggleston, Nottage, Pannell, Parish, Parrish, Patmore, Pegrum, Pilgrim, Pledger, Quilter, Raven, Rickett, Root, Ruffle, Savill, Scruby, Shave, Sorrell, Spurgeon, Staines, Stock, Strutt, Sweeting, Taber, Tabor, Thorington, Tilbrook, Tofts, Tween, Wenden, Wendon, Whitlock.

GLOUCESTERSHIRE

Arkell, Ballinger, Biddle, Blandford, Browning, Bubb, Cadle, Clutterbuck, Comely, Cornock, Croome, Cullimore, Dobbs, Dowdeswell, Fawkes, Flook, Fluck, Flux, Garne, Gazard, Goulding, Goulter, Hanks, Hatherell, Hewer, Hignell, Holder, Iles, Kilminster, Kilmister, Limbrick, Lusty, Minchin, Minett, New, Niblett, Organ, Parslow, Pegler, Penson, Priday, Radway, Ricketts, Righton, Rugman, Rymer, Selwyn, Shields, Shipp, Shipway, Staite,

Stinchcombe, Theyer, Till, Trotman, Tuffley, Vick, Vimpany, Wadley, Werrett, Wintle, Wintour, Witchell, Yeend.

HAMPSHIRE

Abbinett, Amey, Attrill, Ayles, Barfoot, Blackman, Broomfield, Budd, Clift, Cobden, Drewitt, Drudge, Edney, Fay, Fitt, Jolliffe, Lavington, Light, Mew, Poore, Portsmouth, Potticary, Rumbold, Seaward, Southwell, Stares, Stride, Turvill, Twitchin, Whitcher, Witt.

HEREFORDSHIRE

Allcott, Apperley, Banfield, Berrow, Bodenham, Bounds, Bromage, Callow, Eckley, Embrey, Godsall, Godsell, Hancorn, Hobby, Hoddell, Maddy, Mailes, Mainwaring, Marfell, Meadmore, Monnington, Ockey, Orgee, Paniers, Panniers, Pantall, Scudamore, Sirell, Skerrett, Skyrme, South, Tudge, Vale, Welson, Went.

HERTFORDSHIRE

Acres, Ashwell, Bonfield, Campkin, Chalkley, Chennells, Clinton, Hankin, Ivory, Kingsley, Kitchener, Mardell, Orchard, Overell, Parkins, Patten, Sears, Tittmus, Vyse, Walby, Woollatt.

HUNTINGDONSHIRE

Achurch, Bletsoe, Cheney, Corney, Ekins, Humbley, Jellis, Ladds, Lenton, Looker, Mask, Speechley, Spriggs.

KENT

Ballard, Barling, Belsey, Benstead, Bensted, Bing, Boorman, Boulden, Brenchley, Brice, Broadley, Buss, Chantler, Clinch, Coultrip, Coveney, Crowhurst, Curling, Dark, Dilnot, Dungey, Fag, File, Filmer, Finn, Fremlin, Godden, Goodhew, Gower, Hambrook, Harden, Hartridge, Hickmott, Hogben, Hogbin, Holness, Honess,

Hollamby, Hollands, Inge, Jarrett, Kingsnorth, Langridge, Larkin, Larking, Laslett, Leney, Love, Luck, Manwaring, Matcham, Maylam, Maxted, Millen, Milne, Minter, Miskin, Missing, Morphett, Murton, Neame, Offen, Orpen, Orpin, Oyler, Pidduck, Pitock, Pilcher, Prebble, Quested, Rigden, Scoones, Seath, Shorter, Solley, Solomon, Southon, Stace, Stickles, Stunt, Stuppies, Swaffer, Tassell, Thirkell, Tickner, Tomkin, Tompsett, Tuff, Usherwood, Unicume, Vinson, Wacher, Waterman, Whitebread, Wiles, Wyles, Witherden.

LANCASHIRE

Alker, Almond, Alty, Aspinall, Aspinwall, Atherton, Bamber, Battersby, Bent, Bibby, Bleasdale, Bleazard, Blezard, Blezzard, Bonney, Bretherton, Brindle, Bulcock, Butterworth, Caldwell, Cardwell, Cartmell, Catlow, Catterall, Caunce, Charnley, Charnock, Collinge, Coward, Critchley, Crompton, Cropper, Culshaw, Cunliffe, Dagger, Dearden, Dewhurst, Drinkall, Duckworth, Dunderdale, Duxbury, Eastham, Eaves, Eccles, Entwisle, Entwistle, Fairclough, Fazakerley, Fish, Forrest, Forshaw, Gornall, Gorst, Greenhalgh, Gregson, Grimshaw, Hacking, Hakin, Halliwell, Halsall, Hardman, Haworth, Haydock, Hayhurst, Haythornthwaite, Hesketh, Hesmondhalgh, Higson, Hindle, Horrocks, Huddleston, Ibison, Iddon, Kellett, Kenyon, Kilshaw, Lawrenson, Leaver, Lever, Livesey, Livesley, Longton, Longworth, Lonsdale, Lyon, Lythgoe, Maden, Margerison, Margerson, Marginson, Martland, Mashiter, Maudsley, Mawdsley, Mayor, Molyneux, Newby, Nutter, Ollerton, Pemberton, Pendlebury, Pickup, Pilkington, Pilling, Pimblett, Pollitt, Pomfret, Postlethwaite, Rainford, Ramsbottom, Rawcliffe, Rawlinson, Riding, Ryding, Rimmer, Rogerson, Rosbotham, Rosbottom, Rosebotham, Rossall, Rossell, Rothwell, Sagar, Segar, Salthouse, Scholes, Seddon, Sefton, Sephton, Shacklady, Shakelady, Sharples,

Sharrock, Shorrock, Silcock, Singleton, Stanworth, Starkie, Stuart, Swarbrick, Tattersall, Threlfall, Topping, Townson, Tyrer, Unworth, Wallbank, Walmsley, Walsh, Wareing, Waring, Whipp, Whiteside, Winder, Winstanley, Worsley.

LEICESTERSHIRE AND RUTLANDSHIRE

Beeby, Berridge, Branson, Burnaby, Cobley, Dalby, Darnell, Dawkins, Dexter, Dowell, Drackley, Draycott, Eayrs, Eayres, Forryan, Frearson, Freestone, Geary, Gimson, Hack, Henson, Hollier, Jarrom, Jesson, Keetley, Keightley, Kirkman, Lacey, Leadbeater, Leadbetter, Loseby, Macaulay, Mackley, Matts, Musson, Oldacres, Orson, Paget, Pochin, Pretty, Royce, Scotton, Sheffield, Shipman, Toon, Toone, Wilford, Wormleighton.

LINCOLNSHIRE

Anyan, Bemrose, Bett, Blades, Blankley, Border, Borman, Bowser, Brackenbury, Bristow, Broughton, Brownlow, Brumby, Burkill, Burkitt, Butters, Cade, Cammack, Capes, Casswell, Chatterton, Codd, Collishaw, Coney, Cooling, Cottingham, Coupland, Cranidge, Cropley, Cutforth, Cuthbert, Dannatt, Daubney, Desforges, Dook, Dows, Dowse, Drakes, Drewery, Drewry, Dring, Drury, Dudding, Elmitt, Elvidge, Epton, Evison, Forman, Frisby, Frow, Gaunt, Gilliart, Gilliatt, Gillyatt, Goodyear, Goose, Grummitt, Hay, Herring, Hewson, Hides, Hildred, Hoyes, Hoyles, Hutton, Ingall, Ingle, Laming, Lamming, Leggett, Leggott, Lill, Lilley, Lynn, Mackinder, Maidens, Marfleet, Markham, Mastin, Maw, Mawer, Merrikin, Minter, Mowbray, Odling, Overton, Palethorpe, Patchett, Pick, Pickwell, Pocklington, Ranby, Reeson, Rhoades, Riggall, Rippon, Sardeson, Sargisson, Scarborough, Scholey, Scoley, Scrimshaw, Scrimshire, Searson, Sergeant, Sharpley, Sneath, Stamp, Storr, Stowe, Strawson, Stuble, Temple, Thurlby, Trafford, Ullyatt, Vinter, Waddingham, Wadsley, Wass,

Westerby, Westoby, Whitsed, Willey, Willows, Winn, Wroot

MIDDLESEX
Ewer, Woodland.

NORFOLK
Abbs, Amies, Amis, Arthurton, Atthow, Attoe, Banham, Batterham, Beales, Beanes, Beck, Bettinson, Boddy, Brasnett, Bunn, Cannell, Case, Claxton, Copeman, Cossey, Cubitt, Culley, Curson, Duffield, Dyball, Dye, Eglinton, Failes, Flatt, Gamble, Gapp, Gayford, Gaze, Gedge, Gooch, Goulder, Greenacre, Heading, Howes, Huggins, Ingram, Kerrison, Lain, Land, Larwood, Leeder, Leeds, Lewell, Mack, Mallett, Milk, Minns, Mullinger, Nurse, Plumbly, Poll, Purdy, Ringer, Rising, Rivett, Rix, Roofe, Sands, Savory, Scales, Sheringham, Shreeve, Slipper, Soame, Spink, Spinks, Starling, Stimpson, Thrower, Tooley, Utting, Warnes, Whalebelly, Whittleton, Woolston, Wortley.

NORTHAMPTONSHIRE
Aris, Barford, Bazeley, Bazley, Bellairs, Bellars, Borton, Brafield, Britten, Bromwich, Buswell, Butlin, Chew, Dainty, Drage, Dunkley, Gibbard, Goff, Golby, Goode, Gulliver, Hales, Heygate, Holton, Hornsby, Judkins, Kingston, Linnell, Mackaness, Main, Mawle, Measures, Montgomery, Newitt, Panther, Roddis, Scriven, Siddons, Spokes, Stops, Turnell, Vergette, Warwick, Westley, Whitton, Whitney, Woolhouse, Wrighton, Wyman, York.

NORTHUMBERLAND
Alder, Allan, Annett, Arkle, Aynsley, Bewick, Bolam, Borthwick, Bothwick, Brewis, Brodie, Bushby, Cairns, Carmichael, Cockburn, Common, Cowan, Cowen, Cowing, Craig, Dand, Dinning, Embleton, Fairbairn, Gallon, Gilhespy, Glendinning, Harle,

Herdman, Hindmarsh, Hogg, Howey, Howie, Jobling, Laidler, Lumsden, Middlemas, Middlemiss, Morrison, Nevin, Nevins, Ormston, Philipson, Pringle, Renton, Renwick, Roddam, Shanks, Shield, Stewart, Stobart, Stobert, Straughan, Telfer, Telford, Usher, Wanlace, Wanless, Weddell, Weddle, Younger.

NOTTINGHAMSHIRE

Annable, Barrowcliff, Bartram, Beardall, Beecroft, Billyard, Binge, Bingley, Blatherwick, Broadberry, Buttery, Byron, Carver, Challand, Cheshire, Chettle, Collingham, Corringham, Cumberland, Darwin, Derry, Doncaster, Duckmanton, Eddison, Esam, Farnsworth, Fenton, Footitt, Footit, Gag, Gelsthorpe, Gunn, Hardstaff, Harpham, Hempsall, Herrick, Herrod, Hickton, Holbrook, Howett, Howitt, Hurt, Huskinson, Keyworth, Leavers, Leivers, Lindley, Merrills, Millington, Norwood, Ogle, Oliphant, Olivant, Paling, Payling, Paulson, Peatfield, Pell, Pickin, Plumtree, Quibell, Radley, Redgate, Roadley, Selby, Staples, Stendall, Straw, Stubbins, Templeman, Truswell, Weightman, Wombwell, Woombill.

OXFORDSHIRE

Akers, Aldworth, Arnatt, Batts, Blencowe, Breakspear, Buller, Calcutt, Chaundy, Clapton, Clare, Coggins, Deeley, Edginton, Filbee, Florey, Hatt, Hutt, Hobley, Hone, Honour, Loosley, Louch, Lovegrove, Luckett, Midwinter, Neighbour, Nevell, Padbury, Paxman, Paxton, Pether, Pettipher, Rowles, Sabin, Savin, Shrimpton, Spurrett, Stanbra, Turrill, Tustain, Widdows, Wilsdon, Witney, Woolgrove.

SHROPSHIRE

Ashley, Back, Bather, Batho, Beddoes, Benbow, Blakemore, Boughey, Bowdler, Breakwell, Brisbourne, Broughall,

Cadwallader, Cleeton, Corfield, Cureton, Duce, Eddowes, Everall, Felton, Fowles, Growcott, Gwilt, Heatley, Heighway, Hinton, Home, Hotchkiss, Inions, Instone, Jacks, Kynaston, Lawley, Madeley, Mansell, Mellings, Millichamp, Minton, Munslow, Nock, Onions, Paddock, Pinches, Pitchford, Podmore, Ravenshaw, Rodenhurst, Sankey, Shuker, Tipton, Titley, Warder, Wellings.

SOMERSET

Amesbury, Aplin, Ashman, Arney, Baber, Badman, Bagg, Banwell, Barnstable, Barrington, Batt, Bicknell, Binning, Bisdee, Board, Bowering, Brimble, Burch, Burston, Carey, Cary, Chard, Churches, Clapp, Clothier, Coate, Cogan, Coggan, Corner, Corp, Cosh, Counsell, Croom, Crossman, Dampier, Denman, Denning, Derrick, Dibble, Dicks, Diment, Dyment, Durston, Evered, Farthing, Fear, Floyd, Gare, Giblett, Greed, Haggett, Hatch, Hebditch, Hembrow, Hockey, Horsey, Hurd, Hurley, Isgar, Keedwell, Keel, Keirl, Kidner, Look, Loveybond, Lovibond, Loxton, Lutley, Mapstone, Meaker, Oram, Padfield, Perham, Phippen, Pople, Pottenger, Pow, Puddy, Rawle, Reakes, Rood, Rugg, Say, Sealey, Sealy, Singer, Speed, Sperring, Spratt, Stallard, Steeds, Stuckey, Sully, Summerhayes, Swanton, Sweet, Tarr, Tatchell, Tazewell, Teek illey, Toogood, Treasure, Tyley, Vigar, Vigors, Vowles, Walrond, Wescott, Winslade, Winstone, Withey, Withy, Wookey, Yeandle.

STAFFORDSHIRE

Ash, Averill, Bagnall, Bakewell, Baskeyfield, Batkin, Beardmore, Bickford, Boden, Boon, Bott, Bould, Boulton, Bowers, Brindley, Brunt, Cantrell, Cantrill, Chell, Clewlow, Clulow, Clowes, Colclough, Corbishley, Cumberledge, Deakin, Durose, Eardley, Elsmore, Fallows, Farrall, Fern, Forrester, Goldstraw, Hambleton, Hammersley, Heler, Hodgkins, Hollingsworth, Hollins, Howson, Jeavons, Jevons, Keeling, Kidd, Lakin, Lese, Leighton, Lindop,

Lovatt, Loverock, Lymer, Limer, Malkin, Marson, Mayer, Mottram, Myatt, Orpe, Parton, Pyatt, Sharratt, Sherratt, Shelley, Shemilt, Shenton, Shirley, Shoebotham, Shoebottom, Stoddard, Swetnam, Tomkinson, Torr, Tunnicliff, Turnock, Warrilow, Whitehurst, Wilshaw, Wint, Wooddisse, Woodings.

SUFFOLK

Aldous, Alston, Aves, Baldry, Bendall, Blowers, Borrett, Button, Calver, Catling, Cattermole, Cobbold, Colson, Cracknell, Cutting, Debenham, Deck, Feaveryear, Feaviour, Finbow, Fincham, Fisk, Fiske, Flatman, Fulcher, Garnham, Gooderham, Grimsey, Grimwood, Hadingham, Haward, Hitchcock, Hurren, Ingate, Jillings, Juby, Keeble, Last, Meen, Nesling, Newson, Pendell, Pendle, Dawyer, Sheldrake, Sheldrick, Southgate, Squirrell, Stannard, Steggall, Sturgeon, Thurman, Tricker, Whitmore, Wolton, Woollard.

SURREY

Caesar, Charlwood, Chuter, Gosden, Puttock, Smithers, Tice, Wenham.

SUSSEX

Akehurst, Allcorn, Ayling, Aylwin, Barham, Bodle, Boniface, Botting, Bourner, Challen, Chitty, Churchman, Coppard, Corke, Cornford, Diplock, Dumbrell, Dumbrill, Etheridge, Evershed, Fogden, Funnell, Gander, Gates, Goacher, Gorringe, Haffenden, Head, Heaver, Hide, Hoadley, Hoath, Hobden, Hobgen, Honeysett, Hook, Isted, Joyes, Killick, Leppard, Longley, Mannington, Message, Newington, Packham, Pankhurst, Penfold, Pennifold, Rapley, Sayers, Sinden, Sparkes, Stay, Sturt, Suter, Tester, Tobitt, Towes, Tribe, Verrall, Wakeford, Walder, Wickens, Woodhams, Wren, Wrenn.

WARWICKSHIRE

Arch, Boddington, Burbidge, Chattaway, Crofts, Currall, Edkins, Elkington, Fitter, Grimes, Hands, Hicken, Hickin, Hollick, Ibbotson, Jeffcoate, Jephcott, Keyte, Knibb, Ledbrook, Moxon, Murcott, Rainbow, Tibbetts, Tidy, Trippas, Truelove, Warden, Weetman, Wilday, Willday.

WILTSHIRE

Awdry, Beak, Bracher, Breach, Compton, Cottle, Cuss, Cusse, Doel, Eatwell, Frankcombe, Francome, Freegard, Freeth, Garlick, Ghey, Greenaway, Greenhill, Grist, Hathway, Henley, Howse, Hulbert, Jupe, Keevil, Kemble, Kinch, Knapp, Manners, Maundrell, melsome, Milsom, Mintey, Minty, Morse, Newth, Ody, Parham, Pickett, Pinchin, Puckeridge, Ruddle, Rumming, Russ, Sidford, Sloper, Taunton, Titcombe, Whatley.

WORCESTERSHIRE

Albutt, Allbutt, Allington, Amphlett, Blakeway, Boucher, Boulter, Byrd, Careless, Cartridge, Doolittle, Essex, Firkins, Follows, Gabb, Ganderton, Granger, Grove, Guilding, Hadley, Halford, Harber, Hemus, Hingley, Hollington, Holtom, Huband, Hyde, Merrell, Moule, Munn, Mytton, Newey, Nickless, Penrice, Purser, Quinney, Quinny, Smithin, Spiers, Stinton, Tandy, Tipping, Tolley, Tongue, Willets, Willetts, Winnall, Winwood, Workman, Wormington, Yarnold.

YORKSHIRE: NORTH AND EAST RIDINGS

Agar, Blenkin, Blenkiron, Bosomworth, Botterill, Bowes, Brigham, Bulmer, Codling, Coverdale, Creaser, Danby, Dinsdale, Duck, Duggleby, Elgey, Elgie, Ellerby, Foxton, Galloway, Garbutt, Goodwill, Grainger, Harker, Harland, Hawking, Hebron, Heseltine,

Hick, Holliday, Holyday, Horsley, Hugill, Iveson, Jacques, Jordison, Judson, Kendrew, Kettlewell, Kilvington, Kipling, Knaggs, Lamplough, Lamplugh, Laverack, Laverick, Leak, Leake, Leaper, Leckenby, Matson, Matterson, Mattison, Medforth, Megginson, Meggison, Megson, Monkman, Nornabell, Nottingham, Outhwaite, Parnaby, Petch, Pickersgill, Plews, Porrett, Porritt, Precious, Prodham, Prudom, Pybus, Raw, Readman, Rennison, Rider, Rodmell, Rounthwaite, Routhwaite, Rowntree, Scarth, Sedman, Sellars, Sellers, Severs, Spenceley, Spensley, Stainthorpe, Stavely, Stockhill, Stockill, Stokell, Stonehouse, Sturdy, Suddaby, Suggett, Suggitt, Sunter, Tennison, Tweedy, Tyerman, Tyreman, Ventress, Ventris, Weighell, Weighill, Welburn, Wellburn, Welford, Whitwell, Wilberforce, Wilberfoss, Witty, Wray, Wrightson.

YORKSHIRE: WEST RIDING

Addy, Ambler, Appleyard, Armitage, Balmforth, Bamforth, Barraclough, Batty, Battye, Beever, Beevers, Beevors, Bentham, Binns, Blakey, Bottomley, Bramall, Brear, Brears, Broadbent, Broadhead, Butterfield, Capstick, Clapham, Clough, Cockshott, Crapper, Crawshaw, Demain, Demaine, Denby, Denison, Dibb, Dyson, Earnshaw, Emmott, Feather, Firth, Garside, Geldard, Gelder, Gledhill, Gott, Haigh, Hainsworth, Haley, Hampshire, Hanson, Hardcastle, Helliwell, Hepworth, Hey, Hinchcliff, Hinchcliffe, Hirst, Hobson, Holdsworth, Houldsworth, Holroyd, Horsfall, Houseman, Ingleby, Jagger, Jowett, Jubb, Kenworthy, Laycock, Lodge, Longbottom, Lumb, Mallinson, Mawson, Midgley, Moorhouse, Murgatroyd, Myers, Newsholme, Newsome, Noble, Peel, Popplewell, Poskitt, Ramsden, Redmayne, Rishworth, Rushworth, Robertshaw, Roebuck, Sedgwick, Shackleton, Sheard, Stansfield, Sugden, Sunderland, Tatham, Teal, Teale, Thackery, Thackray, Thackwray, Thornber, Thwaites, Tinker, Townend, Umpleby, Utley, Varley, Verity,

Wadsworth, Watkinson, Weatherhead, Whiteley, Whitley, Widdop, Widdup, Woodhead, Wrathall.

NORTH WALES
Bebb, Bellis, Colley, Foulkes, Ryder, Tudor.

SOUTH WALES
Beynon, Duggan, Harry, Matthias, Mordecai, Ormond.

MONMOUTHSHIRE
Crowles, Duckham, Ellaway, Gwynne, Jeremiah, Moses, Rosser.

SCOTTISH BORDERS
Aitchison, Armstrong, Beattie, Bell, Calder, Carruthers, Douglas, Edgar, Elliot, Grierson, Hogg, Hope, Hyslop, Little, Maxwell, Milligan, Moffat, Nicholson, Nicolson, Oliver, Purves, Purvis, Rae, Richardson, Robson, Rutherford, Scott, Tait, Turnbull.

SCOTTISH LOWLANDS
Adamson, Aitken, Allan, Arthur, Baird, Barbour, Barclay, Barr, Bell, Blair, Boyd, Brodie, Brown, Buchanan, Cairns, Caldwell, Cowan, Craig, Crawford, Cunningham, Currie, Dalgleish, Dalziel, Dick, Dickie, Dickson, Dodds, Dods, Dunlop, Dunn, Dykes, Findlay, Finlay, Forrest, Forsyth, Sullarton, Fulton, Gemmell, Gibson, Gillespie, Gilmour, Graham, Gray, Hall, Hamilton, Hood, Howie, Inglis, Jack, Jackson, Johnston, Johnstone, Kay, Lang, Laurie, Lawrie, Lawson, Lennox, Lindsay, Logan, Lyon, McCulloch, McKie, Mackie, McNeil, McNeill, Mair, Marshall, Martin, Morton, Muir, Murdoch, Neil, Neilson, Nisbet, Nisbett, Orr, Park, Paton, Pollock, Pringle, Rankin, Richmond, Scott, Shanks, Sloan, Smith, Somerville, Steel, Stevenson, Stoddart, Struthers, Swan, Templeton, Tennant, Thomson, Tod, Todd, Turner,

Waddell, Wallace, Watson, Welsh, White, Whyte, Wilson, Young.

CENTRAL SCOTLAND

Balfour, Baxter, Burns, Cameron, Campbell, Dawson, Dewar, Dickson, Donaldson, Drummond, Drysdale, Duff, Duncan, Edward, Edwards, Finlayson, Forbes, Galbraith, Galloway, Gordon, Gow, Graham, Hall, McArthur, McDougall, McEwan, McEwen, McFarlane, McGregor, McIntosh, Mackintosh, McIntyre, McLaren, Maclaren, McClean, Maclean, McMillan, Macmillan, McNab, Macnab, McNaughton, McNeil, McNeill, Marshall, Menzies, Ogilvie, Ogilvy, Paton, Sharp, Stirling, Tod, Todd, Wallace.

THE HIGHLANDS

Cruikshank, Cumming, Duncan, Farquhar, Farquharson, Forbes, Geddes, Gordon, Grant, Innes, Low, Lumsden, McDonald, McIntosh, Mackintosh, McKay, Mackay, McKenzie, Mackenzie, McKie, Mackie, McLeod, Macleod, McPherson, Macpherson, McRae, Macrae, Middleton, Milne, Munroe, Rennie, Ross, Stephen, Strachan, Sutherland, Urquhart, Watt.

THROUGHOUT SCOTLAND

Adam, Alexander, Anderson, Baillie, Ballantyne, Black, Bruce, Burnett, Carmichael, Chalmers, Christie, Clark, Crichton, Davidson, Donald, Ewing, Ferguson, Fisher, Fleming, Fraser, Gardiner, Gardner, Gibb, Gilchrist, Glen, Greig, Grieve, Guthrie, Hardie, Harper, Harvey, Hay, Henderson, Hill, Hunter, Hutchison, Jamieson, Kennedy, Kidd, King, Laing, Lamont, Law, Leslie, McAdam, Maitland, Malcolm, Matheson, Mathieson, Meikle, Millar, Miller, Mitchell, Moir, Morrison, Muirhead, Murray, Nicol, Nicoll, Paterson, Patterson, Philips, Ramsay, Reid, Ritchie, Robb, Robertson, Rodger, Russell, Shaw, Shepherd, Simpson, Sinclair,

Stewart, Stuart, Taylor, Thom, Walker, Webster, Weir, Wilkie, Williamson, Wood, Wright, Wylie, Wyllie.

APPENDIX 3: FIFTY MOST COMMON SURNAMES

	ENGLAND AND WALES	USA	SCOTLAND
1	Smith	Smith	Smith
2	Jones	Johnson	Brown
3	Williams	Williams	MacDonald
4	Taylor	Brown	Thomson
5	Davies	Jones	Wilson
6	Brown	Miller	Stewart
7	Thomas	Davis	Campbell
8	Evans	Wilson	Robertson
9	Roberts	Anderson	Anderson
10	Johnson	Taylor	Johnston
11	Robinson	Moore	Miller
12	Wilson	Thomas	Murray
13	Wright	Martin	Scott
14	Wood	Thompson	Reid
15	Hall	White	Clark
16	Walker	Harris	MacKenzie
17	Hughes	Jackson	Paterson
18	Green	Clark	Taylor
19	Lewis	Lewis	MacKay
20	Edwards	Walker	MacLean
21	Thompson	Hall	Young
22	White	Robinson	Ross
23	Jackson	Allen	Walker
24	Turner	Young	Mitchell
25	Hill	King	Watson
26	Harris	Nelson	Morrison
27	Clark	Wright	MacLeod
28	Cooper	Baker	Fraser

29	Harrison	Hill	Henderson
30	Davis	Scott	Gray
31	Ward	Adams	Cameron
32	Baker	Green	Graham
33	Martin	Lee	Duncan
34	Morris	Roberts	Hamilton
35	James	Mitchell	Kerr
36	Morgan	Campbell	Hunter
37	King	Phillips	Davidson
38	Allen	Carter	Ferguson
39	Clarke	Evans	Simpson
40	Cook	Turner	Martin
41	Moore	Collins	White
42	Parker	Parker	Kelly
43	Price	Murphy	Allan
44	Phillips	Rodriguez	Grant
45	Watson	Edwards	Bell
46	Shaw	Morris	Black
47	Lee	Peterson	Wallace
48	Bennett	Cook	Russell
49	Carter	Rogers	Marshall
50	Griffiths	Stewart	MacMillan

Collins Dictionary of Curious Phrases
by Leslie Dunkling

The essential guide to the origins of metaphorical phrases in common use, from 'The Full Monty' to 'Shaggy Dog Story'. Published to huge acclaim in Spring 1998, Leslie Dunkling's highly entertaining and informative guide to those curious phrases which have established themselves in our everyday speech is a 'must have' for anyone interested in our language, literature or culture.

ISBN: 0 00 472060 1 Price: £6.99

Collins Dictionary of Allusions
by Julia Cresswell

Why did Tony Benn called Harold Wilson the 'Archie Rice' of politics and why should someone describe Nastassia Kinski as a beautiful 'woodentop'? If you have trouble with these references, or can't remember who 'Skippy' was, or who children mean by the 'Demon Headmaster', help is at hand in this highly entertaining guide to allusions in everyday speech, from classical times to 'Power Rangers'.

ISBN: 0 00 472054 7 Price: £5.99

Collins Dictionary of Slogans
by Nigel Rees
'What passes for culture in my head is really a bunch of commercials' -
Kurt Vonnegut Jr

This classic guide includes unforgettable slogans from the worlds of advertising, politics and cultural history, from 'I'd Love a Beer' and 'Black Power' to 'You Too Can Have a Body' and 'A Diamond is Forever'. Compiled and researched over many years by the broadcaster and author Nigel Rees, this is an indispensable reference source for trivia, crossword and quiz buffs.

ISBN: 0 00 472042 3 Price: £5.99